From the Marne
to Verdun

From the Marne to Verdun

The War Diary of Captain Charles Delvert, 101st Infantry, 1914–1916

Translated and with an introduction by Ian Sumner

Pen & Sword
MILITARY

First published in Great Britain in 2016 by
Pen & Sword Military
an imprint of
Pen & Sword Books Ltd
47 Church Street
Barnsley
South Yorkshire
S70 2AS

Copyright © Pen & Sword Books Ltd 2016

ISBN 978 1 47382 379 2

Typeset in Ehrhardt by
Mac Style Ltd, Bridlington, East Yorkshire
Printed and bound in the UK by CPI Group (UK) Ltd,
Croydon, CR0 4YY

Pen & Sword Books Ltd incorporates the imprints of Pen & Sword
Archaeology, Atlas, Aviation, Battleground, Discovery, Family
History, History, Maritime, Military, Naval, Politics, Railways, Select,
Transport, True Crime, and Fiction, Frontline Books, Leo Cooper,
Praetorian Press, Seaforth Publishing and Wharncliffe.

For a complete list of Pen & Sword titles please contact
PEN & SWORD BOOKS LIMITED
47 Church Street, Barnsley, South Yorkshire, S70 2AS, England
E-mail: enquiries@pen-and-sword.co.uk
Website: www.pen-and-sword.co.uk

Contents

Translator's Introduction

'Your book will give future generations a faithful portrayal of the war, one neither too massaged nor too dark – each fault as dangerous as the other when the extremes of militarism and pacifism are on the rise.' So wrote Jean Norton Cru, reviewing Charles Delvert's compelling first-hand account of French front-line infantrymen in the First World War. The diary kept by Delvert throughout the conflict first appeared in 1918 as *Histoire d'une compagnie: Main de Massiges – Verdun: novembre 1915–juin 1916: journal de marche* (Paris: Berger-Levrault). The revised and extended edition presented here was first published as *Carnets d'un fantassin* (Paris: Albin Michel, 1935). This also recounts Delvert's experience at the battles of the Frontiers (August 1914), the battle of the Marne (September 1914) and the Main de Massiges (July and August 1916). The immediate appeal of the book is evident from its initial print run of 3,000 to 5,000 copies, extraordinary by modern standards; its enduring interest is revealed by the five subsequent editions published in 1966, 1981, 2003, 2008 and 2013. Now, for the first time, the *Carnets* are made available in translation to English-speaking readers.

Charles Laurent Delvert was born in Paris's 3e *arrondissement*, on 27 April 1879, the son of shoemaker Antoine Delvert and his wife Anna Servant, a jewellery polisher. A talented student, he was awarded a bursary to attend the elite Lycée Charlemagne, before proceeding to the École Normale Supérieure, where he graduated in history in 1901. He later became a schoolteacher.

Like all his male contemporaries, Delvert saw service in the army, volunteering in advance of the call-up to reduce his time on active service. He was posted to 46th Infantry on 10 November 1899, promoted to corporal on 26 May 1900, discharged from active service on 26 September 1900, and promoted to sergeant in the reserve on 1 May 1901. Moving around the country in 1906–10, he was on the books of regiments in Lille, Narbonne, Béziers and Lyon, receiving his commission as a sous-lieutenant on 16 December 1908. By January 1911, Delvert was back in the Paris area, posted as a reservist to 101st Infantry, which maintained its principal depot at Dreux (Eure-et-Loir) and a detachment at Saint-Cloud (Hauts-de-Seine). He was promoted to lieutenant on 16 December

1912. During his time in the reserve, he also received at least two substantial periods of training, participating in the annual autumn manoeuvres in 1902 and 1912.

Recalled to the colours on the outbreak of war, on 1 August 1914, Delvert was given command of 2nd Platoon, 4th Company, 101st Infantry (part of 7th Division). The regiment soon saw action, suffering a heavy defeat in a small encounter battle around Ethe (Belgium) on 22 August 1914. Delvert was wounded during the long retreat from the frontier – at Marville (Meuse) on 25 August – but refused to be evacuated. On 3 September 1914, his division travelled north-east of Paris to reinforce Sixth Army on the Marne (6–9 September 1914), 101st Infantry arriving just in time to participate in the final actions of the battle. Throughout September, the regiment followed the Germans through the Aisne and the Somme in what became known as the Race to the Sea. Delvert was evacuated after suffering a serious thigh wound at Champien (Somme) on 23 September. He was later mentioned in divisional orders for his leadership during these actions: 'Remained alone with his platoon in their assigned position, although the rest of the battalion had withdrawn behind the village [of Ethe]. Wounded at Marville on 25 August, but refused to be evacuated. Wounded again on 23 September at the head of his company.'

After a long period of convalescence, Delvert eventually returned to his regiment in November 1915. During his absence, 101st Infantry had served with 7th Division around Roye (Somme), and in Champagne, before transferring in June 1915 to the newly formed 124th Division, where it took part in the autumn offensive in Champagne, serving in the Aubérive-sur-Suippe sector (Marne). The regiment suffered heavy losses in the opening attack on 25 September and was withdrawn from the front line the following month.

Delvert rejoined the 101st on 11 November, now in command of 8th Company. In early December the regiment returned to the front at the Main de Massiges, in Champagne, where it remained until April 1916. Delvert was promoted to the temporary rank of captain on 19 December 1915. In May 1916, the 101st moved to Verdun, where Delvert's company suffered very heavy losses in defending Retranchement R.1, one of a line of four small redoubts covering the north-western approaches to Fort Vaux. Thanks to Delvert's spirited defence, Retranchement R.1 was the last to fall to the German attack of June 1916, enfiladed on both sides.

Delvert was appointed a chevalier of the Légion d'Honneur for his leadership during the battle. Army orders of 20 June 1916 read: 'twice wounded at the start of the conflict, returned to the front before he was completely recovered, played his part in checking violent German attacks on an adjoining sector, strongly attacked in his turn, placed himself at the head of his bombers, determined at all costs not to cede an inch of ground. Inflicted very heavy losses on the enemy and maintained his position intact.'

On 3 July 1916, 101st Infantry returned to the front line in Champagne, again in the Main de Massiges sector. On 4 July Delvert was confirmed in his rank of captain, but five days later he was wounded by a German grenade, then again on 16 August by a Minenwerfer. Unfit for further front-line service, he saw out the war in a variety of staff posts: from 14 September with Fifth Army, where he served in April 1917 during the Chemin des Dames offensive; from 20 July 1917 with First Army, where he was on hand for the Flanders offensive; and from 4 August 1918 with the French army in Italy.

Following demobilization on 15 March 1919, Delvert resumed his teaching career at two prestigious Paris institutions, the Lycée Janson-de-Sailly and the Lycée Henri IV. Still a reservist, he was promoted to the rank of major in 5th Tirailleurs in 1925, and officer of the Légion d'Honneur in 1927. He stayed in contact with many of his wartime comrades, but does not appear to have participated in the politics of the French veterans' movement, nor in the pacifism it later espoused. After marrying Andrée Leduc in Paris on 28 June 1920, he devoted a considerable amount of time in the next two decades to writing and travelling, including a round-the-world voyage. He died on 10 July 1940, from the long-term effects of his wounds. Charles and Andrée had four sons: three fought with the French Resistance – two escaping to join the Free French, while the third took part in the liberation of Paris; the youngest was still under age in 1945.

Charles Delvert was awarded a further honour on 12 December 2013. Each annual intake of the Fourth Battalion of the French military academy, the École Spéciale Militaire de Saint-Cyr, now based at Coëtquidan (Morbihan), chooses a name for their class among French battles and distinguished officers. The Fourth Battalion (composed primarily of cadets destined for the Engineers and supporting services) maintains the traditions of the reserve officers' school, and the class of 2013–14 chose to commemorate Charles Delvert.

Delvert was a prolific author. His first book, *Quelques héros* (Paris: Berger-Levrault), a collection of factual accounts of gallantry at the front, was published in November 1917, going through at least six editions within a year. The author cites just a few of his own experiences, all of which reappear in other works. In December 1920, Delvert made use of his later diaries, drawing on his period of service on the staff of Fifth Army to produce *L'Erreur du 16 avril 1917* (Paris:

L. Fournier) – a bird's-eye view of the unfolding disaster on the Chemin des Dames from his position with XXXII Corps at Point 186, west of Cormicy (Marne).

In January 1921, Delvert provided the text accompanying reproductions of fifty-nine paintings by Joseph-Félix Bouchor, published as *Verdun* (Paris: L. Fournier). Once more he provides little personal information, although he does include a section on his role in the defence of Retranchement R.1, outside Fort Vaux. His next book, *Les Opérations de la 1re armée dans les Flandres*, appeared in June 1921 (Paris: L. Fournier) and again is based on his diaries. As a staff officer on the attacking force, Delvert details the build-up and progress of the offensive of 31 July–2 November 1917 across the river Lys towards Houthulst Forest.

Delvert then temporarily abandoned military history. His next published work was a speech delivered at a prize-giving at the Lycée d'Amiens in 1924: *Discours prononcé par M. Charles Delvert, professeur agrégé d'histoire, à la distribution des prix, le samedi 12 juillet 1924, sous la présidence de M. Armand Tumel, avocat, président de l'Association des anciens élèves* (Amiens: Imprimerie du Progrès de la Somme). *L'Algérie* (Paris: Hachette, 1930) was informed by his round-the-world trip, and that same year he also published a school textbook designed for *baccalauréat* students: *Memento: Histoire contemporaine depuis le milieu du XIXe siècle, 1848–1920* (Paris: Émile Croville).

In 1932 Delvert returned to his wartime service, contributing the Verdun chapter to *La Guerre racontée par les combattants* (Paris: Flammarion), using some of his front-line experiences to illustrate a more general account. *Carnets d'un fantassin* (1935) was his final major work.

Delvert was by no means unique in keeping a diary and using it as the basis of an autobiographical memoir. Yet so succinct was his writing that it required little further editing. There is no question of 'horrors recollected in tranquility'. The majority of the printed text is exactly as written at the time, supplemented only by material added by the author in 1917. Delvert even records the moment a shell exploded and made his pen jerk, producing a blot on the page.

Such immediacy and authenticity made an instant impression. The writer Henry Bordeaux borrowed Delvert's diaries for two pieces on the fall of Fort Vaux, first published in the *Revue des deux mondes*, October 1916, and later as *Les Derniers Jours du fort de Vaux* (Paris: Plon, 1916). Bordeaux used the diaries almost verbatim, making changes only to further his propagandist aims. Jean Norton Cru, the compiler of the critical bibliography *Témoins* (Paris: Les Étincelles, 1929), believed that memoirs and novels, if exaggerated or untruthful, served only to disguise the reality of war, making it almost attractive to those ignorant of its true nature. In comparing Bordeaux's work with Delvert's original, he was scathing in his conclusions: 'Henry Bordeaux's book has received a number of glowing reviews. However, its worth depends entirely on his borrowings from the vivid writings of Delvert and the work of the abbé Cabanel.[1] Adapted to the public taste by a propagandist like Bordeaux, the vigorous, lively and honest text of a combatant emerges emasculated and distorted. Sadly, readers and critics are much more familiar with the Bordeaux version than with Delvert's original, serving only to conceal the merits of one of the best author combatants.'

Cru continued to champion Delvert's diaries. Their value, he argued, lay in their faithful reflection of life in the trenches. Delvert *was there*; Bordeaux was not. 'I have my own definition of a "war book",' wrote Cru, 'one that no other review, newspaper or elsewhere, has come up with: [that is,] a book by a combatant describing his own experiences. We are hypnotized by historical novels and histories, by the books of Madelin Le Goffic, Bordeaux, Victor Giraud, not to mention types like Mangin and all the other brass-hats and Young Turks. Why speak to the saints when you can address God? [The accounts of actual combatants] are what matters. Ask the eyewitness, not the bystander.'

When reviewing *Témoins* in the *Revue des deux mondes*, 1 December 1929, Delvert admitted the difficulty of preparing his diaries for publication and doubted the appetite of the reading public. '[There are] too many myths, too many preconceived ideas for [eyewitness accounts] to achieve acceptance. Once upon a time, the [public] wanted a romanticized version of the war, flags fluttering in the breeze; today it wants something no less fictitious, trenches filled with grotesque, grimacing corpses ...'

Delvert believed some authors took advantage of the editing process 'to spin things out, to develop and dilute. The firm, direct language of the front line disappears, to be replaced by its polar opposite – a language allusive and refined, that of the modern novelist. The truth – literary and historical – emerges primarily from rough notes, which reveal life as it appeared to the combatant, as participant as well as eyewitness. Edited notes resemble a painting completed in the peace of the studio. Raw notes are a canvas painted *en plein air*, infinitely more evocative than a more considered work.'

---

1. Translator's note: Cabanel was padre to a battalion of chasseurs alpins at Fort Vaux and author of *Avec les diables bleus* (Paris: Beauchesne, 1916).

This is one reason for the use of contemporary memoirs in my previous works, *They Shall Not Pass* and *Kings of the Air*. Contemporary eyewitness statements are of inestimable value, simply because they are contemporary, unmodified by later opinion and 'found' memories. In *14–18: retrouver la guerre* (Gallimard, 2000), Stéphane Audoin-Rouzeau and Annette Becker underplay the role of eyewitness accounts, arguing that it is impossible to disentangle them from the culture that produced the individual soldier. But this is to throw the baby out with the bathwater. Eyewitness accounts should be treated as sources like any other, to be interpreted within their historical context, not discounted or ignored.

The names of trenches (*tranchée*), communication trenches (*boyau*) and geographical features (for example, *côte*/hill, *ferme*/farm) have been retained in the original French. Delvert anonymizes many individuals in his narrative, referring to them by a single letter, asterisk or combination of asterisks. Individuals have been identified wherever possible, while a glossary of personal names provides supporting biographical information. A glossary of place names is also provided, with a note of the modern *département*. All names are alphabetized by the first significant word. Delvert's original footnotes have been supplemented where necessary to elucidate points unclear to the modern Anglophone reader. The opportunity has also been taken to correct some misspellings and minor errors in dates. All insertions by the translator are enclosed within square brackets.

My thanks go to my wife Margaret for her translating and editing skills, as well as my commissioning editor Rupert Harding and copy editor Sarah Cook for their help and apparently limitless reserves of patience. The translator and publishers are most grateful to Vincent Delvert for the support he has given them during the translation of his grandfather's diary.

Preface

The time has come when authentic first-hand accounts of the First World War can be published. It is over seventeen years since the armistice. A new generation has reached maturity. The agonizing slaughter of Humanity already belongs to the past. A plethora of works on the conflict has since appeared. Few would satisfy the historian, but the controversies they have provoked have at least prepared readers to accept the truth.

That truth will be found in the day-by-day diaries of eyewitnesses.

The undisputed model for this type of publication are the *Carnets de Gallieni*. The Grand Old Man of colonial soldiering and victor of the Marne kept a diary almost daily from 1 January 1914 to 19 April 1916, recording anything he judged significant with a view to later writing his memoirs. Messrs Gaëtan Gallieni and P.-B. Gheusi have edited the three volumes with scrupulous care, simply adding explanatory notes where necessary – a decision that works admirably.

Although not directly inspired by their example – for I, too, have always thought this the only way to proceed – I have adopted the same method for these diaries of a humble infantryman. I was mobilized as a reserve lieutenant, and the seven diaries presented here cover my service from Friday 7 August 1914 to Wednesday 16 August 1916, with a gap from Saturday 26 September 1914 to Wednesday 10 November 1915, after I was seriously wounded following the battle of the Marne, at the start of the 'Race to the Sea'.

Book 1 runs from 7 August to 25 September 1914. It is a 14.5cm x 9.5cm notebook. It contains 76 pages – some written in pencil, others in ink – and was carried by me as commander of Second Platoon, 4th Company, 101st Infantry.[1]

---

1. Translator's note: Delvert's platoon consisted of c.60 men, divided into four sections, each commanded by a corporal. Two sections formed a half-platoon, commanded by a sergeant. Each platoon was commanded by a commissioned officer (lieutenant or sous-lieutenant) or warrant officer (adjudant), four platoons forming a company. Each company was commanded by a captain, four companies forming a battalion, each commanded by a senior captain or a major. 101st Infantry contained three battalions. The regiment was commanded by a colonel, assisted by a lieutenant colonel, two regiments forming a

It also includes the nominal roll by section of the two half-platoons, plus tenting and tool-carrying arrangements. For use as a diary I simply turned the book over and started from the other end.

The other six diaries are all written in ink: Book 2 (11 November 1915–25 March 1916, 17cm x 10cm) contains 170 written pages; Book 3 (26 March–20 April 1916, 14cm x 9cm), 58 pages; Book 4 (21 April–30 May 1916, 14cm x 9cm), 78 pages, plus a continuation sheet attached to the page for 5 May; Book 5 (30 May–2 July 1916, 16cm x 10.5cm), 50 pages, plus six loose sheets attached as follows – two to 1 June, one to 3 June, two to 4 June and one to 5 June. Book 6 (3 July–15 August 1916, 14cm x 9.5cm) is bound in mauve. It contains 84½ pages, initially written in black ink, then in blue. Book 7 (14cm x 9cm, 15–16 August) is written in blue-black ink and like the first five volumes is covered in waxed black cloth.

The handwriting is small and fairly neat throughout. My pen slipped when a shell exploded on 2 June 1916, scratching the paper and causing a blot, but the writing then resumes as fluently as ever. The few instances of crossing out and overwriting are all contemporary. A handful of faint pencil instructions were added by the typist who typed up the diaries.

The text is divided into three sections. Part One, 'Early Battles', contains the whole of Book 1 and describes the covering operations in the Hauts-de-Meuse (Mangiennes, 10 August 1914), the battle of the Frontiers (Ethe, 22 August 1914), the retreat, the battle of the Marne and the initial stages of the Race to the Sea. Part Two, 'History of a Company', comprises Books 2, 3, 4 and 5. It tells the story of 8th Company, 101st Infantry Regiment, re-formed after the Champagne offensive of 25 September 1915 and wiped out while defending Fort Vaux (1 June–5 June 1916). Part Three, 'In a Quiet Sector', comprises Books 6 and 7, which kept me going in the trenches of Maisons-de-Champagne, supposedly a quiet sector in the summer of 1916.

[My diary entries are supplemented by a number] of later additions. In 'Early Battles', these provide extra information drawn from a version of the diary based on the original and written in 1917. I was still very close to the events, and my memories were fresh and wholly reliable. ... The additions gradually tail off and eventually disappear entirely: I had trained myself to record events in full at the time. 'History of a Company' includes a handful of additions. They too date

---

brigade. 101st Infantry was part of 13th Brigade. Two brigades, plus supporting artillery, formed an infantry division. 101st Infantry belonged to 7th Division until June 1915, then 124th Division until the end of the war.

from 1917, just a year after the events described, and are, I believe, relatively trivial: by then I was an experienced diarist, accustomed to noting what I saw. 'In a Quiet Sector' is just the original text.

Finally notes have been added to cover points since remembered or requiring further explanation.

I can thus now lay before the public a series of wholly authentic war diaries for the two greatest battles in history – the battle of the Frontiers/battle of the Marne and the battle of Verdun.[1]

A simple, factual account.

Charles Delvert

'We will leave our dead in the trench as a reminder. There they are, stiff in their blood-soaked tent sections. I recognize them still: Cosset, in his corduroy trousers; Aumont, poor soul; Delahaye, the red-haired "Bamboula", who extends a waxy hand, so wonderfully adept at grenade-throwing; and many more – fierce, sombre guardians of this corner of French soil, seemingly eager, even in death, to bar it to the enemy.'

Captain DELVERT
Trenches of Fort Vaux
5 June 1916

---

1. Approximately 315,00 men were killed during the battle of the Frontiers/battle of the Marne (August–September 1914); around 400,000 at the battle of Verdun. These encounters alone account for over half the French war dead.

Book One

Early Battles

They grumbled but still they marched.

IN THE EVENT OF MY DEATH, I LEAVE THIS DIARY TO MY COMRADE
H. FOCILLON, 7 RUE DE L'ESTRAPADE, PARIS, PROFESSOR AT THE
UNIVERSITY OF LYON.[1]

Friday 7 August 1914
2.30pm. Left from Saint-Cloud.[2]
Women with drawn faces, no more tears to shed. 'Au revoir! Au revoir!'
Handkerchiefs wave half-heartedly. The countryside looks splendid. Sky grey. It
rained all morning and throughout our embarkation. Very forlorn for troops who
are victory bound. Everyone was cheering us on. Sèvres, Ville-d'Avray, wooded
hillsides. All in full bloom. Amid the greenery, villas with carefully tended gardens.

Saturday 8 August
Arrived Reims, 4.00 am. Directed to Dugny, outside Verdun.

9.30 am. At Vienne-la-Ville. A halt. The sun has come out. Beads of water
sparkle on the leaves. Two horses graze peacefully in a bright green meadow. A
flight of pigeons over by the tall poplars. The harvest is almost home.

---

1. Now at the Sorbonne.
2. We arrived at 101st Infantry's depot at Saint-Cloud on Sunday 2 August. No stone had
   been left unturned to ensure the mobilization proceeded according to plan, and it all
   went like clockwork. The early August weather was idyllic. We lieutenants and sous-
   lieutenants strolled down to the Pavillon Bleu each evening for an aperitif. Many believed
   the war would never happen: 'They'll keep us here for a month or so, then send us home.'
       I disagreed. I had noticed the ambition and bellicosity of the German people when
   visiting the country a few years earlier.
       'Then the war will be over quickly – a month, six weeks at most.'
       'No,' I replied. 'It'll be a long one. Three months at least.'
       I – like most Frenchmen, I believe – never dreamed that, after forty-three years of
   preparation, the opening battles would show us so inferior in ideas and resources, that ten
   départements would spend four years under enemy occupation.

Sunday 9 August

Disembarkation, followed by a gruelling 28-kilometre march from Dugny to Brabant-sur-Meuse. Left in full sun at 1.00 pm.[1] Slow progress with endless hold-ups. Finally arrived at 10.00 pm. The last two hours were dreadful. The men were worn out, dragging themselves along in total chaos. I wondered what would happen if we were shelled. It would produce a mad stampede.

Today is Sunday. Gorgeous countryside: all meadows and orchards. Bright with sunshine and greenery, full of birdsong.

We're billeted with Pa and Ma Hyacinthe. Cagey peasants, aged around 50 or 60. He's a scrawny fellow, thoroughly henpecked. All you can hear are her shrill tones: 'Hyacinthe! Hyacinthe!' Every time she turns her back, he grimaces. 'Hyacinthe!' she shrieks again – and the poor fellow shrugs and follows orders.

Monday 10 August

In a wood in advance of Haut-Fourneau, the Bois de Billy-sous-Mangiennes. Artillery fire. Beautiful sky. Amid the thunder of the guns and the crackle of rifle fire, two butterflies are chasing each other.

At each of the three exits from the wood we have built a log abatis reinforced by support trenches.[2] It is 3.00 am. We're waiting. The gunfire is unremitting. The band, colour and transport of 102nd Infantry pass on the road from Billy-sous-Mangiennes to Haut-Fourneau. Three batteries from 26th Artillery take up position at the edge of a wood to our right. Two guns remain buried up to their axles in the soft ground. More teams are quickly summoned as reinforcements. The guns are dragged out. They fire.

Lieutenant Colonel Ferran orders me to take my platoon and go protect the batteries on our right. I skirt the edge of the woods. When I reach the guns, the artillery captain asks me to cover a ravine. We drop down through the wood. It's full of hoof-prints but not from our horses. I send patrols to investigate.

I settle my men at the edge of the wood, opposite the hillside descending to Billy-sous-Mangiennes. We have an extensive view ahead of us. To the

---

1. In an infantry company only the captain received 1:80,000 maps. Platoon commanders were given 1:200,000 scale – admittedly right up to the Rhine. This shortage of maps hampered us immediately, especially after our captain was wounded and evacuated on 22 August. A few days later I had to assume command of the company and lead it without adequate maps.

2. The men were still in the habit of using trenches. Not so their generals, as will soon become apparent.

north-east, the villages are burning. One, two, three, four columns of smoke rise into the sky. Behind us the rumble of the guns. Plumes of white smoke billow out, marking the fall of shells. Night falls over the countryside – a lovely, still summer evening. I hear the artillery captain order the limbers brought up. He comes to tell me to withdraw.

Back at the entrance to the wood, the first wounded. One has his head wrapped in a bloodstained bandage. No transport to evacuate them. They remain calm.

We dine in front of a tumble-down house, in the pitch dark, lit only by the fire burning under a cook-pot sizzling with boiling oil. Sleep in the hay with my men, still in my boots.

Tuesday 11 August

Wake at 4.00 am. Billeted in Le Fourneau. Nobody gets washed. Everyone is cheerful, cracking jokes. Such insouciance!

Some of the wounded pass by. 'What does it feel like?' ask the men.

'A brief sting, that's all …'

They make it sound quite natural.

Around 9.00 am we pull back to Azannes. The heat is already oppressive and makes the march tough going. Retreating through the woods we crossed yesterday is very demoralizing. 'It's a manoeuvre,' I say. 'The generals want all their troops on hand.' But the men are not convinced by my explanations.

It's been confirmed that yesterday's battle was very hard. Two battalions of 130th Infantry were really put to the test. According to a sous-lieutenant from 14th Hussars, one battalion was surprised by a hail of shells while taking a meal break in a field. The other was ordered to advance 800–900 metres and attack a machine-gun platoon.[1] The men arrived exhausted at a ditch full of water and were mown down. He says 80 were killed and 250 wounded, a figure confirmed by a maréchal des logis who saw them burying the bodies.

We're billeted in Azannes. I hurry to find somewhere to cook, introducing myself to a lady who offers me her kitchen and dining-room. She's no 'Madame Hyacinthe'. A lieutenant from 115th Infantry stayed with her three days ago and she asks anxiously after the regiment. I have no news.

Sent to cover the intersection of the Mangiennes and Montmédy roads. [Lieutenant] Le Roch, who is holding the Mangiennes road, has ordered his men to dig two trenches. I do likewise on the Montmédy road. Endless columns

---

1. The criminal lunacy of this manoeuvre is clear. After the attack failed, we opened up with our guns and reduced both machine guns to scrap metal within minutes.

of wounded pass by, bouncing around in haywains on a thin bed of straw. A young graduate of Saint-Cyr, like de Bragelongne or de Laval[1], lies senseless, his body quivering with every jolt of the cart. He has a bullet in his head.

Wrapped in my waterproof cape, I sleep under the stars, on a bale of straw in a ditch. Woken all night by cries of: 'Halt! Who goes there?'

'France.'

'Advance with the password.'

'Nevers.'

'Pass.'

Wednesday 12 August

Weather still glorious. Rolling hills covered in crops, wooded valleys.

11.00am. Installed as advance guard in the Bois des Nouelles. Dense stands of oak slumber beneath the blazing sun. On the main road all is quiet. Just the odd whinny of a horse or glimpse of red uniform trousers to show these are extraordinary times. In the woods behind the trenches, the men have fashioned shelters out of branches. They sleep oblivious to the death awaiting them just a few kilometres away, anxious only to 'dodge the column' as if they were still on the ranges at Garches.

The French soldier may be steady under fire; he may have plenty of 'go'. But he talks too much, he doesn't take things seriously. He refuses to believe we're not on annual manoeuvres. In short, he hasn't been trained properly.

We covered 28 kilometres on the first day, and almost as far again (22 kilometres) on the second. All you could hear was moaning. I know the heat is terrible, but still ... Then some great, slack-jawed buffoon of an MO came to tell the colonel that the regiment is being overworked! ... I suppose things will settle down after a few days on campaign.

Thursday 13 August

We camped in the Bois des Nouelles, in shelters made from branches. Mine is conical with twigs concealing the entrance. The sun filters in, making the

---

1. Two sous-lieutenants in our battalion, both fresh from Saint-Cyr. 'They handed us revolvers and sent us to the front.' And they did initially carry a revolver, unholstered, stuck into their belt. Both were killed: Laval on 22 August 1914; de Bragelongne on 31 August 1914. I cannot say whether or not they donned white gloves on 22 August. [Note: a reference to an oath sworn by some Saint-Cyr cadets in 1914 to wear their uniform white gloves when they first went into action.]

dew glisten on the leaves. Salvoes are audible ahead and to our left, north of Mangiennes. Wagons passed us yesterday, bringing back the rifles and packs abandoned by 130th Infantry.

The guns have been rumbling all night. We must be moving forward.

This wood is delightful. Beyond our outpost line, all is silence, shade and brilliant light. The birds are singing somewhat nervously; their sanctuary has been disturbed by uninvited guests.

The French soldier is an extraordinary fellow. Some men have brought a fishing-line from Paris: they have cut a thin branch for a rod and are fishing in a pond. Each is fully equipped, ammunition pouch around his waist, since the enemy is only 2 or 3 kilometres away. We can hear the odd burst of rifle fire and must be ready to move as soon as we receive the order.

They see me passing: 'Fancy a fry-up, sir?'

Must thought and action always be incompatible? Unlike my two comrades, both regular officers, military matters are not my only preoccupation. Right now, the sweetness of this beautiful summer morning suffuses my entire being. The campaign is far from my mind.... But on picket duty yesterday I could think of nothing else.

Friday 14 August

Yesterday we returned to Azannes for a rest! The village is vile. Dung-heaps in front of every door, pools of liquid manure.

'How can you live with this stench, *madame*?' I asked one local.

'What do you expect, *monsieur*? We need a proper downpour to wash it away.'

I think of the villages in occupied Lorraine, now so clean and tidy under German administration. Despite our coming victory, I hope we will follow the example of the vanquished.

The room we slept in was vile. I flung myself fully clothed on the mattress, but it did nothing to stop the fleas.

This morning – through a curtain of gauzy pink mist – we returned to the edge of the Bois des Nouelles and the trenches we occupied yesterday. I am on the left. The trenches are camouflaged with branches.[1] In front are lines of barbed wire. I have them reinforced with entanglements. The rest of 1st Battalion is further forward at Mangiennes.

---

1. General de T[rentinian], divisional commander (7th Division), made us fill them in again: 'What have we got here? ... Trenches! ... To hell with that! They'll hold up our offensive!'

Lieutenant Sivan returns with a Bavarian boiled-leather shako. Excellent. I'd rather one of those than a kepi.

A hundred metres beyond the Bois des Nouelles, a farm has been ransacked. Wardrobe gutted, linen soaked in blood, mattress and bedstead upside down, broken glass and china on a torn satin dress. In the other room, a brand new engine in pieces. A ginger cat stalking through the wreckage ran off at our approach. The culprits were a platoon from 115th Infantry. Apparently the farmer's wife told them she wanted to save her wine for the Prussians. It's the umpteenth time I've heard this tale. No one has ever said this to me personally, but I've seen houses stripped, nay plundered, everywhere we go. How are these poor souls to live? The soldiers are incredibly stupid in their demands. They insist on wine in a region that doesn't produce it.

Saturday 15 August

Bivouacked at the entrance to Mangiennes. Arrived in the darkness, lit by the flames of the cooking fires. I slept rolled up in my waterproof cape beside the straw bales commandeered earlier by Captain [Cauvin], Lieutenant [Bourguignon] and [Lieutenant] B[enoit].

In the morning we found billets in Mangiennes. Dung everywhere, like every Lorraine village.

Yesterday we fired on a Taube. Of course, we missed it. Lieutenant [Bourguignon] was so thrilled with this feat of arms that he went to report it to Major [Lebaud].

'I know,' said the major. 'I wasn't best pleased either. The men just blazed away. All they did was reveal our position.'

Quite so.

Lieutenant Bourguignon was livid: 'I'm sorry my first *initiative* doesn't meet with your approval, sir.'

Initiative!

He must be barmy.[1]

---

1. Nevertheless, a sound chap and very brave soldier. A heavy-jawed colossus. Tawny hair; small, twinkling blue eyes; a tough 'wild boar of the Ardennes', whence he came. He was one of those bright young working-class boys ('I'm a mechanic by trade,' he often confessed) who stayed on after discharge and made his career in the army. He was a lieutenant at Saint-Cyr when war broke out and joined us in his *garance* trousers with their sky-blue stripe down the outside of each leg. His party piece (he was famous for it) was fencing against a bayonet with his infantry officer's sabre. Our ideas of combat were

His comrade Lieutenant Benoit is 27 or 28 years old. Trim, fair, thin moustache, pince-nez. He was a quartermaster when I first got to know him during the 1912 manoeuvres. When war broke out, he was at Saint-Maixent. He was commissioned as a sous-lieutenant and sent to join the regiment. He is still full of the teachings of the École (with a capital É). 'At the École,' he says constantly. He expounds on strategy, especially when I'm around. Such innocent conceit is a delight to behold, if a little wearing after a time.

Smiling wryly, Captain [Cauvin] lets him rattle on. The captain is a zouave who has already seen action. He's 40, average height, close-cut brown hair, handlebar moustache; regular features, prematurely lined; strong chin; pale complexion. He's trim, aloof and unemotional, although his careworn expression occasionally dissolves in a roar of youthful laughter. He seems thoughtful, solid and cool. A natural leader, the type who inspires confidence. Over dinner he told us the old chestnut about Christ and Mohammed crossing the wadi: Christ on a donkey, Mohammed on a lion.

I managed to keep a straight face.

Sunday 16 August

It rained this morning. Wagons pass piled high with the equipment of the two battalions of 130th Infantry wiped out on 10 August. Left for Pillon at 11.30 am.

Called at the Red Cross post in Mangiennes yesterday. Saw a hussar who had been captured by the Germans. He was tied between two horses and forced to run like that for 150 metres before his squadron rescued him. He was writhing on the bed, weeping and shouting[1] 'I want to kill the lot of them.'

Saw a German from 13th Hussars, pale from loss of blood, a bullet in his chest. I asked him if he was glad to be fighting us.

'*Ach, nein!*'

He was a Saxon. Nothing like our men! Cooler, thinner, harder features perhaps. Our men seem more cheerful, even the wounded.

---

so deluded that we expected soon to be following suit. Almost everyone had taken his weapon for sharpening, including me. 'Just watch,' [he] said. 'I'll show you what to do.' But he never got the chance. The battle of Ethe a week later put an end to any interest in sabres and bayonets. Our sabres were relegated to the company transport and remained there for the duration. They only came out for parades.

1. Eyes closed, punching the mattress, crimson with rage.

(Lieutenant Bourguignon came in too when he heard about the 'Fritz'. Of course he got the wrong man, picking out a little bloke from 14th Hussars just because he was fair.)

Billeted that evening at Pillon. The Germans have literally ransacked the place, emptying out any bottles of wine and spirits they left undrunk. They raped the women,[1] burned down the houses. All the walls are scorched and crumbling. On the charred wall of the post office is an enamel plaque – all that remains of the 'Telephone Booth'. Poor folk reduced to the clothes on their backs wander distraught through the wreckage. It looks like a horde of savages has passed this way. The world must be told that the Germans have transgressed the bounds of humanity. By all reports they were using some kind of accelerant to make the houses burn faster.

'They threw pellets through the door,' said one man. 'A minute later the whole place was on fire.'

I stopped one wretch stumbling from house to house. Tall, scrawny, unkempt grey hair, oily skin, clad only in trousers and a dirty, half-open shirt, feet bare in shoes without laces.

'They took everything, lieutenant. They stripped me naked and threw me outside.' He pointed to the rags that covered him. 'A neighbour gave me these.'

Monday 17 August
Billeted at Pillon.

According to the locals, the Prussians marched through the village boasting 'Verdun in three days, Paris in five.' They were rather less cocky after the battle of Mangiennes, tossing aside their equipment, lances and rifles as they fled ...

We're billeted in one of the few houses to remain intact. The husband, wife and children move about in total silence, eyes darting everywhere. They seem haunted by fear that the savages will return.

'Not a word! Let's not put ourselves in danger! What if "they" come back!'

Spend all day on picket duty in a farm.

The green fields slope down to a stream running slowly between the willows towards the Othain.

---

1. I approached a woman of 40 of so – tallish, brown hair, still pretty. After a brief conversation, I asked her gently if the rumours were true. I can still see her shake her head sadly. 'I mustn't say anything ...' she whispered. 'It would be wrong ... It happened to us all.' The tone of her voice was enough to tell me that 'all' brooked no exceptions. Similar enquiries conducted by the Abbé Lelièvre produced vigorous denials (see Cru, Jean Norton, *Témoins*, p. 174). This explains why.

A beautiful summer day, restful and calm. Blue sky, glorious sunshine – hot but not oppressively so amid the greenery. The leaves of the tall poplars quiver in the light breeze. Beyond a culvert, a red patch in the grass: the trousers of the sentry guarding the exit of the narrow track climbing from the south-east, through the Bois de Warphemont.

Tuesday 18 August

Left Pillon for Villers-lès-Mangiennes. The whole army must be moving north. Our troops have reportedly captured Mulhouse and abandoned it again. Depressing. I won't mention it to the men.

At the cemetery in Villers-lès-Mangiennes, I spot the new grave of Sous-lieutenant Marcadet of 91st Infantry, 'killed in action'. I swallow hard, feeling instinctively for my identity disk … I return to our billet: window open on a garden bright with greenery and sunshine.

Nabbed for a game of poker. You can only admire the carefree good cheer of my comrades. Lieutenant Bourguignon is seated at the table with Captain Ségonne and Sous-lieutenant [Glandaz] of 2nd Company. I make up the quartet. Lieutenant Bourguignon drinks, smokes and honks like a seal. He 'shuffles' the cards with his big fingers, mopping his brow with the heat. His hoarse voice dominates proceedings.

'Fold … I'll open with ten … Ten more … Pat?'

Ségonne and G[landaz] hold their tongues, like real club-men.

All we're worried about right now is a full house, a flush or four of a kind.

Wednesday 19 August

Billeted at Villers-lès-Mangiennes. A horse wounded by shrapnel had been lying there on its side since the battle on 10 August. Poor thing. It tried to stand, flayed and pathetic. A bunch of soldiers were gathered round, pulling on its mouth with morbid curiosity.

The nag was chewing miserably on some straw. I sent its tormentors packing, and it fell down dead. Tomorrow we'll cover it with straw and bury it.

Our billet is a low room with scorched beams, cheap religious prints on the walls, piss-yellow beds full of vermin. These houses in Lorraine are indescribably filthy inside. The people wallow like pigs in muck … Our presence scares them stiff. Although they've been assured that they'll be resupplied from the rear, they won't give us a thing. They want to keep something back for the Prussians.

Thursday 20 August

Still at Villers. When will we move forward? Beautiful sky. The red roofs of Villers huddle among the trees. Flowers – purple, white and yellow – fill the fields running down to the Loison.

At the foot of the hill, soldiers in red trousers mill around between stream and houses, calmly doing their laundry as if they were on manoeuvres. On the tops, the harvest is drawing to a close, war or no war ... But for the occasional dull rumble of distant guns, no one would believe we are at war. A deep silence envelops the woods, the fields, the little village and its pointed steeple, bells ringing as they did in happier days.

Why did Germany embark upon a war she could have avoided until the very last moment? I accept that it is useful, necessary even, to human progress.[1] But to Germany herself? A certain fatalism governs the affairs of men. The world was growing accustomed to brutal Teuton hegemony. Her current regime could have lasted for years. With a few conciliatory measures in Alsace, Schleswig and Poznan, a little moderation of her demands, a few concessions over arms, the Kaiser's government – representing authority, conservatism, the enduring power of the old noble and military oligarchies – could have maintained its global power indefinitely.

This war will mark the end of the counter-revolution. The forces of reaction will be defeated. Germany, like the other nations of Western Europe, will become a parliamentary democracy. Good or bad? I don't know, but it's a fact. It breaks my heart to see regular officers fighting a war that will sooner or later result in arms limitation and universal peace; i.e. whatever the compensations, in their own demise.[2] And the most extraordinary aspect of this wholly extraordinary crisis is that many would agree with this sentiment.

Friday 21 August

Marching towards La Tour. Cloudy skies. Heavy atmosphere. Gun and rifle fire all day. We're pushing back hostile elements, probably withdrawing after the battle of Dinant.[3] A prisoner, a reservist from 2nd Württemberg Uhlans, seemingly pleased with his fate. He's a factory hand from Stuttgart, a big soft lump of a lad. He slumps on a pile of straw. The Germans are in Warsaw, he

---

1. Discounting German brutality. We were all confident of victory: our preparation, our 75s, our allies ... Britain's declaration of war had removed the last lingering doubts.
2. This naturally seems rather less certain today (1935).
3. We had heard vague rumours of the battle. Of course we believed it a French victory.

says, and cholera is rife in the Russian army. 'Germany has set up a cordon sanitaire' so it can turn all its forces on France.[1]

Torrential rain leaving the Bois de Charency.

Arrive at Malmaison, evacuated by the Germans, at 9.00 pm.

We're exhausted. It's pitch black. The quartermaster takes us to the barn assigned to our platoon. The corporals light their lanterns. The four sections divvy up the billet, three sleeping downstairs while the fourth climbs a ladder to a loft above some sort of stable or storeroom.

A corner has been set aside for me.

We need fresh straw: that used by the Germans is a stinking mess. Then all we want is something to eat. A problem. All the troops passing through have bled the place dry. [Lieutenant] Benoit (our mess officer) and I each take a different direction and between us manage to scare up a dozen eggs, a few rashers of bacon and a big round loaf. At midnight, by the light of a candle planted in the neck of a bottle, we devour the last omelette we will eat in France.

Saturday 22 August
Leaving at 3.30 am.

It is still not quite daylight. A damp, grey dawn. The nights are getting colder already. I rub my eyes, a few taps to shake the straw. I button my tunic, holster my revolver with a flick of the wrist, buckle my belt. I stow my forage cap in my pack and set my kepi, in its blue cover,[2] on my head.

'Chevalier! Take my greatcoat.'

Chevalier is my orderly. A beardless youth from the class of 1913. Somewhat below average height, but stocky and strong. Regular features, handsome enough. Chestnut hair. Very brown eyes, unremarkable, but wily nonetheless. A farmer from the Mayenne, rather soft and slow, but tenacious. Gets the job done without fuss. He takes the waterproof, rolls it up carefully, cinches it with the belt from a soldiers' greatcoat and sticks it beneath his arm.

'My sword!'

'Here, sir.'

---

1. Cholera apart, his information was correct. The Germans were planning to combine their forces, crush the French army, then turn and face the Russians.
2. We later had blue overtrousers to conceal our red ones. Eventually, we received our new pattern uniforms.

That's the sum total of my ablutions. We're ready for the off. Ready to march to victory.

Outside, I can already hear the orderly sergeant: 'Fall in!'

5.00 am. The road is climbing. The sun rises in a halo, its dazzling rays tinting the thin mist pink. This is beautiful rolling country. Wooded hilltops, valleys swathed in mist, green slopes beneath a blue sky.

We cross the Belgian frontier. We've left France behind. My heart sinks, something I've never experienced crossing the border as a tourist.

On the downhill road, the regiment forms a long dark ribbon, streaked by silver glinting off the mess-tins.[1]

6.00 am. Arrive at Grandcourt. A decent enough road – wide, smooth, no ruts, densely shaded by trees. We stop at the entrance to the village. Some gunners pass by. They got here yesterday evening. The Belgians greeted them enthusiastically, handing out bottles and cigars. They do the same for my men, who are delighted by the windfall.

We rest behind our piled weapons.

'The French are here. I can stop worrying now,' says a woman in a house by the road, in advance of the village. 'I slept with my window open last night.'

Her son is a tall, slim 18-year-old, dark-brown hair, placid and slow moving. He watches quietly from the front door, hands thrust deep in his pockets.

I get my men to pass him a few buckets so he can fetch some water. He hurries away, but he's much less elated than his mother.

'Have the Germans been here?'

He nods: 'They were round here a fortnight ago.'

'Pah! We'll give 'em what for.'

A whistle blows. 'Packs on!'

We're off again.

'Au revoir! Au revoir!'

I turn round. The woman is waving her handkerchief.

We march towards Ruette. The fog is still with us. In fact, it seems to be growing thicker.[2] We cross the railway line. 26th Artillery is now on the right

---

1. The Germans bronzed their mess-tins. A seemingly minor point. Wrong, a very important detail. How many reliefs were annihilated, betrayed by their glinting mess-tins? I return to the subject, 17 May 1916.
2. The 'Ethe fog' remained notorious within the regiment. We blamed it for our bloody defeat on that dreadful day.

of the road, while we are on the left. We come to the first houses of Gomery. With the column of guns and ammunition wagons alongside us we're too tightly packed to move.

Suddenly artillery and rifle fire. The rattle of machine-guns in the fog. A murmur spreads through the ranks: 'The Germans are 200 metres away!'

Pandemonium among the artillery.

Orders go back and forth.

The batteries want to turn round. But how? One gun flips over while crossing the roadside ditch. The drivers shout, the horses shy. Through the fog, the gunfire redoubles in intensity.

'Forward!'

The road swings up and left through Gomery. A hussar captain shouts at us as we enter the village: 'Go get 'em!'

'We'll aim for the base of the target,[1] sir.'

Horses streaming with crimson blood are blocking the main street. We grind to a halt. In an open barn to my left, a hussar is lying on a stretcher, very pale, tunic unbuttoned. His shirt is damp with big red stains. Another has his foot up on a post. He has ripped open his breeches and is bandaging a thigh wound with the help of a comrade.

We exit the houses and deploy[2] in a field bordered by a hedge. The artillery and rifle fire is deafening. Battle must be engaged right along the line. The captain is standing, arms folded, very calm and composed. I think he looks paler than usual, the lines on his face more pronounced. He never stops chewing his moustache. Inside, his mind must be racing.

'Delvert,' he barks. 'Bring up some ammunition!'

I call one of my corporals: 'Nicole, take eight men, two per section, and go back to the wagons.'

My heart had skipped a beat when I heard the captain's orders.[3]

Nicole returns with his men, bowing beneath the heavy cases.

'Come on! Four packets a man! Move!'

Nicole is a good chap, scarcely over 1.55 metres tall. Thin face, brown hair, black eyes, guttural Beauce accent. Not robust, but unrivalled energy and courage.

---

1. In accordance with regulations.
2. Fortunately, our battalion was leading the column. We could deploy easily.
3. Only then did I 'realize' battle was imminent. I had great respect for the captain as a leader with experience of action, and his order suddenly concentrated my mind on the dread unknown.

The distribution is soon complete. I snatch a few packets and stuff them in my pocket.

A runner approaches the captain.

Now is the hour: 8.30 am.

The captain gives his orders: [Lieutenant] B[enoit] will go left; [Lieutenant Bourguignon] right; Adjudant [Bes] will follow Lieutenant B[enoit], while I follow Lieutenant [Bourguignon].

'Maintain an interval of 300 metres.'[1]

We move forward. Vive la France!

We set off in columns of two, passing Colonel Farret at the corner of the cemetery. Short, stout, pince-nez, an ex-colonial. 'Go on!' he mutters. 'Forward!'

'Yes, sir!'

In bounds I reach the forward edge of the wood occupied by the remnants of Nth Infantry. The ridge is under particularly heavy fire so we have to cross in a single bound. We make it between two volleys.

Bullets whine on all sides – first a whine, then a whiplash.

I deploy my platoon beyond the forward edge of the wood, below the ridge. The right decision. Ten paces to the rear are shrapnel, bullets, etc. An ear-splitting din. The men remain quite calm, Boitier munching away beside me.[2] Behind us are the awful moans of the wounded. What madness possessed those who unleashed this war? The fields we crossed are stained crimson. Ahead of us the meadow descending to Ethe is filled with bodies clad in red trousers.

Gomery was full of wounded hussars, their horses drenched with crimson blood as if they had been in a bullfight.

What carnage! Hours pass. The deafening gunfire never slackens.

We can hear the cries of the wounded. A harrowing, drawn-out 'Here, sir! Here!'

---

1. This was too far apart; the platoons lost sight of each other. All movements were performed according to regulation, despite the myths that have since gained credence – some military men claiming that early in the campaign the platoons deployed either too close together or not at all.

   'During the battles of the Frontiers the infantry attacked in a gaggle – just like those nippers,' a regular officer told us one day, pointing to some children playing in a yard.

   'What regiment were you in?'

   'Me? I was the vet in Nth Cuirassiers.'

2. 'Damn it!' he said. 'I must have something to eat. Want a bite, sir?' He offered me half a loaf, which I accepted because I was ravenous.

Prone on my right, Corporal Chapelain, class of 1913,[1] fires away. Suddenly he drops his rifle. His head slumps forward. He moans softly.

'Oh, oh!'

'What's up?'

'I'm hit.'

'Where?'

'In the shoulder. Can I go back, sir?'

'Not now! Wait till I tell you!'

Behind us the music is louder still. The shrapnel shells are falling with the crack of huge hailstones.

Now isn't the time to go that way.

And still the gasps of the wounded.

1.00 pm – a lull.

'Chapelain! Go! Now! … Leave me your rifle.'

The poor lad crawls away.

'Thank you, sir!' he murmurs.

The Germans are retreating up the hillsides behind Ethe.[2] They are visible as dark lines in the fields. I issue my orders: 'Volley at 1000 metres! Ready! Fire!' The lines are flattened by a hail of gunfire. We've clearly halted them. The exchanges continue for another half hour. The enemy reform at the far left of the village and concentrate on our left. They infiltrate the woods. I spot a platoon directly in front of me, just 400 metres away.

'Ready! Fire!' Just a handful of men remain standing.

A lieutenant from 102nd Infantry comes to join me. This is a splendid vantage point. He's a machine-gun lieutenant. Average height, trim build, dark hair; calm, mild face. He has a white cloth around his neck: boils.

'My platoon is over there,' he says. 'Did you send out that patrol just now?'

'Yes!'[3]

Footsteps sound on the broken branches behind us. It's Adjutant [Bes].

'Where did you spring from?'

---

1. Tall, ash blond, very mild mannered.
2. So, at one point or another, both sides pulled back. We had also been told to retreat, but we were still unaware of the order, my captain having suffered wounds in both legs right at the start of the action. 7th Division inflicted such heavy losses on the enemy that the opposing V Corps was withdrawn from the line the following day.
3. I had despatched two patrols to check my position: one went right and found 102nd Infantry; the other went left and found no one.

'I followed you, sir.'[1]
'Where's your platoon?'
'There, 30 or 40 metres back.'
'Fine!' ...
The lieutenant from the 102nd departs.
'Sir! Sir! There! Opposite! They're heading for the wood.'
Adjudant [Bes] is behind me. He points to a skirmish line exiting a farmstead halfway up the hill. They're heading in single file for the trees.
'Volley fire! 400 metres! ... Between the farm and the wood! ... Aim! Fire!'
The mouse-grey uniforms hit the ground but are soon back on their feet.
'Fire at will! Same range!'
I grab Chapelain's rifle and fire along with the rest.[2]

4.30 pm. A sergeant runner from 102nd Infantry arrives to tell us his regiment is falling back, leaving my right flank in the air. My platoon and I are alone in the wood. Adjudant [Bes] is positioned to my rear, and I order him to cover the retreat. We leave the edge of the wood in a skirmish line, in textbook order, each sergeant in the centre of his half-platoon.
Bullets whistle by.
'Get down! Face the enemy! Fire!'
We retreat in bounds across the ground we covered that morning.
We make it back to Gomery and I lead my platoon in good order to Colonel [Farret].[3] He sends me forward to pick up some ammo from the 102nd. I am the only officer from 101st Infantry left in Gomery. I call everyone together.[4] I must appear confident.

---

1. He had got mixed up. He was meant to be supporting B[enoit].
2. In my eagerness to do my duty I didn't lie down all day. I ordered my men to adopt the prone position, but I remained kneeling – and I even felt guilty about that. I thought, perhaps justifiably, that lying down would damage my reputation in the eyes of my men. We were still unfamiliar with battlefield conditions, and our main summer manoeuvres had been a pretty poor training ground.
3. Colonel Farret was then in Gomery. I chanced towards the cemetery and found him where I'd left him that morning. 'You're all I have left,' he said. 'Go and deploy ... we must stop any pursuit.'
4. On the main street of Gomery I pulled together the stragglers from all four regiments in the division – the 101st, 102nd, 103rd and 104th. I can still see the sun-drenched road and the men forming up in front of the houses. I had almost 200, including my own platoon. I ordered the sergeants to step forward and organized three more platoons. So I set off in

A runner arrives with the colonel's orders. 'Fall back by the Ruette road. You're covering the retreat.'

Fine.

We reach the road. The guns are booming louder than ever. Their heavy artillery is hounding us. We can hear the odd shell rumbling through the branches before falling like a huge *marmite* [cauldron][1] in the fields around. A battery of 75s manages to get off four rounds before it is spotted and destroyed.

Colonel [Farret] is at the Ruette crossroads, Lieutenant Colonel Ferran beside him. [Ferran] stands erect – tall, sharp features, small drooping moustache. His face is ashen, expression strained. I spot the dressing on his left leg. He's been wounded.

'Nothing to worry about,' he says. 'Only a scratch.'

The road starts climbing. The setting sun bathes the hillside in a tawny glow. The colonel is marching beside me ...

Stretcher-bearers ... carrying the captain. I haven't seen him since this morning. He looks extremely pale.

'I'm sorry to meet you again in these circumstances, sir.'

'Not at all! Not at all! My pleasure.' He smiles.

'Goodbye, sir.'

'Goodbye, Delvert. And good luck!'

Grim, to be retreating like this. We recross the Belgian border. This time all the shutters are closed.[2] But the men know they have come through their baptism of fire and given a good account of themselves. At dusk, approaching La Malmaison, they raise their heads despite the dust and the fatigue.

'Halt! Left face!'

'Fall out! Pile weapons!'

Sous-lieutenant Thibaut, our signals officer, appears on the road. He gives me a hug. 'We thought we'd lost you for good, old chap. We thought you were dead like the rest! Serve, killed; Bonnieux, Tisserand, de Laval, Vallet, Battesti, Molinier, Schoenlaub, all dead. Ségonne wounded ... 2nd Battalion only has eighty men and two officers left.'[3]

---

good order, placing two platoons on the right and two on the left, while I stood in the middle of the road directing the retreat in echelons, one platoon firing while the other fell back. The Germans came no closer than 800 metres. They just pursued us with their artillery.

1. A name [for a heavy shell] that quickly became commonplace.
2. Even those of the woman who had greeted us so warmly that morning.
3. I spotted Lieutenant Dutrey, the senior of the two, silent and dejected, leading the remains of the battalion. By 23 August, 2nd Battalion comprised just two officers and 229 men,

A complete massacre!

He tells me what happened. The division was surprised in thick fog (I knew that already), forcing the cavalry to charge to disengage the general.[1] Lieutenant Colonel Hauteclocque was killed, two of his squadrons cut to pieces.

'But didn't they report yesterday that there was nothing in front of us?'[2]

'Yes, I can't understand it at all.'

The reconnaissance failure of the hussars before the surprise attack at Wissembourg on 4 August 1870 springs unbidden to mind. I wasn't expecting a repeat performance.[3]

---

i.e. not one officer had returned from the firing line. The regiment as a whole had lost a third (1,046) of its 3,300 men and 27 of its 62 officers, i.e. a half of all officers, excluding non-combatants – medical officer, bandmaster, signals officer, supply and administration officers (Colonel Lebaud, *Actes de guerre*, p. 39). Infantry losses remained proportionally higher among company officers than ordinary soldiers throughout the war, despite the claims made by some authors with little or no combat experience.

1. General Trentinian – small, trim, still a magnificent horseman at almost 80 – was renowned for his courage. As a young captain in 1893, he was first into Ouagadougou, the capital of Mossi, beating the English column by several hours to make sure we took possession of the country. At Ethe – our customary name for the battle of 22 August – he was part of the division's advance guard. 'The general will march with the advance guard,' stated his order from the previous day. He later told me that *'regulations demanded it'*. I believe him, but I'm not sure he was right. At 8.00 am, he was in Ethe with his escort, surrounded by the enemy. Colonel de Hauteclocque, commanding 14th Hussars, was forced to take two squadrons and charge to disengage him. It was almost noon by the time the general returned to 7th Division, which was thus left leaderless throughout the morning's battle.

   The order to withdraw was also given at noon. Did the French high command have sufficient information to take this decision?

   The diary (see above) shows that at 1.00 pm the Germans also withdrew.

2. In front of us was the German Fifth Army under the Crown Prince: V Corps, XIII Corps, VI Reserve Corps, XVI Corps and V Reserve Corps; i.e. three active corps and two reserve corps. The first two corps were opposite our Third Army (General Ruffey); the next two were opposite General Maunoury's reserve divisions; while V Reserve Corps was at Bettembourg, further to the rear. Enemy elements had been in the area for a fortnight. How did our cavalry miss them? Were our hussars too ... high and mighty? The only way to obtain information was by talking to the locals, who were pretty taciturn – as we have already seen.

3. Inevitably, 1870 came to mind. 'Our field army must avoid a disaster like 1870,' wrote Gallieni in his diary for 25 August (p. 40). 'We have to protect our lines of communication with the Loire, Saône and Rhône.'

We regain Charency in pitch darkness, then Villers-le-Rond. Roads jammed. Retreating like this gives you an inkling what a total rout might look like. I was lucky to escape with nearly all my men. One offers me a celebratory cigar. According to the colonel, I've 'done very well'.

Sunday 23 August
Bois de La Taillette. Moving forward again towards Charency. The battle yesterday lasted all morning. The battalion was annihilated, almost every captain and platoon commander killed or wounded. We're now part of the reserve.

Lieutenant B[enoit] and I are the only officers left to command the company.

11.00 am.
Halt in an orchard with Nicolas, captain of the adjoining [3rd] company, and his surviving sous-lieutenants, de Bragelongne and Lée.

Bright sunshine. We lie down on the grass, beneath the apple trees, enjoying the gentle heat. The blue sky gleams between the branches, the light shimmering with silver shards. A warm breeze caresses us. The distant golden fields sleep in the infinite azure peace.

Lée is telling the tale. He's tall and heavy, rather awkward in his blue cadet's tunic with its single strip of gold [rank] braid. He has thick fair hair, a high domed forehead, a broken nose and an enormous but fragile-looking jaw – rather like his frame, which is large but not terribly robust. He comes from Lorraine. Very keen. Perhaps a little too keen.

A big devil comes walking up the hill towards us, waving from some way off. His head is swathed in a white bandage. It's Lieutenant [Bourguignon]. A bullet has ploughed a furrow in his skull.

'The impact stunned me. It knocked me out. I didn't know where I was. I was taken to Longuyon. "I'm not staying here," I said. "I want be back with my regiment."'

In the afternoon, Captain Nicolas's 3rd Company and our own, much reduced, 4th Company enter the woods right and ahead of Charency to maintain contact with V Corps.

'We won't be seeing any action,' explains Major [Lebaud]. 'Our task is simply to maintain contact with V Corps.'

We pass through Charency.

3rd Company takes up position as advance guard. We follow at a hundred paces in line of platoons at two-pace intervals. We stop in a shallow bowl of a clearing: to our right is the edge of the Bois de Mény, which prolongs the Bois de La Taillette south-east along the ridge; to our left, the Bois de Vezin.

The clearing is all pasture, climbing towards a broad notch of blue sky between two shady, wooded crests. The major orders us to halt behind a thick hedge. Suddenly shots ring out. We look at each other. Maintaining contact with V Corps may be harder than we anticipated.

Nicolas appears, loping calmly down the hill.

'Bumped into some Prussians at the exit to the Bois de Vezin, sir!'

He wipes his chin with his handkerchief. A bullet has quite literally given him a close shave.

'Right,' says the major. 'Delvert, take your platoon. Go search the wood. Hold up the enemy and protect our left.'

Forward!

Patrols despatched.

Nothing.

I place a sentry at the point where a steep path through the woods emerges to join a dirt track running down to Charency. Suddenly a line of skirmishers exits the Bois de Vezin and swarms over the ridge, while another emerges from the Bois de La Taillette. The two groups combine in a textbook manoeuvre. Some go right; others, left. A line of flat caps is silhouetted in the dip between the wooded crests.

Bang! Bang![1] They swing into action immediately.

They advance in parade-ground formation. I hurry my men into a trench – a ditch that prolongs the steep path beyond the junction, cutting across the hillside. '800 metres, volley fire … Aim! Fire!' A patrol from 3rd Company hurtles towards us. 'Cease fire!' I shout. A hail of bullets whistles round our ears. At the far right of our line panic ensues at the sudden appearance of red trousers. The men clamber from the ditch, each sticking his kepi on the end of his rifle, removing the cap-cover to show the red beneath.

They think everyone in front of them is French.

'Hold your fire! Hold your fire!'[2]

---

1. Not the 'Boom! Boom!' of our rifles, but a sharp crack.
2. The man who shouted was one of those puny types from the Paris *faubourgs*. [Note: the *banlieue*, or suburbs, typically the working-class districts of the city.] We had a few in our battalion because the law allowed married conscripts to choose where they served. A real conundrum for both sexes! The poor lad was average height, but pale and sickly, with hollow cheeks, round shoulders and a squint. He had climbed on to the parapet. I got him down again.

'Chumps,' drawls a man from 3rd Company, dropping into the ditch beside us. 'Can't you see they're Germans?'

A hail of bullets confirms the misunderstanding. Behind and to my right I can hear Lieutenant [Bourguignon]. I rally my men under a hail of bullets – French and German – and return through the woods to Charency. Just one casualty; Sergeant Feugère is wounded.[1]

Lieutenant B[enoit] has to be evacuated. He's twisted his leg and broken it again.

Fall back from Charency towards Villers. Arrive in the dark. The men haven't eaten, drunk or slept for over twenty-four hours. Neither have I. We halt to await developments, but light no fires. Conscious of our retreat, of the enemy in hot pursuit, dog tired, hungry, in the dark without a fire, beside a road jammed with convoys, the men are edgy. The divisional commander is on the road trying to rally his troops. Suddenly horses appear at full gallop: utter confusion. The men panic and run for their weapons: 'Uhlans! Uhlans!'

I get knocked over, trampled underfoot. Orders go unheeded. Eventually calm is restored. Just a few stray horses,[2] but clearly we must fall back again to the hills south of the Othain.

We reach Marville at 1.00 am after an interminable eight-hour march, full of stops and starts. The men are dozing, bumping nose first into the pack of the comrade in front of them, dropping like dead men into the ditches. I'm constantly pinching my legs to stop myself from nodding off. After one halt, I succumb to temptation and sit down on a milestone. I wake up again ... No company. The march has resumed ... The men have followed. I catch up 500 metres further on. Rest for an hour. In the silence and the darkness, the long column sets off again, staff officers moving back and forth with lanterns.

Monday 24 August

Reach Marville at 1.30 am, off again at 4.00 am.

We're holding the sides of the Othain valley. The guns have been thundering since dawn. We're in the rear, overlooking the Delut road. Clear skies, a deliciously crisp summer day that already hints of autumn. On the white road a

---

1. He had been defending himself very bravely, moving from tree to tree, revolver in hand.
2. The men were demoralized. They began to see spies everywhere. Some men came to point out some lights on the horizon. Then the adjutant did likewise. Signalling to the enemy, they said. In fact it was just farmhouses deep in the countryside, lighting their lamps as normal at dusk.

cart moves slowly uphill, bringing in the harvest. Meanwhile, a few kilometres away, the 120s and the 155s are spitting out their load of steel, the men on both sides butchering each other, screaming as they fall.

Every battle opens with an artillery duel. The artillery's role is to destroy the enemy guns, allowing the infantry to advance and gain victory.[1] Casualties during an advance are few. Men are more likely to be killed when retreating. Our check at Gomery can largely be explained by the overwhelming superiority of their heavy artillery.[2]

They had got their sums right.[3]

I go down into Marville with my orderly, the faithful Chevalier. Streets deserted, silent as the tomb under a blazing sun. Next to the church is an aid post run by nuns. The sister apparently in charge – her wimple framing a strong, kind countrywoman's face – invites us to sit down.

'Poor boys! Come and rest a while. Look, lieutenant. Have you seen the state of our ceiling?'

The sky is visible between the beams. A shell of one calibre or another. That apart, this gallant lady does not seem too concerned.

---

1. The experience of the front-line infantryman immediately belied the assertions of the 1913 Artillery Regulations: 'It is recognized today that the primary role of the artillery is to support ground attacks ... the artillery *no longer prepares attacks*, it *supports* them.' 'It is recognized today.' By whom? On what grounds? This phrase appears often in military regulations and instructions with no greater justification than here. 'The phrase "It is recognized today" is one for the psychologist to ponder,' remarks General Gascouin (*L'Évolution de l'artillerie pendant la guerre*, p. 52). 'How often it appears in military history! Within a month of the outbreak of war, what the infantry was demanding – and quite rightly too – was an accurate, intense and prolonged artillery preparation before any ground attack.' As late as 1917 I heard senior staff officers say: 'We must leave some work for the infantry.' Our high command displayed a quite extraordinary ignorance of the power of matériel.
2. Compare the heavy artillery available to the two sides in August 1914. France had 300 pieces: 120s (Baquet) and 155s (Rimailho). Germany had 3,500: 2,000 heavy howitzers, mortars and long-barrelled guns, and 1,500 105mm light howitzers. Our guns had a maximum range of 5.5 to 6 kilometres, while theirs varied in range from 6 to 14 kilometres. Consider also the comment made the following day by an artillery captain commanding a battery of 75s. 'The Germans are flattening us from 10 kilometres, while our maximum range is 3.5,' he complained. We did not yet know that the 75 was capable of much more than this. 'Our infantry was immediately struck by this disparity,' noted General de Fonclare (*L'Armée française à travers les âges. L'infanterie*, p. 124), 'and by the dramatic impact of the large-calibre enemy shells.'
3. This answers my earlier question (20 August): 'Why did Germany embark on this war?'

Sitting round the table, the orderlies are eating cabbage soup. My stomach rumbles greedily. It looks delicious. No culinary masterpiece has ever affected me more. I'm literally dying of hunger. It must be plain as day, because the good sister sets two bowls on the table and fills them to the brim.

'Dig in, lads. I'm sure you haven't eaten.'

'Thank you, sister. It's very kind, but really I couldn't.'

But I soon let myself be persuaded. Chevalier, meanwhile, just dives straight in.

Afternoon, 2.00 pm. Heading north–west to Flassigny – a village nestling in a bowl, a handful of red roofs among the greenery.

Major [Lebaud] is glad of the chance to relax for a while. Small, trim, bright eyed, ever cheerful. He leans his elbows on a sort of stone parapet running beside the road. He rests his eyes on the green fields sloping away to the dense mass of trees and bushes that mark the banks of the Othain. In the distance, the light blue hills doze in the sun. A golden day. It feels good to be alive.[1]

'We'll be fine here, I reckon. It's pretty much out of the way ... they'll forget all about us.'

A hussar lieutenant rushes up.

'Here comes a comrade with news ... Well?'

'Enemy reported. Right bank of the Othain, sir! You're to cover these two fords. Colonel's orders.'

He points them out on the map.

'Get moving, Delvert,' [says the major]. 'A platoon from 1st Company will cover the ford on the left, you take the one on the right. You're in command of the sector.'

'Yes, sir!

The platoon from 1st Company is commanded by Sous–lieutenant Loriot, a young teacher just finishing his six months' probation, splendidly staunch and brave. I order him to hold a position 100 metres from the left-hand ford. Hidden in a wheat-field, he can cover the whole crossing. A wooded spur overlooking the valley seems perfect for my company, and I send a small detachment to establish a picket ahead of and slightly below us. We immediately dig in along the spur, opposite the enemy, with abatis of branches to hide the trenches and serve as a parapet.

---

1. I used to tell Major [Lebaud] that my men were poor shots. 'Do you know how often they've been on the ranges this year?' he replied. 'Twice!' Cf. General Gascouin (p. 71): 'Our infantry were poor shots.'

Having made my dispositions, I find a sergeant and go to reconnoitre the riverbank.

Tuesday 25 August

I made my reconnaissance yesterday evening amid fields of oats and wheat, divided by hedgerows and copses. Delightful walk: sunken lanes full of marjoram and mallow ... But I could hear the rumble of the guns, and my hand reached occasionally for the butt of my revolver.

Spent all night in our positions. Slept for an hour, lying on the parapet.

The guns begin to thunder at 4.00 am or 4.30 am. By 7.20 am the concert is deafening. To our right the battle has begun. I manage to forget how hungry I am, even though it's two days since our last distribution of rations.

The fog has reduced visibility to 600 metres.

Around 9.00 am I receive orders to pull back to Flassigny, below us and a magnet for shells. Why, when we're in such a good, elevated position? We follow a narrow sunken track. As soon as we emerge, we can see the huge shells of the German heavy artillery pounding both sides of the valley. Major [Lebaud] is holed up in a farm that has just been destroyed. He orders me to stay behind to support the battery of 75s still above us on Côte 316.[1]

I return to my men. I order Sergeant Gallas[2] to go and check the ridge.

The guns have gone.

But how are we to get back to our regiment? Shells are falling all around. Eventually I find a path slanting across the hillside and set off, followed by my men. A piece of the shrapnel peppering the ridge hits me in the left leg.[3] The barrage is deafening. My thigh hurts. The enemy holds the edge of the wood opposite. I fall back in echelons towards Remoiville, my designated line of retreat. Halted by the divisional commander, who orders us to support the artillery from the edge of Remoiville Wood. Major Lebaud positions us, then continues on to Brandeville.

---

1. 'We can't abandon the guns,' he said. 'It's a matter of military honour.' We would hear this phrase repeated time and again during the campaign.
2. Class of 1909. Gallas had been recalled on the outbreak of war, just a year after his discharge. Brown hair, prematurely grey; average height, solidly built and exceptionally strong, a former regimental boxing champion. Decent, energetic and resourceful, he was the best sergeant in the company and very popular among the men.
3. It was just a flesh wound. The ball passed straight through.

We reach Brandeville at 5.00 pm. The hills of the Hauts-de-Meuse loom darkly above the Woëvre.

I overhear the men chatting.

'Are we really stopping here?'

Lieutenant Bourguignon is back with us, more passionate than ever.[1]

'Perhaps not,' he butts in. 'We're heading to the rear to re-form. But the Boches are in for a shock when they get here.' He gestures towards the formidable heights. 'They are all crammed with artillery.'[2]

At 8.30 pm, night march towards Brieulles. My leg is hurting so badly that Colonel [Farret] has me put on a machine-gun cart.[3]

The march is interminably slow, with a halt every couple of minutes. The men are exhausted, but above all demoralized. An army sensing defeat, and one impossible to combat – at the mouth of a howitzer. Our artillery only fires a handful of salvoes, withdrawing the limbers so the batteries cannot be spotted. But the enemy knows exactly where they are. A German Taube has been overflying our lines for the past three days.[4]

We finally reach Brieulles-sur-Meuse at 4.30 am. Until now we have been retreating in reasonably good order. But what suffering, what chaos! The units are all mixed up. Underlying it all, a certain softness and indiscipline. Men are grumbling about lack of wine (!) and sleep. 'They should have left us at home in peace.' Still, this flight by night *is* extremely demoralizing, surrounded by shoals of poor folk escaping with their beasts and a few meagre belongings – the girls, in their Sunday best and extravagant hats, sitting on straw in the carts.

Run into our brigadier, worn out, the long face of a halfwit. He is busy arranging stabling for his horses. The other brigadier is a hapless old stick, completely drained of all colour. He stands there flexing his knees, pince-nez perched on his nose.

---

1. He was suffering physically from his head wound and psychologically from our defeat.
2. He turned to me and repeated his claim. [In fact] there wasn't a single gun. Our men were very demoralized when we surrendered these heights without a struggle.
3. I first approached a nearby artillery captain from the 26th, who very kindly offered me a lift. When our own machine-gunners appeared, the colonel stopped one of the carts for me. The artillery captain was as distressed as everyone else by our retreat: 'The Germans are flattening us from 10 kilometres, while our maximum range is 3.5.'
4. 'German aviation was a real surprise, a ghastly revelation ...' (Gascouin, p. 75).

Wednesday 26 August

Brieulles-sur-Meuse. Have my dressing changed. Our current billet is the filthiest yet. The layer of dust covering the furniture in our 'bedroom' would befit a house that's stood empty for years.

Afternoon, sunshine and cloud.

Walk with de Bragelongne, fresh from Saint-Cyr, class of Montmirail. A stocky little fellow, big head, close-cropped fair hair, blue eyes. He takes a philosophical view of life. Right now, his main worry is getting hold of some socks. All I want is a pair of drawers. The ones I have on are fit only for the bin.

But where are we going to find socks and drawers?

'At the grocer's, *monsieur*,' says a little girl.

We track the place down, not without difficulty.

'Sorry, *messieurs*. I'm clean out.'

Marvellous!

Left for Épinonville around 4.30pm. The women weep to see us go.

Dark sky above woods and rolling pastures. Long grey clouds full of rain. The half-light of dusk, the dark green fields, the distant blue of the woods, the sombre column of men – all combine to lend this march a funereal air.

It's dark when we reach Épinonville. All the officers in the battalion dine together: nine of us in total, including the doctor.[1] We rehearse the twists and turns of the battle. Count the dead and the wounded. These meals lack a certain gaiety.

We try to snatch some vital rest. In 4th Company, just 127 of the original 262 men remain, plus two of the four officers, both wounded.[2]

Artists depict war as an angry woman surrounded by fiery serpents; or as a dashing young cavalryman sounding a trumpet, while mothers bewail their dead children beneath a tragic sky thick with the smoke of distant fires. The reality is more awful and less picturesque. For a subject, I might suggest Gomery, with its chaos of dismembered horses awash with crimson blood; hussars, cut or stabbed, staunching their wounds; fields of stubble puddled with gore. Or a green pasture strewn with the bodies of poor red-trousered *pioupious*, face up, greatcoats open, arms outstretched. But no. Instead I will offer them Flassigny, the valley sides devastated by the huge shells of the German howitzers, hitting

---

1. From a total of fourteen. Our [1st] Battalion had got off more lightly than the 3rd, and in particular the 2nd, which only had two officers left. Remember this is only 26 August.
2. One of whom, Bourguignon, would be evacuated the following day.

the ground like meteors, long trails of black smoke mounting to the heavens, echoing with a fearsome clap of thunder.

Thursday 27 August
A beautiful morning.

We're at rest in a meadow, our weapons piled at the edge of the Bois de Montrebeau.

A transport column fills the dusty road below. The vehicles are stationary, bathed in sunshine. The men are asleep beneath them or sitting on the banks, eating slowly, knives in the air. Lieutenant Bourguignon arrives. He rips off his dressing. His wound is turning septic. It looks ghastly.

'It's festering, old chap. I've a headache too. I'm being evacuated. Here are the company funds.'

He hands me a sheet of paper showing the company accounts, as well as our funds – 350 francs in cash – which I plan to entrust to David, my sergeant-clerk. David is a regular NCO. Twelve years' service, I believe. Small, clean shaven, blue eyes, a lisp, a constant worrier, tireless if physically rather frail. The war has upset all his meticulous peacetime routines. He can't bear to show me the books.

'Wait till we get a few days' rest, sir. I'll put things straight then.'

A few days' rest! He'll be lucky. We'll both be dead before I get to see the figures.

2.00pm. At Exermont, north of Apremont. The troops are resting. The men have found some wine in the village. Three-quarters are blind drunk.

8.00 pm
After dinner we gather round the table while Major [Lebaud] compiles a list of possible mentions in despatches.[1] He says Colonel Farret has sent him a note: 'Don't forget Delvert. I want to put him forward for a captaincy.'

Friday 28 August
Leave at first light.

---

1. N[icolas] suggested Y. 'We must put his name forward. He's a regular. It will help his career.' Humble reservists [like me] normally didn't stand a chance. We were ignored except for 'missions of honour' – hence Major [Lebaud]'s surprise on reading the colonel's words.

We're advancing towards the Meuse again, but further north this time – between Dun and Stenay.

Billeted at Villefranche. Pretty village, abandoned by most of its inhabitants. The men divide up the houses and empty the cellars, in other words loot the place.

To the outpost line. My orders are to cover the Meuse crossings. Reconnoitre along the river, through tall grass and scattered hayricks. The rays of the sun glint off the clouds of dust. The whole valley glows red. On the golden road along the far bank of the Meuse, a cavalryman. The enemy. He looks, turns and gallops off.

I deploy two outposts, each a half-platoon strong: one downstream, opposite a known ford; the other opposite a point where a branch of the river is narrowed by an eyot to just 3 or 4 metres. With a little daring, a passage might be forced here.

Place one platoon on grand guard by a hayrick 150 metres from the eastern exit of the village. Two pairs of sentries from this platoon will maintain contact with the outposts. The other two platoons will remain under my command, ready to intervene as necessary. Haywains, ploughs and harrows block the roads into the village, each barricade further protected by a barbed wire entanglement raised 30 centimetres off the ground. If the uhlans get this far, their horses will catch their hooves in the entanglements. Then we'll take over.

Evening falls peacefully on the valley.

Saturday 29 August
Pulling back through Beauclair, Tailly, Barricourt. Struggling with the heat. The men are demoralized. Reach Bayonville at 11.00 pm, leave again at 3.00 am. Our obsession with finding billets is hopeless. Bivouacking out of doors would be much less tiring in this fine weather. Lack of sleep is the real killer.[1]

Sunday 30 August
Tough going through the Bois de Vieux-Billecoq.

Reach Halles via Beauclair.

---

1. 'The most urgent human need is sleep' (Blaze, *Souvenirs d'un officier de la Grande Armée*, p. 38).

Monday 31 August

Entered Tailly around 6.00 pm yesterday evening. Leaving the village, saw a German cavalryman lying face down in the ditch; his cheeks were green, clotted with blood from a head wound. He had a stripe of silver braid.

Passed through Beauclair on the *route nationale* and entered Halles in darkness, bayonets fixed, with orders not to shoot. Immediately blocked the exit routes. The company halted in the first road on the right as you enter the village from Beauclair. We laid straw on the footpath. The light was fading fast. I placed one platoon with Adjudant [Bes] at the Beauclair exit to the village. We blocked the road with an upturned cart and a few ploughs and harrows, leaving a chicane for passage.

The north-west exit to the village is defended by a proper fortification: piles of logs with loopholes created in between. My orders are to cover this exit too. I billeted the three remaining platoons nearby, in a barn opening directly onto the street.

Returned to my other platoon.

My wound was bothering me. I was thirsty. I really needed a drink – I didn't care what. A door was ajar. A light. I went inside. Five or six people were gathered, men and women. They offered me a glass of plum brandy.

Suddenly from the street came cries of panic, growing louder: 'Stand to! Stand to!'

Chaos. Galloping horses. Shots.

I grabbed my revolver and headed for the door. The occupants of the room instantly huddled in a corner. 'This man's going to shoot us,' said one.

This man. They meant me.

'Don't worry,' I said.

I went outside. Shadows were moving in the street. I ran to the barricade.

'Two uhlans, sir! Coming up the road. We fired. They ran off.'

A big fellow appeared. 'Uhlans! … Uhlans! … Idiots, the lot of you! That was me, sir. Bringing up the colonel's horses. They fired at me! Imbeciles! They made me drop my sword.

'They were uhlans, sir!

The supposed uhlan was incandescent. 'Uhlans, I'll give 'em uhlans!' He bent down abruptly. 'What do you call this, then?'

He was brandishing a sword, definitely a French light cavalry pattern.

'This is what was dropped by your uhlans! … It's mine, sir. I'm an old chasseur d'Afrique. Six years' service.

And off he went, chuntering to himself.

My adjudant is a little unstable. He had fired on some mounted orderlies, mistaking them for uhlans. The war has completely unhinged the poor chap. About to retire after seventeen years' service, he finds himself in a living nightmare. And he's not the only one.

'My throat's dry,' says Lieutenant [Hillère]. He's lost his voice. His tongue is swollen.

Everyone complains about bad breath. It's nerves, although they'd rather blame the food. Most of the men are suffering from diarrhoea. Not hard to guess why. It's ghastly to watch them returning from the firing line. Most are distraught.[1] Souls in torment.

Dinner with the mayor, a bossy little fellow, aged 60 to 70. His daughter, whose prematurely white hair gives her a dowager air, is wife to the assistant headmaster of the Lycée de Toulouse. He's an academic, a greying, rather pompous man, deliberate of speech, quite obviously terrified. He's here on holiday. What a place to choose! He said the Germans had passed through. Their commander requisitioned all the bread, collected up the firearms and completely banned the sale of wine. Their discipline greatly impressed the locals.

'We have no bread,' said the mayor.

'You can have some of ours,' [I replied].

As we said our goodbye to these good folk, the woman took me aside on the doorstep. 'There's going to be a battle, monsieur. Our cellar is sound. When should we take cover?'

'At dawn, *madame*. Perhaps even earlier.'

I went to inspect the sentries at the two exits to the village, then returned to my men in the barn.

This morning, the regiment left for Beauclair. 4th Company and I are staying behind to defend Halles from the east (the only side under direct threat), while 1st Company watches the western edge of the village.[2]

I place plenty of men in the south-east corner. This is the weak spot. The enemy will definitely attack from this direction.

---

1. There were some exceptions. Apart from a frown and slight pallor, Gallas, for example, was as chipper as ever. So, too, were the runners. Georget (see below) was imperturbable. If he ever felt any emotion, he never showed it in my presence.

2. A half-platoon was detached from 1st Company and given to me. It was led by Sous-lieutenant Loriot, that young teacher and outstanding soldier mentioned in similar circumstances on 24 August.

Two roads intersect here. Enemy troops crossing the Meuse at Saulmory will use the one from Montigny-devant-Sassey; the other turns into a dirt track which emerges on the Wiseppe road – another possible line of attack. My most urgent task is to reinforce the barricade on the Montigny road. Once that's done, and Sergeant Dufrenne's platoon installed, I set off downhill on the road leading to the dirt track.

A local man approaches me: 'Excuse me, sir. I may be able to help. I'm a veteran, 50 now, too old for the call-up, but I know this area like the back of my hand. You can rely on me.'

He seems a sound chap, so I decide to listen to what he has to say.

'If they do attack here, they'll come up through this dip that I'll show you.'

I follow him.

He's right. This dip is a sort of sunken track which emerges in the village, just behind the crossroads!

I summon the half-platoon from 1st Company assigned to me as reinforcements and deploy them in the orchards so as to enfilade the valley. I send a half-platoon commanded by my best sergeant, Gallas, to hook to the left to outflank the enemy, and another half-platoon, facing north-east, to cover the slopes descending to the Ruisseau de Wiseppe. My final platoon I will keep in reserve, along the road leading to the Bois de Halles, our line of retreat if necessary.

I will remain at the crossroads with my four runners, Georget, Pinel, Guignol and David – all aged from 22 to 26.

Georget is a big lad, 1.75 to 1.8 metres tall. Ash-blond hair, blue eyes, gap toothed. Tireless, brave, staunch and oblivious to danger. Pinel is a Parisian: below average height; brown hair, squashed nose, bright eyes. Very full of himself. Guignol is from the Beauce, tireless and cool under fire. David is a small, black-haired Breton with laughing bright eyes.

Sergeant Gallas has gathered his men together. His sleeves are rolled up, revealing his strong wrists. He was regimental boxing champion in 1913 and it shows.

'Right, sir!' he shouts in passing. 'We'll give 'em a pasting!'

'We certainly will,' I reply with a laugh.

The sun is shining brightly.

At 6.00 am, gunfire. The medics and the band have only just left. The Germans are advancing up the sunken way covered by Sous-lieutenant Loriot and his half-platoon, with Sergeant Gallas in support on his left. Our fire is deadly. The Germans whirl and fall. They withdraw quickly, pursued by our bullets.[1]

They relaunch their attack, methodically this time, deployed as skirmishers, but they shoot too high, leaving us unscathed. The bullets whistle harmlessly over our heads, level with the first floor of the houses.

'They're aiming for the supply wagons,' quips one wag.

Our men excel themselves, aiming as coolly as on the firing range. So grumpy on the march, here they are calm and composed.

9.00 am. The German attack is checked. Prompted by Captain X., Major [Lebaud] orders us to pull back. Loriot is in despair. 'Why? When it's all going so well. They'll say we're cowards.' He leads his men back into action and carries on fighting. But we're coming under fire from the right and from the rear. We must withdraw. Gallas is engaged furthest forward, so I order him to start the movement, followed by Loriot, then Dufrenne.

I'm bringing up the rear. Loriot enters a lane to our right to check that we aren't surrounded. When I reach the corner of the lane, we meet head on. All that remains now is to get out of here.

The village is deserted, deathly quiet. It's almost 11.00 am. The sun is beating down on the white road. The little church, the square, the road climbing towards the wood, all are empty under the blue sky.

Scarcely past the last house, the bullets begin to whine.

Over there, at the crossroads, Germans!

We're in the wood. Instead of deploying and adopting retreat formation, the men have run for cover. We'll have to work our way uphill under a hail of bullets. Loriot makes superb use of the terrain, moving from tree to tree, turning each time to face the enemy. One particular skirmisher really takes a shine to us, his bullets whistling constantly round our ears. Halfway up, we finally meet more elements from the company with Adjudant Marçay (1st Company), a reliable sort with a firm grip on his men. Fifteen years' service but looks younger; brown hair, stocky, good natured, solid as a rock.

A battery of 75s has just occupied Côte 210, less than 300 metres from the village. We're close enough to see the four flashes from the firing shots. The din of the explosions is quite hellish.

---

1. That's how to conduct a pursuit. It would have been madness to fix bayonets and send my handful of troops charging after the enemy. All we needed to do was raise our sights: bullets travel much faster than legs.

We pull back slowly.

The bullets are still whistling past. A body: face waxen, eyes glassy and purple rimmed. It's Private Loriot from my company. Poor lad! Over the hill, we find Major [Lebaud] and [Captain] X. The major orders me to take the Rémonville road. We halt at the Bois de Barricourt. The men are exhausted. They've been fighting and marching non-stop since early morning, with almost no chance of a drink.

Forward again, towards Tailly. Now, colonel's orders! Major [Lebaud] instructs me to wait while he checks with the colonel that these still hold. A staff captain (Lepetit) turns up to confirm it is so. He also threatens us with a court-martial.[1] Return to Tailly. A dreadful sight. Pools of blood everywhere. A house devastated by a shell. A dead horse in a pond. My orders are to take up a defensive position at the entrance to the village.[2] The sun is setting. The gunfire starts to slacken.

Our orders are to bivouac on Côte 292 behind Tailly. A night beneath the stars. 3.00 am, reveille. We're used to it by now.

---

1. Note the readiness of our high command to threaten ordinary soldiers – the 'rank and file' as dismissed by the general staff – with a court-martial (i.e. a firing-squad). I can still see Captain Lepetit, average height, stocky, pencil and notebook in hand. 'I have orders to take your names.' He didn't dream of asking what orders we had each received. (There were three of us: Major Lebaud, Lieutenant [Vinerot] and me.) I had followed the orders of my immediate superior, Major [Lebaud]. 'So that's how we're treated,' he remarked. 'Officers, too! ... Delvert behaved splendidly at Halles this morning.' That 'Officers!' rather upset me. It would be no more acceptable to treat ordinary soldiers this way. I expected him to add: 'Delvert was following my orders.' But in vain. [Lieutenant] [Vinerot] was livid. 'Do you know where I was?' he said, pointing to the map. 'The Bois de Dieulet, that's where.' He stomped back into the trees south of the road, hand shading his eyes. 'Disgraceful! Disgraceful!' he shouted. I stayed perfectly calm, confident I had nothing to hide. I consulted Major [Lebaud], got my company moving again and left for Tailly beneath the scorching sun.

   'All we ask is that you perform your military duty,' snapped Lepetit.

   'That's exactly what we are doing,' I replied. 'But it isn't easy to identify amid all the orders and counter-orders.'

   I heard no more of the matter.

2. Immediately after our arrival, Captain Gérard of 102nd Infantry – a friend of [Jean] Jaurès and informant for the latter's *L'Armée nouvelle* – ordered me to fix bayonets and occupy the edge of the village facing the enemy. I think he'd just been ordered to take up this position himself.

Tuesday 1 September

Marching towards Andevanne and Landres. Refugees are jamming the roads.

Yesterday was awful. Macler (lieutenant machine-gunner) and young Bragelongne (chatting to me only last Wednesday at Brieulles) are both dead; Lée is wounded.

The regiment now consists of just 15 officers and 780 men.[1]

Another glorious day.

Halt at the entrance to Saint-Juvin in a field sloping down to the river.

Reinforcements arrive from the depot at Dreux.

Big D. walks up to me, tapping his riding crop rhythmically against his boots. 'So let me get this straight. If you lie prone you get it in the head ... And if you stand up you get it in the legs?'

Wednesday 2 September

March to Vienne-le-Château, via Cornay, Chatel and Binarville, crossing the Bois de Chatel. Glorious morning. Copses of oak and elm. Clear sky, greenery. It feels good to be alive. The guns are still sounding to our left. Over towards Grand-Pré men are killing each other.

On the road, the troops are nattering cheerfully enough. Their ordeal is forgotten. The veterans are recounting their exploits to new arrivals desperate for information. Men are chatting, weapons jangling, the hubbub echoing through the dark depths of a wood alive with the song of the nightingale.

We reach Vienne-le-Château.

Spend the night on grand guard in the Bois de La Gruerie, at the intersection of the Binarville and Servon roads. Between us and the entrance to Vienne-le-Château lies a real gypsy encampment. The refugees have drawn up their carts and are huddled miserably around huge fires, making soup or brewing coffee in the dark.

Thursday 3 September

4.30 am. March from Vienne-le-Château to Sainte-Ménehould. The little town is packed with soldiers from all arms-of-service. At the department store I run across some of our 'big brothers', the cuirassiers.

'Has your regiment suffered many losses?' asks a lieutenant.

'Three-quarters of our effectives, unfortunately. What about your lot?'

---

1. From a total of 62 officers and 3,300 NCOs and men. Almost none were taken prisoner apart from the wounded left behind on the battlefield.

'None so far! But when we do go into action, there will be nobody left to tell the tale.'

That old chestnut! Does he expect an order to charge the machine guns as at Reichshof[f]en?[1]

Halt for a meal by a factory outside town. Beautiful weather. We're moving on by train. Destination unknown. Distant gunfire.

7.00 pm. Embark by train. A Taube flies over our heads.

Friday 4 September
On the train, destination Troyes. Interminably slow journey.

Saturday 5 September
Terrific racket just before our arrival in Brienne. A crash (the engine-driver was drunk). My company's carriage was in pieces. I don't know what's become of my officer's trunk.

The train is still making slow progress. I'm using the time to rest and to nurse my wounds. On board, the main preoccupation is grub. My travelling companion is Sous-lieutenant G[landaz], from 2nd Company. Small, trim, aged 24, dark-brown hair, slightly aquiline nose, heavy eyebrows that meet in the middle. As a Parisian from a well-to-do family,[2] some of his requirements are quite hilarious. The menu is never sufficiently elegant for his taste, so two days on our current diet, rolling along without any exercise, have really upset his stomach.

He's decided that milk is the cure.

'Grazof,' he called to his orderly earlier. 'Fetch me some milk.'

'How much, sir?'

'As much as you can find ... 10 litres!'

Grazof gave him an old-fashioned look and set off without enthusiasm.

He returned with half a litre.

---

1. The 1912 regulations did, in fact, state: 'The mounted charge with arme blanche is the only method of attack that produces a quick and decisive result. Accordingly it remains the cavalry's main mode of operation.'
2. Splendidly brave and cool under fire.

Sunday 6 September
Still on board the train. Learn that the Germans took Montmirail yesterday. Our lack of heavy artillery undoubtedly underlies our defeat. The general staff has been incredibly complacent in this regard.

I recall a woman I met in Sainte-Ménehould. 'I come from a military family,' she snapped. 'A staff captain assured me that our artillery had the beating of theirs.'

'I'm not a captain, *madame*,' I retorted. 'Nor am I on the staff. But I have spent the last three weeks at the front. Up against the German guns, we're like men using knives to fight opponents armed with lances.'

Some soldiers are incurably mulish. Take this captain who fought alongside us and should know better: 'All we need to gain the advantage is for our infantry to engage theirs.' Fine, in principle. But how can we do this when their artillery is holding us at bay? At Ethe, and again at Marville, the enemy infantry was shielded by an armour of steel: they scarcely had to show themselves to walk into positions rendered untenable by their guns.

I'm sickened by the attitude of the officers I've met in the rear. All they want is peace, and peace at any price.[1]

Monday 7 September
Disembark at Noisy-le-Sec.
   We're heading for Neuilly-Plaisance.

It's 11.00 am. I'm starving. I don't know why, but the proximity of Paris, and the sight of shops for the first time in a month, has turned my mind to croissants.

I go into a shop.
'We've stopped making them. They're banned.'
Ah me!
We arrive at Neuilly-Plaisance. Find our billets.[2] Leave at 9.00 pm to re-embark.
   I assemble the company at the end of our street.

---

1. It was 6 September, the opening day of the battle of the Marne. The pessimists in question were a reservist politician and some regular officers. They seemed to view the war as a fencing match. 'We've been buttoned. We've lost. Halt the attack.'
2. 'As the battle begins ...', Joffre's famous order of the day, reached us at Neuilly-Plaisance. It arrived at 6.00 pm, the same time as our food, so it was ignored completely. Nor is it mentioned by Colonel Lebaud in his diaries.

'Fall in, 4th Company.'

A woman berates me, beside herself with rage. 'So that's how the men are treated. It's a disgrace, *monsieur*! An absolute disgrace!'

I can still hear her shrieks from some way off. She must think I'm the senior officer keeping the men from their beds tonight.

Embarkation.

'Here you go,' says the railway official, putting us on the train. 'Last leg!'

Tuesday 8 September

4.30 am. Disembark at Nanteuil-le-Haudouin, only just evacuated by the Germans. Run into some cuirassiers.[1] A rosy sunrise in the woods. We can hear the guns. I think of May evenings on the Boulevard Saint-Michel, strolling up the hill to the Jardins du Luxembourg, the setting sun glowing red above the trees.

The birds are still singing despite the guns.

The Germans have ransacked Nanteuil. Drawers were emptied, overturned and smashed. A woman shows me a child of seven or eight. 'Look, *monsieur*. One of them put a gun to his head yesterday.' The little man watches me, eyes bright, mouth agape. He doesn't seem too upset by the experience.

We march under fire all day.[2] What a din! I've never known it go on so long. My ears are ringing. My head is starting to ache. At dusk, around 8.00 pm, we

---

1. 101st Infantry formed part of 7th Infantry Division; 7th and 8th Infantry Divisions together made up IV Corps. Gallieni was expecting IV Corps on 2 September. 'My next task is to ring Joffre,' reads his diary for 1 September. 'He is giving me Maunoury's army ... IV Corps will arrive from Verdun tomorrow.' In fact, we didn't leave Sainte-Ménehould until the evening of 3 September (see above). Part of the division went from Sevran-Ligny and Gagny to Nanteuil-le-Haudouin in the taxis requisitioned by the general; the rest, including 101st Infantry, travelled by train.
2. We moved forward at 6.00 am. Bright sunshine but still cool. The men visited the abandoned farms before we left, searching for any stray poultry and wringing the necks of chickens, geese and ducks. This hunt preoccupied them rather more than did Joffre's order of the day – of which, as we have seen, they knew nothing. Some men went into battle with a bird in their pack, jettisoning it during the day as the struggle continued without respite into the night. Duck and chicken carcasses, cavity uppermost, dotted the fields. We deployed and moved forward in textbook order despite the terrible gunfire: the companies in double columns; each platoon initially in columns of half-platoons, then as a single line of skirmishers; the platoons maintaining an interval of around 50 metres throughout. The shells were landing in groups of four as each of the batteries firing at us was composed of four 150mm howitzers. '*Crump! Crump!* They streamed down

take up position at the edge of a little wood, right of the Bois de Montrolles, which was occupied, but quickly evacuated, by 2nd Battalion and some units of 264th Infantry.

The battalion holds all the rim of the little wood, as well as the ridges right and left. The men have fashioned rough shelters for their heads and are sleeping on sheaves of wheat taken from the fields. Around 9.00 pm, fire to our left: machine guns, rifles and guns. The Germans have launched a night counter-attack against the southern corner of the Bois de Montrolles. Beneath the starry sky, the gunfire seems interminable, penetrating every corner of the line. My throat tightens as the bullets whine, criss-crossing in the pitch blackness.

Eventually silence reigns.

Around midnight I manage to lie down behind the bank marking the left edge of the wood. Only half asleep. Interrupted by orders from 3.00 am onwards.

Wednesday 9 September
8.00 am. Pulling back to Silly-le-Long. Shell-holes cover the plain. Bodies scattered here and there. The corpse of one gunner is already completely blue, covered in flies. '*Crump! Crump!*' The shells dog our footsteps. The lines of four crack against the ridges with a dreadful sound like breaking glass.

Terrifying, this march in full sun beneath a hail of shells. Yet the men advance in perfect order, as if on manoeuvres.

Reach Sennevières, out of the firing line.

---

like a cavalry charge at full gallop. I tried my best to keep my company moving forward outside the line of fire, soon grasping the requirements of this sort of manoeuvre. Over a distance of 10 kilometres, covered in 100-metre and 200-metre bounds, the company was fortunate to suffer just a handful of wounded. But all it takes is one unlucky shell. The adjoining 2nd Company suffered forty-odd killed and wounded from a single explosion. Captain Nicolas (3rd Company) was commanding the battalion. I can see him now, with his long legs, standing to monitor the advance. Again this belies the notion that the infantry attacked without discipline at the start of the campaign. We were, however, far too visible. I can picture the endless line of our red trousers against the green of the fields. As General Fonclare (p. 135) remarked, 'We were dressed like parrots … a dream target'. Moreover our guns were wholly inadequate in number and range. The German 150s shelled us throughout the day, while our counter-battery work had no noticeable impact, despite the admirable dedication of our gunners. The enemy batteries were probably out of range of our 75s.

Everything here has been looted, ransacked, systematically destroyed. The windows are all blown in. The rooms are filled with piles of torn linen, dresses and hats; cupboards and drawers emptied and overturned; smashed crockery.[1]

Nicolas rejoins us after remaining in the Bois de Montrolles until 1.00 am. A hellish night. The wood full of bodies from 316th Infantry and 264th Infantry, the wounded gasping 'Here, sir!' Other soldiers had stripped naked and were thrashing around like lunatics. One man had two broken legs: 'I've been here for three days, sir!' he said staunchly. 'Don't worry about me, though. Give those pigs what-for. They're making me suffer. I want my revenge.'

At every step, [Nicolas] was stumbling over disfigured corpses, guts spilling out. An unbearable stench of shit and putrefaction.

Shit and putrefaction, that sums up the smell of the battlefield. Along with the odour of gunpowder that catches you by the throat and stops you breathing.

Dinner, short commons. Just a crust of stale bread.[2]

After his attempts to scrounge 10 litres of milk on the train, [Sous-lieutenant] G[landaz] is now tucking into the scrapings from a jar of jam he found on a midden in Sennevières. Rumour has it we're marching back to Betz. Nicolas says the Germans have dug three lines of concrete-lined trenches there.[3] I can believe anything of that madman de T[rentinian]. He still thinks he's fighting the Moroccans and it was his stupidity that did for us at Ethe.[4]

---

1. Even the soldiers of the Kaiser, normally so disciplined, could be brazen looters.
2. We had eaten nothing since our coffee at 5.00 am the previous day. The supply wagons couldn't reach us during the battle. Even situations offering little to smile about can have their lighter moments. We enjoyed the sorry expression of the four-stripe major who came to complain to Colonel [Farret] about the rigours of the campaign. He was one of those regulars, thankfully few and far between, who believed that real war was the annual manoeuvres. 'We're always on the move,' he protested indignantly. 'No sooner have we established a position than we're off again. No supplies are getting through; my medical units are under fire. We can't carry on like this.' I can just see him now, small, brown hair, ruddy cheeks, angrily twiddling his pince-nez. In view of where we'd just been, Glandaz and I fell about laughing. We even forgot how hungry we were. 'Our regimental MO kept himself and his assistants well back from the shelling, hiding behind the regulations when we criticized his actions,' writes Colonel Lebaud (pp. 62-3). 'He may have been right in principle, but fortunately not every doctor showed such respect for so misconceived a rule.'
3. The information was false. Strange, too, the idea that the Germans might already have built concrete-lined trenches.
4. We bore a grudge against General de Trentinian, blaming him – unfairly in the main – for our defeat at Ethe. We all applauded the decision to relieve him of his command just

4.00 pm. Moving back towards Silly-le-Long. Our flank is attacked by a reserve division.[1] March until evening. 7.00 pm attack at La Râperie. Bullets whistle past. The Germans have the upper hand. We're being plastered with lead.[2] Major [Lebaud] leans against a hayrick beside the narrow track. 'Forward, the 101st! Forward!'

Lean and decisive, G[landaz] moves in front of me, followed by 2nd Company. Now it's our turn.

'Forward, 4th Company! Forward!

Men are falling right and left. The light fades. The bullets whine faster and faster. In the gathering dusk, all is shouting, the crackle of gunfire, the awful screams of men being slaughtered.

I look round.

'Here, sir!'

It's my runner, Pinel.

The battle seems to be continuing on the left. I have about fifteen men with me. How many from my company? I've no idea.

Shadows flee on the horizon.

'Combat range! Fire at will!'

Let rip with rifle and machine-gun fire until it's too dark to see.[3] Ordered to muster and billet at Plessis-Belleville.

---

twelve days later on 21 September, after the battle of Lassigny.

1. Von Kluck had rushed his troops back across the Marne and was attacking our left wing in an attempt to halt our advance. According to the regimental history, an enemy column was spotted north of Nanteuil around 1.30 pm.

2. We were lying in a beet field. The bullets seemed to be exploding around my head. The laws of physics apparently explain this phenomenon, caused by the high velocity of a bullet at the point of impact.

3. The reader is presented here with a soldier's-eye view of part of the action conducted by Sixth Army in general, and 7th Division in particular, on 9 September. General Gallieni describes that action as follows: 'Sixth Army formed up around its positions. Its dogged resistance allowed it to combine its action with that of the neighbouring British.' In an explanatory note, his editors Gaëtan Gallieni and P.-B. Gheusi add: 'The heroic resistance of 7th Division and VII Corps forced the enemy batteries at Trocy to cease firing.' This is one combatant's view of the 'heroic resistance' mounted by his division. The proximity of VII Corps afforded me a new recruit, a corporal from one of its regiments – 42nd Infantry, if memory serves. He was lost and requested permission to remain with my company. 'My pleasure, lad,' I replied. I sent him to one of the platoons. He was fair haired, just a boy really, but very cool under fire – the prime quality of an infantryman. He rejoined his regiment a few days later. I missed him greatly.

'Which way's that?'

'This way.'

'Are you sure?'

'Yes, sir! We're mustering down there, on the plain.'

Half an hour's march away.

The battalion is there, along with D. and Major [Lebaud]. Small groups are still coming in, the odd straggler.

'Have the companies fall in!'

It's not easy in the dark, but we manage somehow.

10.00 pm. Arrive at Plessis-Belleville.

Village deserted. Bivouac on straw. The soldiers enter the houses. In one farm I find the officers of 264th Infantry, sitting round a table lit by candles stuck in bottles. A plumpish chap tells me that he's a friend of the family. He takes me down to the cellar, methodically cracks open a barrel and gives me several litres of wine which Chevalier takes up to the company.[1]

We eat in the darkness, sitting on bales of straw – a dry crust and a tin of 'monkey'.

Chevalier has laid some straw in the cobbled entrance to the farmyard. That will be my bed for the night.

Thursday 10 September

In position at La Râperie in front of Silly-le-Long. A dreadful return to yesterday's battlefield. The trackside ditches beyond the houses are full of German corpses. One has a bullet in his left eye – awful to behold. Corporal Pluyette finds an unsent 'Postkarte'[2] on his body. The German was telling his family that he was nearing Paris: 'We have all the guns and equipment we need to set fire to the French capital.'

Fool.

---

1. Greatly reduced in size. Over these two days of continuous fighting, the company lost – killed or wounded – almost a quarter of its total strength of c.200 since reforming after Ethe. I was the last remaining officer. Two stragglers joined us the following day, after the worst was over. They had gone to ground during the action. In Napoleon's day, shirkers were forced to run the gauntlet while their comrades beat them on the backside with a metal-soled army boot (Blaze, p. 64). I told this pair what I thought of them and described the fate awaiting them if they absconded again. There was no repeat.

2. He brought it for me to translate. It is a good example of that *Schadenfreude*, or 'delight in destruction', typical of all Germans, not just the Pan-Germanist minority.

Another man must have seen the bullet that killed him. He died instinctively shielding his face with his hands.

The ditch also contains a wounded man, shot in the belly.

'Are you in pain?' I ask him in German.

Wordlessly, he rummages in the back pocket of his tunic, pulls out a wallet and hands me a photograph of himself, his wife and two children.'

'You'll see them again. I'll fetch some help.'

He shakes my hand, fat tears rolling down his face.

Around 5.00 pm, forward march. We recross part of the battlefield; the bodies of men and horses everywhere, the unbearable stench of rotting flesh.

Beneath a starry sky, perhaps the last we will ever see, we advance silently along the edge of the woods.[1]

Billeted at Le Luat. Major [Lebaud], Captain D[idisheim] and I are staying in a house previously occupied by one 'Rittmeister von Neumann'. My compliments! He has completely trashed the place. Everywhere evidence of theft and destruction. Furniture ripped apart, china smashed. One of the bedrooms looks worse still. Mattresses and eiderdown slashed, a blanket of feathers covering the debris-strewn floor. Brigand.

Friday 11 September

March through lovely, rolling, wooded countryside. The Parc-aux-Dames is an elegant château in a delightful situation – redolent of fox-hunting, rides in the woods, a life of elegance and luxury. From an open cellar behind the château, soldiers emerge clutching bottles of wine – reminding me we are at war.

Continue to Crépy in the rain.[2] I'm glad. We will suffer in consequence, but it might also soften the ground enough to hold up our nemesis, the German heavy artillery.[3]

---

1. A staff officer, a cavalryman, drove past us in his car. 'It's going very well,' we heard him say, to the CO, I believe. We were flummoxed. We had no idea we were the victors.
2. We entered Crépy (only just evacuated by the Germans) to be greeted by a woman of 35 or so, brown hair, quite tall, blue apron round her hips.
    'Now then!' she said. 'What can I get for you?'
    'You wouldn't have any bread, would you, *madame*?'
    'Actually, the baker has just taken some out of the oven. It'll still be hot, though.'
    'I don't care. It'll be bread.'
    She ran off and returned with some loaves which the vanguard divided between them. No brioche ever tasted better.
3. 'Our nemesis' – a reminder to military historians. The colonel received a note from GQG describing the impact of the German heavy artillery as 'demoralizing'.

On to Feigneux, Grimaucourt.[1]
From Grimaucourt to Retheuil, action.[2]

Saturday 12 September
To Chelles and Vichelles. Still raining, thank goodness.[3] All day in action. All evening getting soaked while we hunt for a billet in Chelles.

Sunday 13 September
Carrying on to Roylaye. Very hard fighting. Gunfire from dawn.

Pass through Cuise-Lamotte. The women throw us flowers. We cross the Aisne at Lamotte, on a wooden bridge constructed by the Engineers after the Germans blew up the railway bridge. Reach Attichy. The Germans have looted all the silver from the château.

Terrible fighting in a ravine east of La Faloise.

Blazing sun. At 4.00 pm a shell falls on the road, 20 metres behind me. Twenty-three or twenty-four horses killed: two of them belong to the colonel; one to Captain Vallet. Six or seven orderlies and gunners badly wounded.

March across the ravine to the Ferme de l'Arbre, a substantial square structure large enough to accommodate the entire regiment. Almost 9.00 pm. Pitch dark. Suddenly, the distant crackle of gunfire. Shouts can be heard: Forward! The bugle sounds the regimental call of the 102nd: '*Frédéric-François, Frédéric-François-Premier*!' Then the charge.

'*La monteras-tu, la côte?* ...' /
'Will you march on up to the top of the hill?...'

---

1. Passing through these villages, we saw messages chalked on the doors by the enemy Engineers. Some were instructions not to loot. '*Gute Leute, nicht plündern,*' they read. 'Good folk, no looting.'
2. That's all I wrote. I was shattered. I can't convey how tired we were, what with the constant fighting, the long marches, the lack of food and no more than a couple of hours' sleep a night. On the evening of 11 September I was chatting with the battalion medical officer when a man turned up asking to be evacuated.
   'What's up with you? asked the MO.
   'I've a temperature.'
   'A temperature?' sniffed the MO. He looked at me and grabbed hold of my wrist. 'The lieutenant is hotter than you'.
3. We always hoped the mud would slow down the German heavy artillery.

Shouts in the dark …

On the ridge, weapons at our feet, we anxiously await our moment. From here we think we can see bayonets glinting in the first distant light of dawn. The gunfire extends right along the front. Then everything falls quiet: the German counter-attack has failed.

We return to the farm. It's a big one – 250 hectares.

The farmer is a lieutenant serving with the Train in Vernon. His brother is standing in for him. A studious young man of 20 or so – tall, slim, angular, pince-nez. Stoops a little, looks rather tubercular in his thick-ribbed hunting jacket. He shows us around. The Prussians occupied the farm for two days and took everything. Harvest lost, livestock gone.

'The war has cost my brother 90,000 francs already,' he says.

'Yes,' we chorus. 'But at least he knows he'll survive.'[1]

Monday 14 September / Tuesday 15 September

Under shellfire all day, marching towards Nampcel.[2] Brief rest at the gatehouse in front of the Parc d'Offémont. Loopholes in the wall. Firing steps. Everything prepared for its defence. Met some spahis at the farm: red jackets, turbans, carbines by their thighs. Like statues. These exotic cavalrymen are a strange sight in this ultra-scientific, ultra-European war.

2.00 pm. In a double column of half-platoons, we advance towards Les Loges across a shallow valley of meadows fringed with woods.

Lieutenant Colonel Ferran is beside me. He rejoined us yesterday, his left leg still sporting a dressing: 'It's no worse than toothache. If my mother was in danger, I was sure toothache wouldn't keep me from her side. So I came back.'[3]

At 9.00 pm, with the burning villages lighting up the darkness, we reach the Ferme des Loges. We plan to spend the night here. The farm is on a ridge. It

---

1. A cry from the heart.
2. Colonel Farret despatched a cyclist to go on ahead and hunt for candles in the village. He never returned. The Germans had occupied the place and stayed for almost three years.
3. He ordered me to reconnoitre a farm on the right, the Ferme de Quennevières. I was met by the farmer, 50-ish, brown hair, quite tall, thin and slightly stooped. He greeted us like a man waking from a nightmare, mute with joy. Imagine my surprise a couple of hours later to discover that he risked being shot as a spy because a telephone had been found in his cellar. I did my best to rescue the poor fellow, and he was eventually left in peace. I later found out he was a very respectable farmer, long established in the area. The accusation was completely baseless.

seems foolish to occupy this big square building, which must be very easily spotted. The Germans have completely trashed the owners' apartments. The straw they put down in the dining room stinks to high heaven. Colonel Farret, now commanding the brigade, has a simple explanation: 'I smell Prussians!'

Bed down in a sheepfold at midnight. Sleep pretty well until 4.30 am.

Lieutenant Colonel Ferran sends 3rd Company right of the farm, and 4th Company left. I deploy 4th Company along the ridge behind. By 8.00 am we're in position.[1]

Shells and shrapnel come raining down …

Adjudant David is dead. Poor man! Poor woman![2]

More shells fall on the farm. Lieutenant Colonel Ferran is dead, Captains Bégert and Didisheim seriously wounded. We carry them into a cave. Such blood!

Here's my orderly, Pinel. Badly wounded in both legs.

'I shall have to leave you, sir.'

Poor lad!

The fire intensifies as normal at dusk in preparation for the counter-attack. We soon hear shooting, the crump of shells on all sides. The battery to our right falls silent, obviously destroyed by a couple of salvoes. Just imagine, our high command thought the German heavy artillery would only play a minor role! And we're the ones paying the price.

Poor [Lieutenant] Colonel Ferran!

He has paid dearly for a mistake of his own making. The first error was to billet us inside the farm, an obvious target, undoubtedly spotted by the enemy. The general, no great paragon of caution, had ordered the division to look for billets in Puisaleine, but Colonel Farret disagreed.

---

1. According to Colonel Lebaud (p. 79), a German aircraft overflew the farm at that very moment. 'Within ten minutes the first heavy shells began to pepper us, bigger and more impressive than ever. Their aim was perfect: the shells fell in the yard, in front of the gate, on the buildings … The men of 1st Company, guarding the internal wall from positions in the attic, were soon half buried beneath the rubble. They came down on ladders, covered in plaster dust. They looked like clowns, but bloody clowns, their faces and white uniforms spotted with gore.'

    I never saw this plane. The farm – a large one – was on a ridge, in the enemy's direct line of sight. The Germans didn't shell it overnight because they had not yet adopted this tactic.

2. When his wife learned of our arrival at Plessis-Belleville on 7 September, she came to try to see him. I granted his request for overnight leave, on his promise to return at first light the following day.

'I'm at Les Loges,' he told us at dinner, 'and I intend to stay here.'

In another blunder, the men lit fires all night. The farm must have been visible from 10 kilometres away. Perhaps the Germans thought it was burning, or weren't paying attention, convinced that we wouldn't move in until dawn. Whatever the case, it's a miracle we weren't shelled overnight. The lieutenant colonel was brought back soaked in blood, right thigh crushed, femoral artery probably severed. He never regained consciousness. But what was he doing with two companies still inside the farm at 8.00 am?

'Come on,' he said, just before the shell exploded. 'Let's get out of here!'

Too late!

Wednesday 16 September

Desperate fighting on both sides right along the front. Tracy-le-Val, Les Loges, Nampcel.[1] Intense shelling from dawn onwards. Elements of 102nd Infantry advance north of the Bois de Saint-Mard but pull back in disorder; bloodied men stream back to the cave in the quarries at Maison Rouge. N[orth] Corridor becomes an aid post, filled with the blood and moans [of the wounded].

The Germans are evidently trying to halt our advance, while we cling to the captured positions. A constant stream of orders arrives enjoining us to fight to the last man.

Around 1.00 pm we enter the cave for a brief rest. The light slanting through the narrow entrance is catching the flanks of the massive pillars of black rock. We retreat into the deep shadow and grab a quick bite to eat – a burnt chicken with some week-old bread.[2] Silhouetted right and left are the mules of the machine-gunners and artillery. It resembles a gypsy encampment in the brigands' cave.

Around 3.00 pm the gunfire intensifies on both sides. This deafening concert is becoming all too familiar.

After some hesitation, we're sleeping tonight on straw in the galleries of the cave.

Thursday 17 September

I've just received a letter from [one of my friends].

---

1. This front remained static until the Germans withdrew in March 1917.
2. We received only one distribution of fresh bread during the battle, on 12 or 13 September.

I'm speechless!

'War,' he writes. 'I've never believed in it. Such a body blow to idealism! But idealism is the very quality that distinguishes man from beast and is surely now the source of the moral strength that will see us through to victory.'

I'm living under constant shellfire, under bullets that even now are enfilading us. I want more than just fine words. I want some heavy guns. A few arrived this morning. Very heartening for us all.

Friday 18 September/Saturday 19 September

In the trenches yesterday, left of Les Loges. Night. Persistent rain. Nothing but straw to cover us. Blinded now and then by the scary, pale caress of the German searchlights. Then darkness, rain, the red glow of gunfire. I ponder [my friend]'s letter. A volley of heavy shells lands to our right, on the farm. The tree serving as my battle station is cropped to a height of 50 centimetres.

Moral strength! It's not lacking here. We hold our position beneath the torrent of shells. Still, one measly 240mm gun would do us nicely.

Billeted overnight in Puisaleine.[1] Woken by a dreadful racket at 2.00 am, a heavy shell landing in the field opposite my billet.

In the evening, en route to Compiègne.

Arrive in the darkness. The men are all in. They were given wine as we crossed the Aisne – at Berneuil, I think. After so many days of fighting, of incredible fatigue, with nothing or next to nothing to eat, three-quarters are rolling drunk.

In Compiègne. Finally, a bed. A miracle: sheets, real white cotton sheets. A chance for a wash and some sleep![2]

Sunday 20 September.

Billeted in Moyenneville. A rest day at last. Good bed. Beyond the windows, a garden with arbours and flowerbeds. Château life. An oasis in this terrible war.

My room was previously occupied by Captain Berger of 3rd Hussars.

---

1. One unlucky soldier was killed by a so-called stray bullet while standing right next to me, with the enemy 1500 to 1600 metres away. The only men who never hit anyone were those who never fired.
2. We hadn't taken our boots off since 6 September. Our division had been part of Maunoury's [Sixth] Army since 3 September, but on 19 September it transferred to Castelnau's [Second] Army, whose orders were to turn the German left wing. This marked the start of the Race to the Sea.

The men are billeted in a barn. I gather them at the door. 'You're winning the battle, so try to look the part. Clean your weapons and wash your shirts and greatcoats. The weather's fine today. They'll dry in a flash. These ladies (some local women were listening in) will help mend your clothes and replace any missing buttons. Correct, ladies?'

'Of course, *monsieur*!'

Laughter all round.

But my men look sceptical when I talk about winning. A long retreat, fatigue and the dreadful losses (scarcely 60 men left of our original 262) has wiped out all their enthusiasm and good cheer.

'Not one would say no to a wound to get himself evacuated,' whispers Sergeant Gallas, the bravest of the brave.

He's exaggerating. But plenty are clearly itching for a 'lucky wound'.

Back at my billet I run into a fusilier-marin. Open collar and beret.

Monday 21 September

2.00 pm. Canny-sur-Matz. Meet a skirmisher returning from the firing line. A tall, rangy type. 'Go on, the buggers are running away.'

The Moroccan Division arrived yesterday. More replacements are expected. Things are looking up.

We're leading the right-hand column: direction La Potière.

The battalion commander is Captain Seigneur (promoted only a couple of days ago). Tall, trim, ash-blond hair, hollow cheeks, bulging blue eyes – the eyes of a dreamer, or an evangelist.

5.30 pm. Positioned in a T-shape, facing north and west.

We have passed the cavalry. They say they can go no further. They're bumping into the enemy all along the front line.

Captain Seigneur orders me to move up. He's attacking La Potière.

I quickly recall my leading platoon, now in an advanced position at the edge of a wood, 700 or 800 metres to the north.

March towards La Potière.

The light begins to fade.

Runners arrive from 1st Company. Captain Seigneur has attacked with 1st Company, the only troops available. 'The Germans were busy cooking up some grub. We stormed in, bayonets fixed, and caught them by surprise. But as we entered the village, the captain was killed by a revolver at point-blank range. The Germans sent in reinforcements. We had to scarper.'

I despatch one platoon as advance guard and immediately deploy two more.

My dispositions complete, the remnants of 1st Company turn up, led by Adjudant Marçay. He confirms what the runners have told us. Night falls. All I can do now is rally the battalion – once more under my command – and fall back on Fresnières where I'll try to join up with the regiment.

I designate the Ferme-sans-Nom as our rallying point.

We reach Fresnières at 11.00 pm.

Tuesday 22 September
5.00 am. Ordered to march on the Ferme Haussu.

We've only had time for a couple of hours' sleep and a coffee. The men are all in, bellies empty.

They're grumbling.

'Why not shoot us now and have done with it?' drawls Degraf, a pale, puny boy from the Paris *faubourgs*.

We circle the edge of a wood... We're opposite the farm buildings. The bullets start to whine. Complete silence in the ranks. All conversation ceases. Sombre faces. A palpable sense of fear.

10.00 am. South of the Ferme Haussu. Beautiful sunny day; fluffy white clouds, light breeze. A glorious autumn morning, marred only by the whine of the bullets and the rumble of the guns. Ignoring the din, my two runners are snoring away beside me. The nonchalance of the French soldier beggars belief ...

We lost Captain Seigneur at La Potière yesterday. I'll never see those big old eyes again. He was cool under fire, very elegant, exquisitely urbane. Of the officers who fought at Ethe, the regiment now has only six left.[1] As Voltaire once remarked, the trick is to agree what words really mean. Our failure to examine them properly explains why we so rarely perceive military history in all its tragedy. To take just one example: 'This regiment held that position all day.' It seems simple enough, but what is meant by that neutral word 'hold'? I've just 'held' the Ferme Haussu all day, and I know exactly what it signifies. It means remaining in the trenches without moving, ready at any moment to meet an infantry attack with a volley of rifle fire, all beneath a deluge of shot and steel.

---

1. Out of 52 front-line officers. The rest had all been killed, wounded or evacuated. This confirms the appalling number of losses suffered by front-line officers and NCOs in pre-war regiments in the first two months of the war.

Percussion shells, shrapnel balls and machine-gun bullets rain down from 11.00 am until nightfall. The two companies stationed in the farm – why, I wonder[1] – fall back, or more precisely get the hell out of there. I take them into my lines and continue to 'hold' my position. The farm is soon on fire, emitting huge clouds of smoke.

In the evening we lie down on the damp grass, still in our positions. The fire lights up the darkness, silhouetting the black gable of the roof.

Wednesday 23 September
Wake up numb with cold.

Orders to move north (Amy). A shell falls.[2] Hit in the thigh by shrapnel. Sergeant Joseph and two others come to retrieve me. I hand over command of the company and show them what route to follow. The bullets are whistling by. 'Don't worry about me,' I tell Joseph. 'I'm done for. Get back to the others.' I feel pretty bad. I want to be sick, even though all I have in my stomach is coffee. But Joseph stays with me. His two comrades[3] return to Fresnières for a wheelbarrow, load me in and push me back under fire. At Fresnières, they carry me into the *mairie*, where my wound is dressed. Then I'm taken by cart to Roye-sur-Matz.

Friday 25 September
I am now at the Hôpital Saint-Joseph after two dreadful days in transit.

I was initially evacuated to Roye. There, the MO of the Moroccan Division sent me to a little house as company for a tirailleur captain with a foot wound. This captain only disembarked four days ago and already seems sick to death of the war. Clearly, this isn't Morocco.

'We've lost a third of our officers and men already,' he said.

'Hold on, sir,' I retorted. 'We started out with 3,300 men on 7 August; now we've barely 700.'[4]

This clarification did something to temper his bitterness.

---

1. An occupied farm is an obvious magnet for shells. Defenders should be placed around it, not inside.
2. In fact, a shrapnel ball.
3. One is now a notary at Ressons-sur-Matz. I can only express my gratitude.
4. According to the calculations of Colonel Lebaud (p. 120), 4,663 men (3,300 plus 1,363 replacements) and 75 officers (62 plus 13 replacements) served with the regiment between 6 August and 9 October 1914. By then just 1,000 men and 11 officers remained.

Our hostess is an old woman of 60 or so, kerchief rolled into a bonnet round her head. She amuses me no end. As I can neither stand nor sit, I have to lie down. And where else but in bed? But the old girl doesn't want me using 'her' bed. It's dreadful, she says. Not good enough for me. The counterpane's not hers. It belongs to some '*monsieur*', a 'senior officer', an adjudant, an NCO. 'I don't know. I can't tell one from another.'

I lie down anyway. Her sighs are quite pitiful, but she'll just have to grin and bear it. There's a Rimailho battery about 600 to 800 metres away. She trembles with every thud of the gun: 'Dear Lord, this is dreadful! Lord have mercy!'

'But it's one of ours, *madame*!'

'I don't care. It's horrible!' Then she continues quite brazenly: 'The Germans said they were heading for Paris. They should have kept their word and left Picardy in peace.'

We embark from Montdidier at 10.00 am.[1] The 'hospital train' is made up of cattle-trucks covered with a thin bed of straw. We're laid down in rows.[2]

'Room for one more,' jokes the stationmaster. 'Hutch up a bit.'

We limp along at snail's pace. My wound hurts unbearably every time the train jolts or brakes.

Eventually reach Aubervilliers station at 11.30 pm.

---

1. We lay on benches in the waiting room until the train arrived. A kind chap gave me a sip of white wine.
2. By a strange coincidence everyone in the wagon had leg wounds. There was nothing we could do to help one another.

Book Two

Story of a Company

Thursday 11 November 1915

We've arrived in Givry-en-Argonne,[1] where the regiment has been at rest for a fortnight.

I now have command of 8th Company. It has a full complement of 173 men,[2] as well as three sous-lieutenants: T[ramard], A[ubel] and L[ambert]. T[ramard] and A[ubel] were both teachers, while L[ambert] is a former maréchal des logis in the artillery, now promoted to sous-lieutenant in the infantry.

T[ramard] is a big, blond 23-year-old, prematurely bald. He's been doing his military service and will probably remain in the army. A[ubel] is 32. Does he also hope to stay on? Perhaps. Meanwhile L[ambert] is 22 years old. He was preparing to go to Fontainebleau but after fourteen months in the front line requested a transfer to the infantry. He watched comrades back at the depot being promoted to sous-lieutenant, while his name couldn't be put forward. Brown hair, apple cheeks, laughing blue eyes: very tall, but a thin neck and narrow chest − not quite as robust as he looks. Enthusiastic and cheerful, though. He's a bit of rascal, slight lisp, always chipper.[3]

---

1. I had left Dreux with a batch of reinforcements on 8 November. A gloomy farewell. A miserable November day, raining non-stop. The men were cheerful enough when we left the barracks, but their courage began to desert them as we approached the station. Some had been met by their wives, who walked beside them, children clutching their skirts. I was hobbling, leaning on a stick, due to my wounded right leg. As if by design, it hurt more than it had for weeks. It was dark by the time we reached the station. Some comrades stood me a glass of champagne at the buffet. Then the senior officer turned up, a regular Engineers major who hadn't seen front-line action and was never going to. He began to hurl abuse at me. Me, leaving for my second stint at the front, and still unfit for active duty. He had four stripes to my two, so I played the good soldier and kept my mouth shut. Shirkers bullied combatants during and after the war.
2. Those serving with, or attached to, the regimental HQ can be deducted from this total. This left just 131 men in the front line.
3. Died of pneumonia at Verdun, 1 June 1916.

Major [Casabianca] is a Corsican, aged 55 or so.[1] Small, bald and lined; stumpy bow legs; accent sharp as an unripe apple. He's only just arrived with the regiment. His military experience is limited to summer manoeuvres and duties in the rear. He acts like a sergeant-major. He presides over the table. The atmosphere is grim. A front-line mess is normally the soul of good cheer, but all we do here is talk shop. No other topic of conversation is allowed. He rises at 10.00 or 11.00 am, sits down at the table and smokes his pipe or sometimes a cigar.

Monday 15 November 1915
Sent on the divisional company commanders' course at Saint-Mard-le-Mont.

We were welcomed by the divisional commander, [General Dantant]. He told us we have to be trained for the resumption of 'normal warfare'. For this pleasant, courteous man in his 60s, florid face, white hair scraped over his scalp, this clearly means the war of movement. Those good old grand manoeuvres so beloved by our regular soldiers are not yet dead and buried. When will they get the message?[2]

Saturday 20 November
Life is dreary here in this little Argonne village of 300 or so, which has already lost eight or nine of its young men in the war.

---

1. He seemed that age, although he must have been younger. Whatever the case, he was still too old to exercise his command. And by this point in the war there were many battalion commanders in the same boat. Instead of promoting captains (whether regular or reservist) with wartime experience, the ministry persisted in its foolish peacetime practice of appointing older men like him, who proved unable either to adapt to their new life or even to cope with its physical demands. During a crisis like Verdun, the results were catastrophic.
2. We were now fifteen and a half months into the war. We had experienced the bloody failures of Champagne (February 1915 and 25 September 1915) and Artois. This proves how long it took for light to dawn at the highest levels. In the second half of 1917, under General Pétain, these courses became extremely valuable. At the time, however, their only function was to 'bolster morale'. The high command was always ready to attribute the failure of our attacks to a lack of 'offensive spirit' among the rank and file. Our total lack of mortars – the only guns effective against trenches, where the 75 was powerless – was ignored.

Monday 29 November

Leaving for the front-line tomorrow. We're heading first to Dommartin-sous-Hans, and from there to Massiges.

The 131 men present in the company include 15 sergeants and 16 corporals, nearly all with front- line experience. I also have my three sous-lieutenants and one adjudant, the excellent Dubuc. He is 40 or so, brown hair, fresh faced; a former NCO turned local tax official; competent, very shrewd and composed, utterly reliable.

The men come from Le Mans, Normandy, and the Beauce, plus a few Parisians.

The company has a good reputation. It always seems to have conducted itself well. I am its fourth CO: Captain Battesti was killed at Ethe[1] on 22 August 1914; Lieutenant Bernard,[2] at Perthes on 28 February 1915; while Captain Rallier du Baty[3] was badly wounded on 25 September 1915.

We will try to live up to our predecessors.

I've seen Big D. again. He's spent the last ten months in supplies. Not a lot of *marmites*, good food. He's bigger and jollier than ever. The other Sunday, he and I had lunch with the new colonel, Lieutenant Colonel L[anusse], ex-Foreign Legion, a southerner (to judge by his accent).[4] Small and trim, typical of the Armée d'Afrique. A very cheerful affair. D., with his songs, was the star of the show. He belted out '*On les aura! Quand on le voudra!*' / 'We'll have 'em whenever we like!'[5] The colonel loved it, and we all joined in with a will. But a man like D., singing a song like that … I ask you![6]

---

1. Right at the start of the action, by a shell that simultaneously killed Molinier, one of his lieutenants. Captain Battesti was perhaps 36 or 37, average height, slim and elegant. He had very brown hair, fine features and a sparkling smile that charmed everyone he met. In 1900, as a very young man, he had been my – highly popular – sous-lieutenant in 46th Infantry. Molinier was short and stocky, exceptionally agile and energetic. He was always bright and cheerful. And, I must own, he liked a lark. On 21 August, the eve of battle, he turned up brandishing his sabre and made off with my boots. Then he had a fine time watching me turn up late for parade.
2. Tall, no older than 30, slightly stoop, light chestnut hair, full of vim. One of the Saint-Juvin reinforcements (1 September). He had a sweetheart, a poor young woman who spent many months trying to discover his fate.
3. A long-service captain who took over from Bernard on 28 February. He died of his wounds in December 1915.
4. He came from Saint-Bertrand-de-Comminges. A good man, honest and brave.
5. Translator's note: a patriotic song by Rip, i.e. Georges Gabriel Thenon (1884–1941).
6. He always managed to keep out of the firing line.

It was a very convivial group, which included some of my original comrades. They were present because all have enjoyed some pretty cushy jobs – [Sous-lieutenant] T[hibaut] as a telephonist, [Captain] Letondot as the colonel's adjutant, and [Lieutenant] S[ivan] in supplies until May, then machine guns. For an adjutant, Captain L[etondot] has done very nicely for decorations. He has four mentions-in-dispatches – two at army, one at corps and one at regimental level – as well as the Légion d'Honneur. Meanwhile the actual combatants get nothing, the reservists especially.

Thursday 2 December

We travelled to Dommartin-sous-Hans by lorry. What a wonderful way of moving troops! Within a matter of hours a whole regiment can cover 30 kilometres, a long march until now. And on the stinking, muddy roads of the Argonne, who knows what kind of state they would arrive in?

The contemporary French army must look very strange to anyone familiar with it before. While still at Givry, we watched 14th Hussars trot past. I thought of the squadrons who marched alongside us at the start: monocled officers in sky blue tunics, shako with white trim and plume, martingale linked with copper; the men in their red trousers, blue jackets and shakos. It was bold, martial and, we would have said at the time, all very French.

Now cavalry officers and men were all in the infantry greatcoat, helmet and trousers. A silver number on a black badge was the only reminder of the glorious hussars. No, there was something else: their horses. Fine beasts, well tended despite the long campaign. These men were definitely cavalrymen.

Another regiment – coming out of the trenches, if 14th Hussars were going in – the 3rd Chasseurs d'Afrique. Here, too, hardly any *chéchias*. Gone were the wide trousers and short blue jackets fitted at the waist and tucked into a red cummerbund. They were in infantry helmets and horizon-blue greatcoats. Just their wonderful little Arab horses to show they are chasseurs d'Afrique.

We're billeted in Dommartin-sous-Hans, a small village of around 300 inhabitants before the war. No one is left but a few old folk, like the owner of the house where I'm billeted with my three sous-lieutenants. With her grey hair and wrinkles, she seems a bit scatty. 'Please forgive the state of the place, *monsieur*. It's usually neat and tidy, but I've been away for the last fifteen months.'

We never clap eyes on her. She skulks in the depths of the attics like a hunted animal.

The village is a real cesspit, full of miserable, filthy, abandoned hovels. Lurking in the farmyards and behind the barns are pools of liquid manure, dung-heap upon dung-heap – all drowning in ankle-deep mud. The fields are an impermeable marl. Water stays on the surface, so any rain (and it's been pouring down) turns the ground into a sticky dough that makes it impossible to advance.

Trenches have been dug near the village as protection from the shells. A sensible precaution. The shelling is pretty regular.

Clouds still miserable and low, gunfire thundering in the distance. I preferred the two or three days of biting cold we had before leaving Saint-Mard.

Saturday 4 December

Reconnoitred our sector, the Oreille de Massiges. 8th Company is in the second line and will relieve 5th Company in four or five days. These were originally Boche trenches facing Massiges, now turned by us to face the enemy who still occupy the Chenille.[1] Their front line trenches are 500 or 600 metres away, separated from us by a ravine. They are apparently held by machine-guns only but that's quite enough. The guns are very well set up. They are positioned in the bottom of their pits and only uncovered to fire.

The Germans do the job properly.

Not something you can say about us.

We are relieving a regiment of southerners, who themselves replaced a bunch of colonials a week ago. The ground is poor, a yielding green marl that any rain soon transforms into a sticky dough. That said, our predecessors don't seem to have put themselves out much.[2] The trenches and *boyaux* are in a shocking condition – often crumbling, nearly always too shallow, usually flooded. Water to mid thigh, mud up to the knees. The men are nothing but great clods of mud. What a life! Trousers and greatcoats disappear beneath a layer of the stuff: mud on the helmet, mud in the eyes. So clogged are our rifles we can't even open the breech.

The horror begins even before reaching Virginy.[3] Shell-holes all around. Left of the road, a dead horse, belly distended. Virginy is a wreck. Its fine stone church stands on a mound, a gaunt shell, completely gutted. The tower has

---

1. A wooded spur that dominated the flatter ground. The cropped trees resembled the stiff hairs of a caterpillar. Hence the name.
2. We often thought our predecessors had been slacking, perhaps with some justification here. The colonials had courage aplenty but scorned pick and shovel. So too did the southerners who followed them.
3. A village around 4 kilometres from the front-line trenches.

collapsed, the two bells intact beneath the rubble. The houses are just a few scraps of wall. A red-brick chimney is still upright, heaven knows how.

I shudder as I enter the *boyau*. Soon we're on the parapet, concealed by the ridge that once formed the German front line. Ahead are solid barbed-wire entanglements fixed to steel posts. Someone has made a good job of it. Our guns had cut the lot here. Half buried at the bottom of a shell-hole lies one of our own; beside him is his rifle, bayonet fixed, rusting already. All you can make out is a thin frame under a heavy blue greatcoat, probably a colonial infantryman. Face decomposing, bluish purple, streaked with blood.

Further away a skull. I'm surprised by T[ramard]'s morbid insistence on viewing these spectacles and cracking jokes. In the *boyau*, a Boche is being dug out of the mud. A greenish-yellow leg has already been uncovered. I turn away. It's horrible. A group of forty German bodies wrapped in tent sections have been spotted close by. T. goes off to inspect.

No wonder those with recent experience of the horrors of war, like the Greeks, are determined to avoid them this time.[1]

Monday 6 December

Relief. It began at 3.45 pm and finished at 9.00 pm. It rained thoughout.

The Boches bombarded the exit from the village all day. Fortunately most of the shells failed to explode.

A gloomy march in the pitch dark, illuminated only by the French and German rockets lighting up the sky like showers of fireworks. The leading companies, guided on horseback by Captain [Hillère] and Major [Casabianca], went at such a lick that, in third place, I was struggling to keep up. Bétron and 7th Company got lost amid the dark, the mud, and the ill-defined tracks cut by trenches and telephone wires.

'Mind the wire!'[2]

The rain was blinding. After covering 12 kilometres in this fashion, our path was littered with stragglers who had fallen into ditches or shell-holes.

We finally reached our destination. I went to my HQ, previously a German officer's dug-out. A hole 10 feet deep, entered backwards. Then a square room,

---

1. Greece was then hedging its bets, but not for fear of the horrors of war. Prominent politicians like Venizélos wanted the country to join the allies, while the court was subject to German influence, King Constantine having married a sister of the Kaiser.
2. We used to get entangled in the telephone wires. Every poilu will recall this warning.

supported by logs 1.6 metres high. Wooden planks line the walls and ceiling. At the back, a bunk of wood and iron mesh.

I lay down. Rats all night. The occasional shell.

Tuesday 7 December
Better weather.

At 8.00 am I went to reconnoitre Tranchée Balcon, which I am to occupy in a few days' time. It lies opposite the German positions on the Chenille and the Justice. The white lines of the enemy trenches stand out along the horizon.

Intense shelling all day.

We went to explore the ravine leading down to Massiges. Dotted by shell-holes, like a slotted spoon. We find the cemetery of the colonials from 23rd Infantry, a row of crosses in a *boyau* now serving as a mass grave. In a former German trench beyond, around forty Boche corpses have been exhumed. The stench is unbearable. The poilus wander between them, hunting for souvenirs.

Wednesday 8 December
The enemy 105s, 150s and 77s have been shelling us since 7.00 pm yesterday. Our batteries reply. It sounds like they're getting the upper hand. Outside the dug-out, the night is inky black, lit only by the glaring white beam of the searchlights and the ruddy glow of the guns.

What's killing us is lack of sleep. Even if we managed to ignore the gunfire, the rats scurrying and squealing behind the planks would keep us awake all night. And now the lice are starting to torment us too.

3.30 am. The shells were raining down on all sides, the perfect time for Major [Casabianca] to order a night exercise. You'd think we were still in barracks. The men just shrugged. We tramped in the dark through the flooded *boyaux*, sloshing our way through mud knee deep in places.

All because no Frenchman has ever heard of the pump!

Soon, the men – who have had no sleep – will have to work like Trojans to shovel out the mud, only to see it re-form behind them because they have no means of getting rid of the water.

Could you imagine a more pointless exercise!

The patience and stoicism of the poilu will eventually triumph over German science and method, but no thanks to the generals and the Staff.[1]

---

1. Until General Pétain assumed command in May 1917.

Inevitably, the Boche trenches opposite are bone dry – or so a German prisoner told us this morning.

Thursday 9 December

'Are those pigs stupid or what?' asks Bocage,[1] my illustrious runner and liaison with battalion HQ, as he comes diving into the dug-out. 'They haven't got a clue.'

The 105 shrapnel shells are bursting all along the ridge. Bocage looks both ways before setting foot again outside.

The *boyaux* are flooded, totally impassable. I don't know what would happen if I had to support the front line. We only need a couple of pumps to dry them out. For the past two days I've asked for one in my 5.00 am and 5.00 pm reports. The suction pump has been around for centuries, apparently unnoticed by Monsieur Le Bureaucrat. How is the poilu expected to clear, or rather attempt to clear, a *boyau*? That's right, with a shovel! The soil here is so impermeable that any water thrown from a trench runs straight back and hits you in the face. We have a few scoops, but not enough. And the end result is no different.

Major [Casabianca][2] still has not grasped our situation. He must always have been a bit touched, and returning to the front has sent him right over the edge. Yesterday and today he roused us at 3.30 am to proceed to the *boyau* of Captain [Hillère]. A stand-to drill, as if we were in barracks. 'This is a night march!' he said. 'No talking.' Not that the poilus showed any such inclination. They're overworked, then deprived of the chance to snatch a few hours' rest just when the shelling normally subsides. They might well make their disapproval plain.

Lack of sleep is the real killer. We can't even enjoy any brief lull in the shelling; the rats and lice in our dug-outs pick up where the Boches leave off. The two orderlies[3] sleep in the dug-out at right angles to my bunk. Bamboula (Delahaye) is 20,[4] class of 1915 – a big, cheerful, easy-going lad. He waits until I lie down

---

1. Average height, ash blond, slightly stooped. A shop assistant in Paris, with the [characteristic local] drawl and slight lisp. Cool under shelling, funny and brave. He would arrive in the dug-out, out of breath after running through the barrage, collapse on the bottom step and fan himself with his helmet: 'Those pigs haven't got a clue.'
2. Irreverent as ever, the men decided the major's bald head, prognathous jaw and turkey neck reminded them of ... Consul [the Educated Ape]. They never used any other name between themselves, hence its appearance in my diary.
3. One was my orderly; the other belonged to one of the sous-lieutenants.
4. Killed at Verdun on 4 June 1916. In the meantime he had become one of the company's best bombers. Average height, slim, still very boyish. He had curly brown hair and a firm jaw: hence the name Bamboula. Wonderfully brave.

each night before writing to his (only) friend: 'Mlle Marguerite Abrahame, c/o her parents, farmers'. His sole ambition is to be a corporal: 'I'll go on patrol, and the lieutenant will promote me to corporal.' Aubry is older, class of 1908, a Norman from Argentan: small and stout; broad, ruddy moon face; always wears a mucky old blue-grey forage cap set fore and aft on his short black hair. Greatcoat, woollen jumper, *salopette* worn over his trousers, that's Aubry. He's an amiable type, a gallant farmer, very crafty despite his girth.

His conversations with Bamboula alone are enough to earn his keep.

Friday 10 December

The Germans have been shelling us since 9.00 am, when I returned from reconnoitring the lines I am to occupy this evening. They're hitting the Ravin du Médius and the Plateau behind us – a former battery emplacement.

That big devil Lambert is estimating the fall of shells. They're all 105s,[1] from a single battery tucked away behind the Bois de la Justice.[2]

Saturday 11 December

11.00 am. The Boches are shelling my new HQ. 'They always send the cheap rubbish,' says L[ambert]. 'It breaks every time.'

My new HQ is like a ship's cabin. All it lacks is a porthole. Three planks for a bed. T[ramard] is very dejected. It's all a bit too rough and ready for him.

Defensively, our sector is in a parlous state. Absolutely no work has been done. The trenches have no firing step; the barbed wire is loose. Two of our three front-line trenches can be enfiladed from the Chenille. Boyau Eitel[3] is a quagmire in some places, a lake in others. I can't rely on receiving reinforcements. A handful of shells and it would fall in completely.

Sunday 12 December

Pounded by shells of all calibres. Those gentlemen should correct their fire. Some of the shells contain tear-gas. It stings the eyes. Masks on! Now! The irritation stops at once.

---

1. From a 105 light howitzer, firing a 15.67kg shell. In the opinion of General Gascouin, 105mm is the optimum calibre for heavier field artillery. Our 155s fired a 43kg shell but were too heavy to manoeuvre.
2. South of Cernay-en-Dormois.
3. The *boyau* had retained its German name. We soon improved conditions there.

A captain from the divisional staff visited my HQ this morning. Nice enough fellow, 40-ish, crow's feet already, slim and polite. He arrived in leather gloves! I offered him a tour of the trenches, but he was happy to stick with the maps. He came because a Boche was captured yesterday. The prisoner says the Germans are planning to retake the Main de Massiges before Xmas, and the captain seems to believe him. He describes him as a broad-shouldered, bullet-headed giant, eyes gleaming with intelligence.

The captain is obviously concerned. He thinks an attack is likely. I'm not so sure, due partly to the state of the ground – the mud in no man's land is thigh deep in places – and partly to the number of dud shells.

I'm on watch tonight. That big soufflé T[ramard] is exhausted. His spirits are drooping. He needs fifteen hours' sleep a day.

Outside it's a beautiful night. Clear skies, moon and stars. The distant plateau appears blindingly white in the pale light. The *boyaux* are still full of water. Rats jump on the banks at each step. Plenty of 'Gaspards'[1] around tonight! Next time Monsieur Poincaré entertains a dignitary, he should bring him hunting out here; the photographs would be a sensation.

The Boches have a clear view into our *boyaux*. It's bright as day. Their 77s greet me as I pass. I'm flattered. They really shouldn't bother. Unfortunately, they are also firing on the men digging my flanking trench. Rotten luck to have such a clear night when we have so much work to do.

I go to gee up the men in the other trenches, then return to my HQ. My splendid poilus believe this is a much tougher sector than the one we occupied last December.

I found one man standing thigh deep in water.

'What are you doing?' I asked him.

'Trying to get warm, sir!' he replied.

Monday 13 December

Tour the sector around 7.00 am with Major [Casabianca]. He's surprised by the pools of water, thigh deep in places. He'll get an even bigger shock in a minute when the shells start falling. This is a most unhealthy time of day … The Boches don't disappoint us. They can see straight into the trenches and let us have a few whenever they spot any movement.

Shelled throughout the day.

---

1. A nickname for the rats.

Overnight my dug-out is rocked incessantly by Boche Minnies targeting the colonials to our left on the Verrue, as well as my front lines. These Minnies[1] are terrifying. An enormous explosion with a flame soaring 20 or 30ft into the sky. It's a very clear night already and they light it up even more.

Tuesday 14 December

Last night I ordered my men to clean the sector; this morning you could walk around it in your stocking feet.

Life is pretty unhealthy here in the front line, but we get by. Shelling night and day. Work all night. I feel like a ship's captain.

Today is fine, clear and dry. Shells criss-cross the skies, rumbling like wagons on an overhead cable. My sector is just about tenable now. On the night of 12/13 December, we dug a flanking trench heading south-west from the western end of my Tranchée Balcon. Putting it in just below the ridge line was a good idea. The Boches began bombarding the trench this morning but all the shells are falling on the ridge.

Crossfire between this trench and Tranchée Balcon-Ouest will make the ravine impassable.

Last night I ordered my men to drain the trenches and *boyaux*, raise the parapet destroyed by shellfire in Tranchée Balcon, and rebuild a wall of sandbags threatening collapse. Others started work in Tranchée Merlonnée, digging out the hump in the middle that makes it indefensible, and constructing an underground shelter for its garrison of thirty. We have held these positions for three months, yet no one has considered giving these poor devils somewhere to sleep or escape the shells.

All that remains is a link with Tranchée Balcon-Ouest. The Boche machine guns on the Chenille overlook our position.[2] If the Germans attacked, they could block our passage at the elbow where the *boyau* runs downhill to the trench. The trench would be isolated and the men taken prisoner.

I ask for a telephone line ...

---

1. The huge projectiles fired by the German trench mortars, or *Minenwerfer*. The men called them coal-buckets.
2. The enemy overlooked almost all our front-line positions. Much better ones were available just a few hundred metres to the rear, but so timid were our leaders, so obsessed with territory, they would rather inflict unnecessary losses than relinquish a few metres of ground.

We write a daily report covering the previous twenty-four hours. It seems that someone might be taking the trouble to read them. Two days ago I reported the barbed-wire entanglements need reinforcing, starting with Tranchée Balcon-Ouest. Yesterday evening the Engineers sent a working party to tackle the job. If the staff are starting to heed the regimental officers, it would be a revolution.

Wednesday 15 December
The Boches have only fired 500 shells. They just don't have a clue.

Relieved yesterday evening. Replaced by 142nd Infantry, commanded by Captain C. An icy, clear night. Set off at 9.30 pm. Arrived at Dommartin at midnight. Consul got us lost. I can't begin to describe the hardships endured by the men over the past week. They came out from the trenches caked in mud, exhausted, struggling to cover the 10 kilometres between the lines and Dommartin. A lot of frostbitten feet; some will have to be amputated.

Thursday 16 December
At rest in Dommartin. L[ambert] has a temperature. The lad has caught a cold.

Friday 17 December
Old Pa Istria[1] sent L[ambert] a purgative. L[ambert] threw it out of the window and is feeling much better.

Inspect the barracks where my men are billeted: two dark attics, open to the four winds. The straw they are sleeping on is no better than powder and ridden with lice.[2] The poor lads are as miserable as sin. Glum faces, doleful expressions. I hazard a joke or two. It does nothing to cheer them up. But they are still taking care of their weapons. All the rifles are clean, the mud of the trenches washed away. Why? The answer is quite simple. The corporal wants to be a sergeant; the sergeant wants to be an officer; the officer wants to avoid a dressing-down and win an extra stripe. The officers bawl out the sergeants, who bawl out the corporals, who bawl out the men. And the men, hounded to death, rise from their lousy beds and start polishing. Pride also plays its part, not to mention the incredible resilience of the French soldier.[3]

---

1. Médecin-major. A charming fellow, famous for his unflappability and tireless devotion to duty. Unfortunately he soon had to leave us. We called him 'Pa' Istria. So, of course, the battalion MO Boisramé (captured at Fort Vaux on 7 June 1916) had to be 'Sonny'.
2. There was never enough good bedding straw for the men coming out of the trenches.
3. The Frenchman's pride will always make him a good fighter.

Saturday 18 December
124th Infantry captured a man from German-occupied Lorraine the other day. He told us all about the Boche batteries, the regiments in front of us, etc. He says the Boches are worried about a possible French attack, although another prisoner claims they've been ordered to recapture the Main de Massiges before Xmas.

Grey skies here. The weather has turned a little warmer. In their miserable attics, the men doze or polish their weapons. I hold a daily inspection at 3.00 pm.[1] The hours drag by.

A few soldiers are doggedly sweeping the road through the village, pushing the mud towards the boggy channel that was once a roadside stream. The harder they try to get rid of it, the quicker it returns.

One of the sous-lieutenants in 5th Company has a brother in 315th Infantry who says that the men in one of his outposts have been warming themselves beside the same fire as the Boches opposite.[2]

1.00 pm. The colonel has told me that I am now a captain.

Tuesday 21 December 1915
Today I signed the 'Comparative Statement of Sums Advanced to the Company, Third Quarter, 1914'. We are required to return the sum of 45 francs 72 centimes overpaid from 1 July to 10 August 1914! 'Peacetime', it says on the statement in red ink. Monsieur Le Bureaucrat really does take the biscuit! Everyone tries to fleece us. Today I was forced to pay 1 franc 50 centimes for a packet of five candles worth 10 centimes. Our billet is a wretched hovel, where we sleep fully clothed on a bed without sheets. The owner came to visit, a tiny, wrinkled mouse of a woman, 80 or so, who pottered around carrying a tiny hand-warmer. She inundated us with her courtesies and complaints: 'Poor boy, this! Dear boy, that!'

Little and old maybe, but she still has her head screwed on the right way. She was here to offer us the wine sold by her son-in-law at the 'attractive' price of 2 francs 75 centimes a bottle. Nice work if you can get it!

---

1. During rest periods, I never demanded more of the men than some target or bombing practice each morning. Regular target and bombing practice was invaluable. The excellent marksmen and bombers in our company always gave cause for satisfaction, especially at Verdun.
2. *Sé non è vero* ... [If this isn't true, it ought to be]. We never saw anything like this.

Wednesday 22 December 1915
Relieving 142nd Infantry. The captain I am relieving used to be a regimental paymaster. He arrived at the front in late June. He's still vexed that he couldn't stay at the depot. He spent his four days in the second line lying in his dug-out.[1] He's also grumbling that he hasn't been made a chevalier of the Légion d'Honneur.

Thursday 23 December
The Médius, Ravin, Annulaire and Abeilles normally seem deserted. But with every lull in the shelling men pop out all over, like legions of termites.
What a life!
Now and then, however, in the muddy maze of *boyaux* a detail recalls French style: a ramp elegantly cut into steps.

Friday 24 December
Christmas Eve.
In the *boyaux* at 10.00 pm. Long grey clouds slide across the moon. Shells criss-cross the sky with an angry whine. In the distance the rumble of the guns.

Saturday 25 December
4.30 pm. The Boches will soon be sending over their 77s and 105s. If they really knew what they were doing, they'd hold on to the junk.
Mud. During the last relief, reports L[ambert] , Cantenot[2] disappeared up to his armpits on the zigzag path through the ravine.
The mice are running behind the planks in the dug-out, nibbling, scampering, jumping. They sound like birds cheeping. The noise never stops.

Monday 27 December
11.30 pm. The Boche 105s are rocking the shelter. Direct hits, showering my notebook with earth.
A shell has just exploded. The flame shot straight down the stairs of my HQ, almost blinding me.
The whole dug-out stinks of powder.

---

1. 'We're teachers,' he said. 'We're not cut out for this lark.'
2. An excellent soldier from my company. His comrades held out their rifles to him. He grabbed them by the butt and his chums pulled him free.

Tuesday 28 December

Inspection at 2.41pm by General Putz, the army corps commander. He's 55-ish, very long, fair moustache, long, fleshy nose and pouchy, red-veined cheeks. Looks mild enough – a bit of a staff 'dandy'. He's average height, trim and rather elegant. He turned up in a helmet, a short leather coat, and red breeches with a black stripe, sensibly protecting his calves with black puttees.

Alongside him were the colonel, L[etondot] and another silent staff colonel. Behind them came [Major] C[asabianca], [Hillère] and me. We all trooped off to the artillery observation post. L[etondot] pointed out the terrain. A group like this naturally attracted the attention of the Boches. We were right in their line of sight. The shells began to fall. A piece of shrapnel bounced off L[etondot]'s helmet and landed on his shoulder.[1] The general turned and smiled. I saluted him. No, he was saluting [Hillère] behind me. The shell too, I think.

We all moved off …

I return to my HQ. The Boches are peppering the whole *boyau*. A shell has just exploded on top of my dug-out. Seconds later a man staggers in. 'A poilu's just been killed in the *boyau*.'

I go outside. It's Sergeant Janvier. He's lying on his front, unrecognizable, face already white. His belly is ripped open. His guts are hanging out. The shell fell on the edge of the parapet, now spattered with blood. It's blown him limb from limb. We have to lay him in a tent section, scoop up his innards with a shovel. The poor lad was due leave in honour of his Médaille [Militaire].[2] He'd just been to see [Sergeant] Pionnier,[3] thinking he was going this evening.

'No, tomorrow,' Pionnier had told him.

Janvier sought me out to ask if this was right.

The tribe of Béni-Oui-Oui. What a bunch of sycophants!

Shortly before inspecting the artillery observation posts, General [Putz] asked me which units were in the front-line trenches.

'1st Platoon and 4th Platoon, sir.'

'How are they fixed?'

'1st Platoon has a sap with a single entry point. We need to put another in here (I pointed to the plan), leading to the trench. 4th Platoon has nothing.

---

1. He looked up at the general and blushed.
2. Very brave. His splendid conduct on 25 September 1915 had just earned him the Médaille Militaire.
3. A sergeant in the Paris municipal police. Exemplary composure and devotion to duty.

We've started putting a sap in here (I pointed again). It needs two ramps and 15 to 20 metres of *boyau*.'

'How long will that take?'

'An Engineers working party could break the back of it in a night, sir. Then we could finish it off.'

'Mmm! I'm not too sure about the Engineers. They have enough on their plate! What's your barbed wire like?'

'Pretty average, sir.'

'The two platoons are on sentry duty, after all. They can stand guard outside, in the trench.'

Silence!

'I seriously doubt we could withstand another bombardment like yesterday morning's, sir.'

Silence!

Then L[etondot] piped up. 'Our pioneers could handle it, sir. Do you remember the colonel's dug-out they built? The entire army corps admired it.'[1]

We moved on to other matters.

Wednesday 29 December

Janvier's death is still affecting us all. It's on everyone's mind. The *boyau* is full of blood. His twisted bayonet and torn greatcoat, covered in gore, lie on the parapet beside the black hole where the shell exploded.

The men due to go on leave with him came to say goodbye today. A departure cloaked in sadness.

At night I reconnoitre beyond the trenches. Pitch black, slipping with every step, eyes darting constantly from side to side. Unstable ground sticking to my feet. A machine gun starts to rattle. The bullets whistle past. I throw myself to the ground. My hand touches something soft. Horrible! A Boche head, there since the attack of 25 September. No man's land is littered with half-buried corpses.

Thursday 30 December

A visit this morning from Sergeant Savary. He's a packer from the 11th *arrondissement*, lives near the *mairie*. Looks every one of his 40 years. A little paunch, a black goatee, bulging eyes. A decent sort. It's not hard to get him

---

1. Inevitably, the sap was never built. The tribe of Béni-Oui-Oui – the fawners and flatterers eager only to please their superior officers – was the bane of our lives.

talking. He tells me about his home, his wife and his 13-year-old son. 'He's no scholar but he works hard. I'm hoping he'll get his school certificate this year. Then I'll try to find him an apprenticeship. That'll be his best bet.'

He talks and talks, describing all the modest happiness of a careful working-class home. It reminds me of my own childhood. He seems to love every member of his little world: his wife, who he calls 'my girl', his son, his little niece 'who lives with us'.

He natters away cheerfully in the typical Parisian working-class drawl, so familiar and so dear to me. I see the *mairie* with the square in front, the rather pompous statue of Ledru-Rollin, the Rue de la Roquette; then up the hill, in the sunshine, Père Lachaise cemetery, last resting place of the generation of '48: Thiers alongside Casimir-Périer, de Musset, Barbès and Blanqui; the executed Communards beside Clément-Thomas; Michelet beside Laffitte. A motley group, where 'Joseph Prudhomme' rubs shoulders with Lamartine, yet each bathed in the rosy glow of idealism.

Meanwhile I am at the bottom of my hole, 12 to 15 feet underground, in a log-and-plank cabin not 3 metres square. I write at a wooden table covered with newspaper. The only source of light is a candle held by a length of wire twisted five times around its base, then suspended from a nail driven into a plank above my head. The upturned lid of a jam-jar serves as a *fumivore*. Attached to the wall opposite are two rough bunks. Two planks are fixed either side of a central post running from floor to ceiling, and two more nailed to the wall. Three more planks are placed across this framework, a bit of straw and a coverlet. *Et voilà!*

The guns sound over our heads, the distant, huge hammer-blows reverberating through our wooden box. Now and then the insouciance of youth reasserts itself. We joke, we laugh, we play schoolboy pranks on each other. Captain [Hillère], commanding the adjoining sub-sector, sends me a smutty drawing, solemnly despatched, like a state secret, in an envelope. I reply in kind, with equal gravity.

But what a life!

Faces are pale, features drawn. A week in these holes is a week in a dungeon. It gives you some idea of life in an *oubliette*. No water. No chance to wash, not even to think about it. In the room facing me, by the dug-out entrance, the telephonist occupies himself making a dagger. Life in his underground exchange has given him a pasty, hollow-cheeked, anaemic look, as well as a bushy black beard. Muddy haversacks dangle from the wall. On the ground is a pack, cover rolled up, white-metal mess-tin lying askew on the flap. Beside it, a blackened kettle. Outside, the endless 150s rock the dug-out. They're deafening.

The war is throwing up some rum battalion commanders. After a century of absolute power, Monsieur Le Bureaucrat is finding it hard to change his ways. In peacetime and in war he takes the soft option and promotes men purely on grounds of seniority. Consul is a good example. Another is that major from 142nd Infantry who provided our first relief – a singular fellow, recalled after thirty years as a captain in supplies.

Friday 31 December

My poor Janvier will have been given a decent send-off by now. Around 9.00 am yesterday morning I saw a Boche officer in a long coat in no man's land opposite Tranchée Balcon. He was ordering three men about. What could they be doing? He strung the men out in a straight line … They had to be marking out the ground. A battery of 75s is attached to our sub-sector. I got hold of the lieutenant observer, gave him the coordinates, and suggested that the Germans might be planning a trench linking Tranchée Bismarck and Boyau Löbau. The spot is around 500 to 600 metres ahead of Tranchée Balcon and Tranchée Merlonnée, at an acute angle to the latter.

Arthur (the 75) began firing at 13.30 pm. I stole from my dug-out, then went down Boyau Eitel[1] to a breach giving a clear view of no man's land. I kept as low as possible but I was still spotted from the Chenille. A bullet whistled past my ears. I studied the Boches trenches. The rounds from the 75 were landing right in their midst.[2] I nipped back to my HQ and grabbed the telephone.

'Hello! Hello! Get me the lieutenant observer with the 75 battery.'

'Hello! That you, sir? Is that the right spot?'

'Perfect! Fire!'

A stream of salvoes followed, throwing everything into the air.

A repeat performance followed at 7.30 pm, in the pitch dark. Great!

'Raise your sights!'

'That's it!'

'Fire!'

'And again!'

---

1. We had retaken the bulge in the landscape known as the Main de Massiges on 25 September 1915. Like Boyau Eitel, which bisected our sub-sector from front to rear, many elements of the fortifications had retained their German names. There was one major disadvantage. The German guns had all the information needed to shell us, and they used it.
2. They were situated below the position of our guns.

Footsteps on the stairs. Captain B. from 142nd Infantry had arrived to relieve us. I hung up the receiver and gave him his orders, these included.

Left my HQ. Ahead of us, in the distance, Arthur was raging – salvo after salvo. Beneath the barrage, the dreadful sound of Boche screams seemed to reach us on the wind.

And that's how we handed over the reins to the 142nd.

Saturday 1st January

More mud and drizzle. A bit of a shindig this evening to toast my stripes. Any officers' get-together makes an interesting study just now. We come from every corner of France – Normandy, the east, the south, Paris – all with our distinctive stamp and songs. And there are always a couple of old Africa hands who have brought home a few Arabic words and customs.

Our MO, Boisramé, treated us to a wonderfully filthy, but very amusing, medical student's song: [Théophile Gautier's] '*De profundis morpionibus*'. Then [Lieutenant] Blaise[1] led us in 'The Young Man of Mourmelon'. Finally, D. presented his party piece, performing a belly dance with his huge paunch. He certainly has the guts for it.

A very jolly evening. It's hard to believe these young chaps have just spent a dreadful week at constant risk of a – horrible – death from a shell. They've forgotten it already – as have the men.

N.B. The government-issue champagne was appalling.

Sunday 2 January

The German positions at Bouconville came under heavy shelling from 11.00 pm to midnight, and again from 3.00 am to 4.00 am. We fell asleep to the thunder of the guns.

Thursday 6 January
Braux-la-Cohière.

4.00 pm. On the road to Sainte-Ménehould. At the bottom of the hill, Braux-la-Cohière and its church are lost in the mist. Nothing distinct – just grey-painted

---

1. The CO of 7th Company, universally known as 'Le Bon Blaise'. He had just returned to the regiment after being wounded on 25 September 1915. Splendidly brave, 27 or 28 years old. He was wounded again on 31 March 1916.

shapes in the fog. To right and left, the gaunt outlines of the leafless trees. A winter landscape.

They got us moving from Dommartin-sous-Hans at 5.00 am. We're leaving from here for the trenches at 3.00 pm tomorrow.

What kind of rest is this? The gentlemen of the general staff clearly never spend time in the trenches.[1] No billets have been arranged – just some huts, still roofless. For a bed, the greasy, sodden ground.

The band performed *Benvenuto Cellini* and *Lakmé* for us this afternoon. Odd to hear this reminder of a happy, cultured existence amid our current hardships ...

'*Lakmé, ton doux regard se voile!*' / 'Lakmé, your tender gaze is hidden!'

I studied the audience. Faded greatcoats, motley headgear: kepis, helmets, forage caps. Men unshaven, uniforms shabby, buttons missing. Mud everywhere.

Such joyous, sensual music feels very strange in these surroundings.

Friday 7 January

This evening, the relief. The regiment is returning to the trenches. Leave Braux at 3.00 pm. Night is falling. Grey sky, fine rain. The muddy road stretches into the thickening darkness. The wind is spooking the horses. The rain is blinding us. Tobie shies, refuses to go further. I have to dismount. At the exit to Maffrécourt I send the horses back – much to the delight of Eustache.[2]

Night has fallen. I can't see more than three steps ahead of me. I stay at the rear of the company with Doctor Boisramé and L[ambert]. The rain falls harder still. The north wind drives it into our faces. Hailstones seem to be pricking my skin. My sodden greatcoat slaps round my legs. Close by, a soldier is bent beneath the weight of his pack, miserably dragging his leg.

'What's up with you?'

'I've been sick for three days, sir!'

---

1. One of the most shocking features of the first three years of the war was the callous disregard of the generals for the humble infantrymen bearing the full brunt of the fighting. Conditions only improved for these pariahs with the appointment of General Pétain.

2. The orderly who looked after the horses. Class of 1903. A sturdy peasant farmer from the Beauce. An ex-cuirassier who had transferred to the infantry. With his helmet and long blonde moustaches, he reminded me of the Gaulish warriors of the history books.

'What with?'

'The runs.'

'You've got your flannel belt on?'

'Yes, sir. Tied tight as well!'

He sounds so weary, I content myself with a few encouraging words. That was tiredness speaking. I don't have a vehicle to carry his pack. He'll have to suffer to the bitter end. Then the major leading the column loses his way, taking my poor men an extra 1.5 to 2 kilometres through Dommartin. The halt never comes. My leg hurts dreadfully. Each time my right foot hits the ground, it feels like I'm pressing on a decayed tooth.

At last, a halt.

Now it's my turn to lead, regulating our pace to maintain contact with 5th Company. Ahead of me the indefatigable Champion[1] stretches his long legs, rifle slung over his left shoulder, stick in his right hand. The rain redoubles in intensity. The storm is growing, slapping the rain-sodden flaps of our greatcoats against our legs. The long line of silent sufferers straggles more and more along the road. Men are falling into the ditches. Their chums continue without complaint – feet bloody, legs stiff, faces scoured by the rain. Despairingly I realize that while we've covered 12 kilometres, there still another ten to go.

To add to our misery, a constant stream of convoys is passing in the opposite direction – 142nd Infantry coming out of the line. With the customary disdain of drivers for the infantry, compounded by the cavalier attitude of the southerner, the vehicles shove us into the ankle-deep mud on the verges, drive over our poor feet. The wind and rain are howling. We're reeling like drunks, blinded by the storm. Then we hear the whistle of the shells – right, left, ahead of us. They pierce the air, rumbling like railway wagons. '*Crump!*' They burst around 100 metres away. The din is deafening. The line of poor automatons continues its hallucinatory march through the blackness ...

Houses, a few lights: Berzieux. Still 5 kilometres to go. Flames streak through the darkness – rockets and gunfire. Hunger begins to torment me. The men ate before we left, but we've had nothing since midday ...

Bright spots of light at the foot of a dark slope: 26th Artillery. One group begins to fire. If the Boches reply, we're done for ...

The road bends towards Virginy. More flooded fields reflecting the glow of the rockets; more leafless trees in gaunt outline. On a mound, Virginy church: a

---

1. The bugler. A strapping lad, ash-blond hair, ruddy cheeks, as good as he was strong. Now a builder in Maintenon.

tragic, tall, shell-pocked carcass, like the skeleton of some huge beast. We march past and turn right. This is the road to Massiges, with its famous tall trees, some ravaged and felled by shells.

Our torment is nearly over.

'Company, halt! Fall out. Packs off!'

We're in desperate need of the break. Our stragglers are still in Virginy.

'Ah, there you are, Delvert. What are you up to?'

'A few minutes' rest for the men, sir!'

'Always a free spirit!'

The men slump exhausted on their packs, draw food from their knapsacks, gulp down some *pinard*. Within minutes tongues begin to wag. The officer of the day arrives to say that everyone is back together.

'Another five minutes, then packs on!'

En route for the trenches Tosca's lament comes to my lips:

'*O doux baisers, délicieuse ivresse!*' /
'Oh, sweet kisses, drunken with delight!'

'Goodness, there's someone singing! Ah, it's the captain.'

Brave Paré[1] has arrived, here to guide the company to its new positions. The men are already forgetting their fatigue. I can hear them laughing, singing, telling jokes. They'll fall silent soon enough, without any orders from me, but for now they can shake themselves out a little. I ponder the strength derived by we French from our wonderful good cheer. These men will hold the line staunchly until the next relief.

When the Kaiser was plotting our destruction, he reckoned without French *joie de vivre* and the infinite powers of resistance it confers.

Saturday 8 January

Bodies from 142nd Infantry lie on top of my HQ.

Pégoud[2] is talking to Aubry:

'What have you done with my pipe?'

'Your pipe? Search me. It'll have gone on leave before you!'

---

1. Scruffy forage cap and curling moustache. Always ready to do his duty.
2. His name was Jégoud, but we started calling him Pégoud after the famous pilot. He was going on leave.

Sunday 9 January 1916

A lovely winter's day, with a whiff of spring already.

Awful night. My HQ is alive with rats. They nibble our trench boots. I suspect the only purpose of these items of kit is providing them with fodder.

We are defending two positions at Massiges, the Ouvrage Martin Saint-Léon and Tranchée Nord. At 8.00 am I go to reconnoitre. The right-hand section of the trench skirts the cemetery (of Our Lady) – a poor muddy plot full of new wooden crosses. Here, a colonial, Picard; and another, Corporal Susini. There, a moving inscription: 'To our father, the 1st Gun', probably a gun commander. Each grave has an upturned bottle holding the man's papers.

Most of the graves are colonials from 23rd Infantry, 21st Infantry and 4th Infantry.

The air is mild, the sun lending the day a festive air. A few birds are singing already. But death moves incessantly through the air. The huge Boche 150s are shelling a 120 battery to our left ... *Crump*! *Crump*! If they hit us, it would take for ever to join the Eternal Father.

3.30 pm. Gas alert. We snatch up our masks. They couldn't be more awkward. The Vermorels are empty. No hyposulphite in the tanks.

We leave the dug-out in a flash.

Two thick clouds are rising from the valley. My eyes sting. Asphyxiating tear gas. The artillery and machine guns rage. The Germans are unleashing a barrage of shrapnel shells over the Médius. They explode in a straight line, as if they're on a string. Splendid work.

3.45 pm. Orders to lead the company to 'the slopes of the Annulaire'. What does the colonel – and Consul in particular – understand by this? They can only mean our trenches. I reconnoitred them this morning and showed my sous-lieutenants the combat positions. I order L[ambert] and T[ramard] to go and occupy them with their platoons. Shells are bursting all round. Shrapnel whistles through the air. My eyes sting even more. In our Tambuté[1] masks we can neither see nor breathe.

The clouds roll in and night begins to fall. A red glow spreads to our left. No question, the Germans are attacking around Mont Têtu with flammable gas and liquid. They use barrage fire to stop us despatching any reinforcements.

---

1. The model of mask then current.

The trench is boxed in by shells: 77s and 105s. A terrifying whistling and roaring. The blood rushes to my head. I expect to be blown to bits at any moment. The men are quite calm, leaning on the parapet, resting on their rifles. The night is pitch black. The hellish din continues. Towards 7.00 pm a lull. The order comes to pull back.

The gas has gradually dissipated. 7th Company has arrived as reinforcements. We don't know what to do with them. The gunfire continues non-stop. In our flimsy shelters – 3 millimetres of corrugated iron covered by a handful of logs – a 105 would make mincemeat of us.

Consul summons me to his HQ. Consul, [Hillère], Le [Carré], Blaise, Bétron, Adjutant Leroy and I are all downcast. The telephone brings news that Sous-lieutenant Fétu from 4th Company is dead. Some men were killed too when a shell fell on their dug-out.

I invite Le Carré (from 7th Company) to dine with me. We eat in style, squeezed around the scruffy deal table in the dug-out. The Boches have started firing 210s, which strike with the sound of a cavalry squadron at full gallop.

Non-stop shellfire from both sides throughout the night.

At 4.00 am the rifles start up again. Another attack has been launched.

Monday 10 January
The shelling begins at 2.45 pm. Behind Virginy, our 55s get things under way. The Boches reply with their 210s. Terrible, a living hell. It's unbearable, even for those with nerves of steel. In the dug-out last night L[ambert] tossed and turned like a sheep with the staggers.[1]

Tuesday 11 January
Pretty quiet after midnight. Our guns start up again at 11.00 am.

At 3.00 pm the Germans reply. A deafening din, joined around 4.30 pm by the sound of a grenade attack. The crackle of gunfire. Our big guns thunder non-stop. Around 5.30 pm, close to Mont Têtu, a white rocket soars like a shooting star into the sky. A request for artillery support. A second, then a third star follows the first. Then, from the plain – from Massiges, Virginy, Berzieux, Côte 181, Côte 191 and Côte 138 – our batteries start firing in unison: a blinding

---

1. He had just come from a battery of 75s so he was used to explosions. The life of the front-line infantryman is impossible to comprehend unless you have experienced it.

stream of thunderbolts in the night. From the observation post on the road in advance of my HQ, it's a magnificent, if terrible, sight. The northern extremity of the Médius appears to be in flames.

The whistle of a 77 tears me from my contemplations.

Things seem to be settling down. The distant shell-bursts reverberate like huge hammer-blows. And here we are – in our dark, corrugated-iron tunnel – completely oblivious to it all. L[ambert] is fast asleep. The orderlies are discussing the serious matter of fetching dinner.

Wednesday 12 January

Fog this morning. T[ramard] and I go to supervise the men marking out the route to be followed on relief at 2.00 pm. The sun rose around 8.00 am, blood red in the mist. It's fine and clear now. All our troubles are forgotten. The men are outside. They're cheerful. They're singing.

'Threshing-machines,' they call the machine guns.

While I lay on my palliasse after dinner this evening, the orderlies took our places around the table. They decided on a hand of manille. Paré had his back to me, so I could see nothing but his cards and the tips of his fair moustache; Guibout (who has replaced Jégoud) was hidden by the post. Facing me in the candlelight, firmly settled, fist on thigh, was good old Aubry, ample of stomach, forage cap set squarely above his round, ruddy face. Three Normans! A tricky one to call!

'40.'

'45.'

'Take, then!'

'Never, lad! ... Oh, go on then. Would you believe it?'

The pack is faded and filthy, drained of colour. It doesn't matter. Paré amuses me particularly with the careful way he spreads his cards. They play three or four hands. Paré goes to join T[ramard], then Guibout and Aubry slide beneath my bunk.

We put out the lights.

Now the '*gaspards*' (rats) and '*totos*' (lice) take command. The rats come and go incessantly, nibbling, jumping, running, tumbling from plank to plank, squealing behind the corrugated iron of the shelter. I constantly expect one to land on my nose. Then the lice and fleas begin to tuck in. At midnight, just as I'm nodding off, a dreadful din makes me jump. Artillery, machine-gun and rifle fire. The Boches must be attacking again in front of Mont Têtu. Around 1.30 am things seem to be settling down, then at 2.15 am it starts up again, this time with terrible violence. The whole earth is rocking. Our guns thunder non-stop. At 3.00 am the shells slacken off, then gradually all falls silent.

I nod off and wake again at 6.00 am. And so do the rats and lice. A return to consciousness means a return to misery. Our heavy guns boom, reminding me the lice and rats are not alone: the shells are waking up, too.

Thursday 13 January

Rained all morning. At 1.00 pm, a ray of sunshine. I set off with Consul and [Hillère] to reconnoitre the Cratère sector. Return via the cemetery, crossing no man's land. Back safe and sound, but it was a close-run thing.

Not a wink of sleep tonight. It's cold. The rats are everywhere, the shelling relentless.

Saturday 15 January

'It's the relief.' 142nd Infantry is replacing us, under Sous-lieutenant L.

We leave at 8.00pm. Sous-lieutenant L. says he has it from a friend, who had it from Sarraut, that the war will be over by late February or early March. He's brisk and jovial. 'I'm not from the Midi,' he explains. 'I'm from Tarbes.'

The colonel is running out of steam. He's anxious and jittery, harassed by General X.

Sunday 16 January

The band entertained us with [Lalo's] *Le Roi d'Ys* – Sellé singing the aubade – and [Lecocq's] charming *Petit Duc*.

This brief escape into city life always makes me pensive. Today it makes me conscious of our plight in this muddy cesspit of a village.

A few lucky ones are managing quite nicely. S. shows off the work he's had done on his hut. Bed, dressing-table, desk: it wants for nothing. With planks from supplies, and sappers providing the labour, it all looks wonderfully elegant and smart. The bottom of a bottle serves as a vase, and the upturned neck as a bouquet-holder.

Monday 17 January

The truth this morning in this article by Lucien Boyer, 'Among the Sparrow-hawks'.

'[Flying] is nothing. If we fall, we do so in daylight in full view of both armies. My comrades and I all agree that the only man worthy of veneration is the poilu, the humble trench infantryman suffering at his loophole and dying unheralded at his post.'

The poilu is an extraordinary fellow. After midnight – i.e. after the attacks – all the Boche guns, bar none, were firing pretty sporadically. Every time a shell fell in front of the dug-outs, the poilus rushed straight out to hunt for the fuse-cap, to get hold of the aluminium. They're obsessed with making rings at the moment. They've finished a very pretty one for me.

Our dinners have been much cheerier since Consul went on leave. 'The Young Man from Mourmelon' and 'The Return from Piedmont'[1] appear at every dessert. Afterwards we play dominos.[2] We forget about the Boches, so near, and the shelling we have just endured. We don't even talk about it. This selective amnesia is quite remarkable. The essential *joie de vivre* of the French character makes us surprisingly resilient. I would never have dreamed the army could be so strong at this point in the war.

Tuesday 18 January

Eustache and I went riding this morning. Before we mounted, good old Tobie kicked me in the shins, an exceedingly unfriendly act, apparently at odds with his normal good temper. I was to blame. I tried to walk behind him without prior warning. He brought me to order.

Whenever I'm out of the front line, I seem to end up limping. S. very kindly helped me to the divisional aid post. A fine one-stripe MO poked around a bit, pronounced a very complicated diagnosis that went straight in one ear and out the other, and bandaged me up with lashings of tape and cotton wool.

---

1. And another song whose refrain brought all the diners together in chorus. A fine tenor sang the first couplet in solemn and sentimental tones:
   Soldat courageux / Soldier so brave
   Soldat téméraire / Soldier so bold,
   Sous les blancs rayons de la lune claire, / Of what do you dream
   A quoi rêves-tu? / In the silver moonlight?
   Then we all thundered back *basso profundo*:
   Je pense aux bidons remplis de pinard / I dream of the *bidon* full of *pinard*
   Je pense au salaud qui m'a pris mon quart / I dream of the rotter who's stolen my *quart*
   Et qui boit ma gnôle le soir à la brume / Who drinks my rotgut at night in the gloom
   Au clair de la lune / By the light of the moon
   The second couplet followed an appeal to the 'Soldier so brave':
   Je pense au loupiot qui me dira papa / I think of the kid who will call me papa
   Fils d'un embusqué que je ne connais pas / Son of a shirker I don't know at all.
2. A type of card game.

The news spread like wildfire through the ranks, particularly as the regiment is returning to the front line in two days' time. 'Is the captain coming with us?' That's the big question. Do I inspire that much confidence? I don't know. Possibly. The soldier – like the female of the species – is very suggestible. Once he finds a leader he admires, he refuses to countenance any alternative. Very mysterious. In this case, however, there is another reason. The men can't abide the sous-lieutenant. They say that by ordering the relief too early on 14 October 1915 he got seven of their comrades killed.[1] They also accuse him of losing his temper, brandishing his revolver and shouting 'I'm a poilu too. I'll show you what that means when we get to the trenches.' And after all his boasting – if you believe his detractors – he beat a hasty retreat to the dug-out at the first sign of a shell.[2]

Whatever, I'll quietly hand over the reins to L[ambert].

Wednesday 19 January

I definitely could have done without that kick from Tobie. It was nothing at all, but walking is agony. It puts me in the perfect mood to appreciate the full horror of these wretched Argonne villages – exactly like Lorraine. Dung all over. Everywhere ankle deep in greasy, putty-like earth, clinging to your feet and sucking at your boots. No lavatories. You have to cross 30 metres of sticky mud to pull down your pants. Not that my hosts are impoverished. Far from it, they have their land and their animals; they run a business. They're doing very nicely at the moment. But it would break their hearts to spend a sou. They live like paupers. The house is dilapidated, dirty, no creature comforts, running with rats. They don't care. They have their gold and silver. The same is true of France in general. Avarice is one of the abiding sins of our nation.

---

1. Probably wholly without foundation.
2. Wartime command is much easier in some ways – soldiers are always at their most disciplined in action (see 22 August 1914 or 8 September 1914) – yet infinitely harder in others, for the company commander at least. Whether lieutenant or captain, he lives in constant contact with his men. His every word or gesture will be monitored and criticized; and rigorously, too, since 'our master is our enemy'. If he is fearless, unflappable and fair, all will be fine and his men will grow deeply attached to him. The first quality is the essential one, often making up for the others. This was true, for example, of young Sous-lieutenant Rouzeaud, a platoon commander in my company, who sparked feelings of genuine warmth.

Thursday 20 January

I'm lying on my miserable bed. Pale skies and bright sun this evening. I'm enjoying the delights of a winter day already promising spring. A few notes float into the room from the band billeted next door.

My company has returned to the front line without me, leaving a great void in my life. I'm at a loose end, rather off kilter. Some men came to shake my hand, telling me to 'Get well soon'.

I feel abandoned. I don't know what to do with myself.

Touchat came to see me this morning. He's one of the latest batch of reinforcements, hails from the Béziers area. He wanted to change regiments, transfer to 142nd Infantry, where he will find more of his compatriots. He said rather sheepishly that southerners are viewed badly in our regiment. He gets teased when he talks 'half patois, half French'.

I happen to know a few words of his local patois.

'Don't worry,' I said. 'It's nothing!'

Then it all came pouring out. He told me his woes, how lonely he feels ...

I listened patiently.

Morale restored, I offered him my hand.

'Do you still want a transfer?'

'No, sir. I want to stop with you.'[1]

Friday 21 January

I've moved into S.'s hut ... Not as comfortable as it looks. It's horribly damp and I'm coughing from dawn until dusk.

The big story in the press is Montenegro, which is reported to have surrendered unconditionally to Austria. Is this a manoeuvre on the part of the Central Powers? Or by Serbia, seeking to prove to the Italians that she can exact revenge for their desertion? Is she trying to extract a formal guarantee that Dubrovnik will be hers after the war? Speculation is rife. Today the reports are being denied. Whatever the truth of the rumour, it's caused a bit of a stir. *Le Journal* – which jumped the gun – has been caught out. It's breathing fire and brimstone. The whole furore leaves us cold.

---

1. He proved an excellent soldier. I spoke to his comrades and they left him alone. [Note: the huge differences in regional dialect could make men mutually incomprehensible.]

Saturday 22 January
An article by Colette Yver in the *Écho de Paris* praises the courage of those living
in towns like Nancy, close to the front line. She thinks their bravery less striking
than that of the front-line soldier, but in a way even more admirable. How does
this bird-brain imagine the front-line soldier? Does she think we spend all our
time brandishing huge sabres, bellowing '*Vive la France*'? Will the good folk in
the rear ever put a stop to this kind of guff?

Bocage, who I see regularly, says the men are getting very demoralized. Some
are starting to give up the ghost. I shall have to keep my eyes open.

Sunday 23 January
Lunched with Captain M. and his two sous-lieutenants – Reynal, an ex-
cuirassier,[1] and D., a reservist. Captain M. is from Béziers. Very proper, hair
brush cut, nose large and imperious. The rather disdainful reserve of the
southern gentleman. Pleasant and courteous nevertheless. Faguet has already
remarked on the rather Spanish demeanour of the haute bourgeoisie from this
part of the Midi.

We attended a matinée performance staged in a huge barn by 102nd and
315th Infantries. A good crowd. We roared with laughter, especially at the jokes
of a runner from 5th Battalion (315th Infantry). He apparently plays the Ba-ta-
clan and he was absolutely priceless. You'd never think that we're at war. That
four or five days ago these men were just a few metres from the Boches at Mont
Têtu. That in a couple of days' time they'll be at the Cratère. Their ability to
'pack up their troubles' is quite heroic.

La Neuville-au-Pont is a pretty little town straddling the Aisne. An excellent
billet. Gothic church with a late fifteenth-century portal: Italian renaissance
choux frisés, little niches slightly later in date. Late Empire town hall, Louis XIII
style. It's a very welcome change from our muddy hole in Braux.

I came back in a cart that Reynal got hitched up. A huge supply convoy was
blocking the whole road. We almost shed our load twenty times at least.

Tuesday 25 January
Still raining.

---

1. From early 1915 our regiments absorbed a number of unemployed cavalry officers who
   had requested a transfer to the infantry. With very few exceptions those we encountered
   were toffs.

The Boche shells destroyed two mobile cookers on the Massiges road yesterday, between the hangar of my cookers and those of 5th Company. Two horses were wounded. One was brought back here but had to be put down. Our runner Le Masson has been up there and reports both horses have been cut up and eaten. And shuttling as he does between the front line and Braux, he's managed to sample both. He claims the one he ate at Massiges was far superior.

It could be straight out of the Comte de Ségur's *Retraite de Russie*.

Wednesday 26 January

D. and I went to Sainte-Ménehould. Met the local captain of gendarmerie. On the short side, hair almost white, moustache yellowed by cigar smoke. Burly, fit, bright eyed; the slight hoarseness of a man who never says no to an aperitif. We saw him in the patisserie and again in the department store. He was pawing a real peach of a shop assistant, around 30 or so. Then he got back on his horse, a fine steed, as fresh and well fed as its master. His orderly followed him on a mount in equally good fettle.

The war could go on for ever for these folk. They've never been happier.

Then there are the artillery officers strolling about the streets. Impeccable black tunic, close-fitting breeches with the double red stripe down the outer seam, whiling away their time flirting with all the girls.

Inevitably, my thoughts turn to our wretched billets. We poor, bloody, mud-shrouded infantrymen, plagued with lice and rats.

The war isn't equally hard for everybody.

Thursday 27 January

A day of mourning. Five killed, two wounded. The dead include Jégoud, poor old 'Pégoud', who left so cheerfully a fortnight ago to see his Mélanie. He returned from leave three days ago. Like Janvier, his downfall was caused by a walk through the sector in broad daylight. A working party from 117th Infantry, led by their officer, amused themselves by strolling along the parapet at 1.30 pm! Soon afterwards, the shells started up again, apparently over 150 of them.

The Germans don't mess about.

Jégoud met an atrocious end. He was at the top of the steps leading into the dug-out when the shell burst (probably an Austrian 130). He suffered burns to his face. A piece of shrapnel pierced his skull behind the ear, while another tore open his belly and broke his spine. You could see the marrow running through the whole gory mess. His right leg was crushed above the knee. And ghastliest of all he wasn't killed outright: he lingered for another four or five minutes.

Monday 31 January

I fainted twice last night. Nobody to fetch me a glass of water. It's a hard life.

I am reading [Paul] Bourget's *Le Sens de la mort*: 'Delanoë, face mutilated by a grenade while the band of his scapular remained untouched.' And again: 'Did you hear what Le Gallic just said to me? I'll give you three guesses – and he's an officer who was present, remember – our victory on the Marne was a miracle … Why? Because it has no possible strategic explanation.'[1]

Incredible, the variation in conditions between front-line troops. L[ambert] saw his old artillery captain yesterday. 'His dug-out is palatial,' he told me. 'A fireplace, a mirror, a bedroom …'. Better to be a captain in the artillery than a colonel in the infantry. Wait until he sees our miserable hovel! Piss-yellow walls, sweating with damp; rats everywhere. The poor old infantry has more to bear than the Boche *marmites*. We've already been hit a few times by our own 75s and from now on we'll be getting some real poundings. The gunners have been ordered to target the Boche front-line trenches, however close they may be. And here on Mont Têtu they're only 35 metres away.[2]

To pursue my line of argument. Those bearing the brunt of the fighting are the poor bloody infantry. They always get the worst of the billets. And within the infantry, the front-line troops are treated worst of all. A new billet virtually every second relief. And when we come out of the trenches, the few decent billets go to the Headquarters Company who never went in.[3]

A true story. We haven't enough carpenters in the front line to build or reinforce the dug-outs. [But] after our latest spell in Dommartin, the colonel ordered the sappers to stay behind and make him a table, benches, etc. Not that the sappers ever really go into the front line. They remain to do jobs for the Headquarters Company.

---

1. Take this with a pinch of salt. I know how little background information is available to a junior officer trying to make a 'strategic' decision in the midst of a battle like the Marne. And strategically Gallieni's flank attack offers a much more convincing explanation of our victory.
2. Given the flat trajectory of the 75 – and the margin of error either way for projectiles set on precisely the same coordinates – this order doomed our infantry to slaughter by our own guns. And this was exactly what happened. 'Trying to provide close support for the infantry, without accidents, using the flat-trajectory 75 (80, 90, 95, 105 etc.) was a problem akin to trying to square the circle,' commented the artilleryman General Gascouin (p. 122).
3. The Headquarters Company comprised all the 'shirkers at the front' – now often the most vocal in the old comrades' associations.

Tuesday 1 February
Fever.

Thursday 3 February
Brilliant sunshine.

Gallieni faced ferocious questioning in the Chamber of Deputies on Tuesday.[1]
Given a choice between a delegation of Marseilles café owners and the general
who saved Paris, our sea-green incorruptibles never wavered.

Friday 4 February
It's raining again. Slipping and sliding everywhere.

A gas-mask drill under the eagle eye of Consul. He tries to make a speech but
he can't find the right words. He stutters. He gesticulates. The men make fun
of him. He loses his temper and starts to swear: idiots, cretins, oafs, simpletons.
They laugh even harder. He decides to end on a patriotic note: 'We will probably
come under attack. Are you determined to hold on?' Glacial silence. Convinced
that he's failed to make himself clear, he starts again. No better. He decides it's
time to go.

Visit from [General] Gouraud.[2]

Saturday 5 February
Relief. 9th Company (124th Infantry). Lieutenant G., Sous-lieutenant de C.,
Sous-lieutenant R.

Rain in the morning. The weather lifted around noon. Left on horseback in
glorious weather, the sky clear as a spring day.

Arrived at the Verrue HQ.

Lieutenant G. is an old colonial, with the Médaille Militaire and the Légion
d'Honneur. Aged 49, twelve years' service, including Tonkin and Madagascar,
and still no third stripe. Average height, solidly built, white hair, heavy black

---

1. Gallieni (p. 258) … describes it in his diaries as follows: '1 February. Three hours in the
   Chamber. Questions about the cafés. A very stormy session. The [deputies] refused to hear me
   out. I stepped down from the podium without finishing my speech, snatched up my briefcase
   and left. Malvy chased after me and brought me back to the Chamber. Applause on all sides.
   Praised to the skies: they wanted to set me above the fray. But it was a mistake to return,
   despite the motion of confidence and the apologies offered by almost all the deputies.'
      Gallieni was more than 'the general who saved Paris'; he was 'the general who saved
   France'.
2. Translator's note: the war diary dates this visit to 2 February 1916.

moustache and black eyebrows, bright eyes and a strong nose. He seems intelligent, cool and energetic. Certainly an excellent officer.

Young de C., a graduate of Saint-Cyr, class of the *Grande Revanche*, has been at the front since January 1915. He is 21 years old, tall and strongly built. R. is one of the three-year conscripts, completing his engagement at war. He's another youngster, stockily built, curly blond hair.

Glorious sunset. A Zeppelin climbs through the immense red glow.

Sunday 6 February
More spring sunshine this morning. The birds were singing. We're wasting some of the best years of our lives here, I thought miserably.

This evening it rained non-stop. The night was pitch black. We stumbled with every step.

Tuesday 8 February
Reading a chance find, de Montesquiou's *1870, les causes politiques du désastre*.

Last night I toured the *boyaux* – cold, sky brilliant with stars and the odd illuminating rocket. I stumbled along. The *boyaux* are big black holes. You have to tap your stick against the walls like a blind man.

This morning a two-star Engineers general came to visit. An elegant, eloquent individual, escorted by two old buffers, both captains. The Engineers promised some time ago to construct three shelters at the Verrue HQ, where I am at present. We're still waiting. I mentioned it to the general. But this elegant, eloquent individual ignored me. Why not heed a humble infantry captain for a change?

I've ordered my men to dig our own shelter in Boyau 33. They're making good progress. The Engineers might bring us their plans when it's done.

Wednesday 9 February
Tour of inspection around 5.30 am or 6.00 am. Barely light. The Boches must have set up some rifles or machine guns to enfilade our *boyaux*. Each step attracts the whine of a bullet.

I'm worn out. I'm shattered. My ribs hurt and my joints ache. The reason is my bunk – three planks of wood. The lack of sleep is a dreadful bind.

1.00 pm. It's started snowing. You can't see past the end of your nose. Everything is white.

10.00 pm. The sky is full of stars. In the distance, Mont Têtu, the Chenille, the Col des Abeilles and the ravines are bathed in ethereal moonlight. I'm hunting a potential machine-gun emplacement in Tranchée 36, near its intersection with Boyau 33. The parapets are capped with snow. To see out, I have to clamber up and crawl through the icy whiteness. My fingers are all thumbs. I can't feel them any more. I find a spot with a good field of fire, but the night is too bright to start work.

Despite the cold Fritz[1] is as watchful as ever. The bullets whistle past as normal.

Return to the dug-out. Perhaps I'll get some sleep. I've had the planks of my bunk replaced with wire mesh. Sleep still doesn't come. I can hear my orderly scratching away.

Thursday 10 February

The sun rises red in a world of white. An orange glow brightens the eastern sky. In the distance, towards the Chenille, the [Creux de l'Oreille] is buried in snow. It's a beautiful sight. A flock of sparrows climbs through the frigid air. They're not flying high, poor things. They're cold. They're hungry. I pass a group of poilus, already digging. They're cold and hungry, too. All they can look forward to is congealed soup, bread – always heavy and dry – and the inevitable lump of boiled meat. Each head is swaddled in a woollen balaclava with a helmet on top. Poor *biffins*! The heroic untouchables of this war! They're doing all the construction work here at the Verrue: trenches with firing steps, barbed-wire entanglements, machine-gun platforms, even dug-outs – the war will be over by the time the Engineers start work on the three shelters they promised us. So, on top of everything else, my men now face the task of digging and equipping a shelter in Boyau 33.

An article by Urbain Gohier in yesterday's *Le Journal*.

'A deputy listed all the pimps, lodging-house owners, gambling-den proprietors and convicted swindlers engaged to supply equipment, horses, wine, weapons and munitions to the French army. Among a hundred or so cases, he highlighted that of a woman involved in the white slave trade, "supported" by a criminal with twenty-one convictions who also holds an official army clothing contract.' (*Journal officiel*, 15 December 1915)

---

1. 'Fritz' was the German infantryman; 'Müller', the gunner.

Friday 11 February

Snow. No man's land looks ominous at 7.00 am. Grey sky, grey earth. Hazy light. Black stumps extend like caterpillar hairs along the ridge of the Chenille. I'm aware of the German look-outs just a few hundred metres away. They scan the *boyaux* for the slightest sign of movement, ready to contact the batteries lurking behind them and request the salvoes that will send us to our doom.

The mud in the *boyaux* is frozen solid. Constructing our firing steps is slow work. We're having to use sandbags in Tranchée 36. Any excavated earth has to remain within the ramparts. If we throw it over the parapet, it will land on the snow and mark the position of the trench for the *marmites*.

In the gloomy light of this snowy day I continue on my rounds. The deathly cold pierces me to the bone. The barbed-wire entanglements are now in place around the Tranchée 36/Boyau 31 crossroads. A bit more effort and the network will be really solid. Charlot is the foreman, class of 1910.[1] Tall, solidly built, as brave at the loophole as he is tireless at work.

I return to Boyau 33, where the men are still excavating a dug-out, real cavemen's work.

On the left is the flanking trench. Buried at a height of 1.5 metres within the parapet, a pair of Boche feet are sticking out. Beneath the rotted boots, the bare metatarsal bones look like jacks. They're covered in a sticky, greenish substance. Quite horrible. You can tell they're German by the metal treads on the soles of the boots. Ours are a different pattern.

The snow has melted. It's been raining non-stop since midday, turning the *boyaux* into lakes. You plunge knee deep into icy mud. Impossible to get your feet warm again. Impossible to poke your nose out of doors. The Boche shelling is relentless. Shells are bursting all around – on the parapets, in the trenches and *boyaux* – destroying walls already on the verge of collapse.

No one will ever believe what the poilu has to endure here.

This evening, a stand-to order. On our left, 130th Infantry is going to try and retake a trench captured by the Boches from the 317th. Behind us, the battery of 90s fires non-stop from 4.00 pm onwards and continues through the night. At 3.00 am, gunfire. The machine guns start to rattle. As expected, the battle has reached our front.

Quickly to the foot of my bunk.

---

1. Charles Langlois, popularly known as Charlot. One of the best soldiers in the company. He became a sergeant, twice mentioned in corps dispatches. He will reappear often in the course of this diary.

'My helmet.'

'Here, sir!'

Outside, it's pitch black and raining.

'Is the captain here?'

'He's here. Don't panic.'

'Sorry, sir! Didn't recognize you. Not with all the firing ahead of us!'

'Let them fire. Get back in your hole. Your rifle loaded?'

'Yes, sir!'

'Good. Keep calm and await my orders.'

But I reckon the gunfire is only sporadic. Gradually everything quietens down and once more all we can hear is the artillery.

Saturday 12 February 1916

We retook 200 metres of trench yesterday. Deafening shelling since this morning. The machine guns joined in at noon, then the artillery started up again. We have apparently retaken another 20 metres of trench and 10 metres of *boyau* forward of here – all at great cost.

The Boches took their revenge with a furious artillery barrage. Boyau 31, Boyau 33, the bottom end of Boyau 32 and Tranchée 35 have all been destroyed. That'll be our task for tonight.

Beautiful moonlit night. Boyau 31 and Boyau 32 are both impassable. Half a metre of water. The walls have collapsed.

Sunday 13 February 1916

Non-stop shelling, quite deafening. In the evening, a lull.

Relief at 9.30pm. Reached Araja at 1.30 am. The rain soon became torrential. I arrived at Braux at 2.30 am, soaked to the skin. I could hardly bear to put any weight on my foot.[1]

Wednesday 16 February

The storm, which lasted all day yesterday, has continued today as well.

I've just read an article by Henry Bérenger in a recent newspaper. 'We're about to see what the generals have been up to over the winter,' he thunders with a frown. He still thinks France depends on the armchair warriors scribbling away in their newsrooms. He definitely believes it was the diatribes of Hébert

---

1. My wounded right leg had begun hurting again.

and the fine words of Desmoulins that saved the nation in 1793. No, Monsieur Bérenger! It's a myth! Hébert, Marat and their fellow [journalists] did nothing but harm. And the same applies to most politicians who've ever served in the army. Only a few are remembered today. And why are they remembered, Monsieur Bérenger? The answer is simple. Like Carnot, Duquesnoy and Saint-Just, they commanded offensive formations. Spend some time out here, Monsieur Bérenger, discover what life is like in the trenches of Mont Têtu, and stop braying so loudly from your snug Paris office.

Thursday 17 February
Rain, eternal rain.

Friday 18 February
The days pass drearily, like the endless rain. The colonel and the CO have reverted to their old barracks habits, keeping us busy with latrine duty or cleaning the rifle racks. They haven't been reduced to a hairbrush inspection yet, but I live in hope.

Mud, the implacable mud. Every day brings more for us to squelch through.

Briand has been to Italy. As if by accident his trip coincided with the signing of a new treaty. The Triple Entente powers promised for the umpteenth time not to agree peace until Belgium has been compensated and returned to her pre-war condition. Now, however, Italy and Japan – neither of them party to the original treaty guaranteeing Belgian neutrality – have both signed up. Was this a product of Briand's trip? I have an idea that Italy has shown recent signs of a strong desire to conclude a separate peace.

War. It looks so good on paper. In reality, it stinks of shit and rotting flesh.

Saturday 19 February
There are some interesting faces in our mess. One of the most entertaining is our mess officer. He's a sous-lieutenant, aged 32 – a proud Alsatian, tall, strong and brave, with a little pot-belly, receding forehead, jowls and blue eyes. A businessman to the marrow. As soon as the Zeppelins appeared over Paris, thereby threatening his wife, he decided the war had lasted too long. He's a devoted husband. Added to which is an implicit fear for his own life. We all feel this way. 'I got through again,' we think after every relief. But we have to return and a week soon passes. Again, the same dread question: 'Will I be back? If I bet on the death card, might I draw a nine this time?' And you count all the death-traps lying in wait en route to the trenches: Berzieux, completely flattened by

shells; the hill that follows, with its endless bloated carcasses of dead horses; the Ville-sur-Tourbe turn-off; the shell-pocked road to Virginy where our chums die every day; the Massiges road, trees ravaged by shell-bursts; the Decauville [rail track] and the corduroy road – the favoured targets of the *marmites*.

After that the danger is constant!

This terrible war, with its relentless gunfire, exerts such a strain on the soldier that he becomes more, rather than less, apprehensive. This applies to us all. Of course we no longer pay attention to a passing shell or a bullet whistling by. But each time we leave for the trenches, the faces are a little more taut.

Future military historians take note.

Sunday 20 February.

Wonderful weather. A beautiful spring day, crisp and bright, the light suffused with pink. I ride to Valmy, via Dommartin-la-Planchette. All types of vehicle are jamming the roads: a line of motor ambulances travelling in convoy, staff cars, wagons carrying wooden planks and beams. Piles of planks, gabions, matériel of various kinds are heaped up in Dampierre station.

I spot a company from 317th Infantry,[1] newly returned from the trenches. What a sight! The men are dragging themselves along, haggard, filthy, covered in mud, over-long greatcoats flapping like dressing-gowns around their legs. Many are carrying their bayonet upside down, letting it hit them on the thigh, too weak and exhausted to set it right. Long beards, pale cheeks. Poor wretches! The bright sunshine makes the spectacle even more distressing.

Our Alsatian sous-lieutenant regards the war as a business – and an unsuccessful one at that. Just before the Brazilian government intervened to raise the price of raw coffee, he had just concluded a number of deals at the old price. For a time he was selling at a loss and thought about liquidation. He looks on the war in similar terms. He thinks it's time to 'pull out'. Thankfully, neither our rulers nor our poilus share the same view.

Monday 21 February[2]

Glorious morning, with a hint of dry cold. Birdsong all around. Spring is coming.

Alongside our Alsatian sous-lieutenant in the mess is Sous-lieutenant B., promoted to his current rank due to the exigencies of war. He's a rum-looking

---

1. Of course any company coming out of the trenches – infantry, zouave or chasseur – would have looked no different.
2. The opening day of the battle of Verdun.

cove for an officer – small, scrawny and sallow, with a bulging forehead and black hair, moustache and goatee beard. He reminds me of Philip IV's court jesters as painted by Velazquez. He's a timber merchant, long resident in the constituency of [Albert] Thomas. He is virtually illiterate and holds a real grudge against Thomas for not making him obtain his academic qualifications.

It isn't France that's in decline but her bureaucracy. And in a state so highly centralized, where that bureaucracy is all powerful, this naturally leads to disaster. The commanders so carelessly foisted upon us by our military bureaucrats may have been appointed according to regulation, with due regard to seniority, but many beggar belief. How can you describe …? Or …? And many more besides!

And worst of all is that after nineteen months of war we continue to churn out more of the same.

The high command may be starting to get the message. We have just received the *Instruction du combat des petites unités*, dated 8 January 1916. 'Men should not be pitted against matériel,' it states.[1] It's hard to believe it took eighteen months of war to reach this basic truth. Still, better late than never. But how long will it take to penetrate the thick skulls of the preposterous senior officers sent to us by Monsieur Le Bureaucrat? Another eighteen months would be extremely worrying.[2]

At 2.00 pm we watch a big black bird appear very high in the clear blue sky – then two, then three, then a whole flight. Ten, fifteen, twenty, twenty-four: all Taube. They fly through the peace and splendour of the heavens, ignoring the shrapnel shells bursting around them in little white clouds. They're heading for Sainte-Ménehould, probably to bomb the station. A French biplane lumbers from our aviation park, circles a few times and lands again. Clearly, this chicken coop can do nothing to combat these big birds of prey operating at 1500 to 1800 metres. At 3.00 pm a few fly back over our heads towards the German lines. They grace us in passing with three bombs that fall either side of the road ahead of our huts.

Leave on relief at 4.00 pm. Still full daylight, far too early. We proceed at a sensible pace as far as Maffrécourt and the lethal hill to follow. We cross one

---

1. The words of the future Marshal Pétain.
2. It certainly took another fifteen months. Methods changed only after General Pétain was appointed commander-in-chief [in April 1917].

platoon at a time.[1] The sky is already turning purple, mist shrouding the horizon. We're out of danger.

We pass through Berzieux between 7.15 pm and 7.30 pm. The sky is black, lit feebly by the stars and the illuminating rockets that soar into the sky before blossoming in silver shards. The searchlights are casting their dim, blurred beam in all directions: 1, 2, 3, 4, 5. What can it mean? We soon have our answer. In the sky to our right appears a dark shape with rounded ends, like a cigar. A Zeppelin! It seems very high. At least 2000 metres. It's heading south-west, probably towards Châlons. At that height the clusters of light form round spots that seem to swim through the sky. We watch the big cigar pass through them, incendiary shells bursting all around. They're well aimed, passing quite close to the target. One shell in particular appears to go straight through the envelope before exploding. The shells seem to us to be climbing very slowly. Suddenly, through clouds turned silver by the searchlights, a magical sight: the airship shining like a silver fish. Five searchlights now have it in their grasp and do not intend to let go. The shells are bursting all round.

Looking skywards, the men keep bashing their noses on the rifle of the man alongside.

We continue to Virginy, eyes trained. The Zeppelin has finally moved out of range of the searchlights. I hear a shout and turn round: 'Look, sir! Behind us. There, to your right!'

A fire is raging in the sky. An oblong shape is discernible amidst a blazing red inferno, like an iron bar in a forge. The oblong seems to be heading for the ground. The blaze is subsiding. A sudden spurt of flame, then nothing. Gradually all dies down and darkness returns.

Our Zeppelin must have caught fire and fallen near Revigny.

Arrive at Massiges.

The men are all in. My legs are stiff as a rifle barrel. Another Zeppelin appears. A handful of shells and it returns to Boche lines.

Tuesday 22 February

It snowed last night. Today everything is white. I leave to reconnoitre the sector.

Wonderful weather. The Ravin de l'Étang, Ravin du Médius, Médius, Col des Abeilles and Annulaire are cloaked in white – with a sunny blue sky above.

---

1. Maintaining an interval of 300 to 400 metres between platoons.

In the distance, shrouded in a diaphanous veil of white mist, the familiar heights of Côte 181, Côte 202, etc. mark our route as far as Braux. I feel unconscionably cheerful. The day is mild. Tramping through the beautiful white carpet, it feels good to be alive. The distant rumble of the German batteries, probably firing on our lines before Verdun, reminds us that we are at war.

Thibault says we shot down five aircraft yesterday. The Zeppelin fell at Brabant-le-Roi, in advance of Revigny. It was apparently hit by an auto-cannon.[1]

Thursday 24 February

A beautiful sunny day. Sous-lieutenant Bodin[2] and I leave before dawn to reconnoitre the sector. We go back up Boyau Schumann as far as Boyau 31. The *boyaux* are frozen, the weather dry. It feels good to be out and about so early. At 5.30 am the only faint light in the sky is over towards Massiges. By the time we reach the junction of Boyau Schultz and Boyau 31, dawn is breaking We pass the 77 abandoned by the Germans. Opposite are the remains of the German artillery dug-outs, a load of shells still in their wicker baskets. The entrances are so badly damaged that the opening is scarcely identifiable: a platform and two beams buried in the grey earth.

The sun is up now, cheerful and bright. Loopholes have been inserted in the *boyau* overlooking the Creux de l'Oreille to give a distant view. We stop here. No man's land extends before us, white with snow, shrouded in silver-grey mist. The sparkling white snow, brilliant sunshine and fresh air all imbue us with a sense of well-being. Inspect the parapets. In no man's land there's a shell-hole every couple of metres. They literally pockmark the area. They come in all sizes: the small bowls of the 75s, the broad, deep sinkholes of the German 210s. Fittingly, here's an unexploded German 210, blue in colour and at least 80 centimetres long. Quite a lump. The 77 alongside looks like a cigar butt.

We return. The Ravin de l'Étang is bathed in golden light, a thousand motes of sparkling dust dancing in its rays.

Friday 25 February

Miserable weather. Cloudy, cold and sleeting.

If the company commander in the front line is like a ship's captain, in the second line he is the chief engineer, the director of works. He has to arrange transport and labour details, then sort out and allocate the tasks to be completed.

---

1. This is correct.
2. He had just transferred to the company.

We have to clear out and rebuild the damaged telephonists' shelter next to my dug-out. Elsewhere we need to shore up the soldiers' dug-outs and complete the mustering area in Boyau Schumann.

After touring the sector, I reckon it should be pretty nigh impregnable – only the bomb shelters remain vulnerable. The soundest are the German shelters we have cleared out and repaired.

Saturday 26 February

After a stone-splitting frost and a midday thaw the *boyaux* are now rivers of gluey, greasy mud, where you skid with every step.

[Captain] L[etondot] says my leave is no go.[1] I'm apparently going on detachment to Sainte-Ménehould instead. But he seems so hesitant that I suspect not.

Non-stop gunfire last night, on both our right (Verdun) and our left (Tahure). The news from Verdun is far from reassuring, although it could be worse. The enemy communiqués claim the Boches have taken Samogneux on the Meuse. On the eastern flank of the positions they've captured Fort Douaumont. It doesn't look good.[2] They've been shelling our lines again since this morning – proof they are trying to either fix our troops here or deter any possible attack.

It's all very worrying. Now is not the time to let captains go on leave.

Sunday 27 February

A number of mortar bombs have arrived. I shall detail almost half of the company to move them to the front line.

All leave was officially suspended on 26 February. It was no great surprise. From the direction of Verdun, the guns rumbled continuously through the night. The Boches claim to have taken 15,000 prisoners. Our communiqué gives a figure of 7,000 to 8,000. The Germans are replying to our Champagne offensive, on a broader front.[3]

Across the stream behind us, opposite the entrance to our dug-outs, is Côte 181. Two batteries are positioned here, one of 90s and one of 75s. Both are being sprinkled with 105s, 150s, 77s, 88s: a proper blessing. While in the vicinity, the

---

1. All leave had been suspended due to the situation at Verdun.
2. Quite right. The situation at Verdun on 26 February was most alarming. This was the day General Joffre authorized General Castelnau to give General Pétain command of its defence.
3. And much better resourced.

Boches also drop the odd shell on the Decauville [rail track] and the corduroy road, which pass 15 metres from our dug-outs in general, and mine in particular.

Unhealthier still, a 77 could walk straight into my dug-out as if it was at home.

Two telephonists are attached to my HQ: Corporal Marius and Corporal Choquet. Both are Parisians, with the accent to prove it. Choquet is particularly admirable. I heard him respond to a call from one of his chums just now: 'You're being hit by 150s. That's nothing, pal. They could be even bigger!'[1]

He's a typical man of the *faubourgs* – a joker, an extrovert, a grumbler and a braggart.

'101st Infantry is a regular regiment,' he told a man from the 142nd. 'We're rock solid.'

'Chocolate-box, more like,' came the reply.

'Chocolate-box! I'll give you chocolate-box! Our regiment has seen much more action than yours. Our flag's riddled with bullet-holes. Something to be proud of. Not like the 14th or the 7th: they lost theirs to the enemy.'[2]

Our sector is ideally positioned. If Verdun is under the hammer, we're on the left flank. If discussions are under way in Champagne, there we are again on the right. It's a very special spot. I explained this to my men this morning. It made them laugh. Excellent. They will hold out to the last man. Laughter is underrated as a means of command. There is no better tonic.

Monday 28 February

I need fifty planks. I requested them at 6.00 am. They're in Virginy, twenty minutes away. They should have arrived by 7.00 am at the latest and be in place by now. But it's 10.00 am and still nothing. Just getting hold of them involved submitting a chit counter-signed by the colonel. It's enough to make you weep.

Tuesday 29 February

The reason behind the German advance at Verdun is simple enough. We didn't have enough shelters.[3] Experienced troops sheltering in dug-outs can definitely

---

1. His chum must have been protesting at the other end of the line. 'Alright! Alright!' I heard Monsieur Choquet reply. 'Keep your hair on!' And he hung up.
2. The Frenchman, cocky as ever. Unsurprisingly, I can't guarantee that the Germans captured these two flags. It could have been one of Choquet's tall stories.
3. There were none at all. It's true we didn't have enough sappers. No surprise there! In the first twelve months of the war, from August 1914 to September 1915, we had needlessly killed the bravest and the best by giving them impossible tasks like cutting the enemy barbed wire with scissors.

withstand a 72-hour bombardment with no loss of morale – as long as they don't suffer a direct hit. The Germans probably had around 700,000 miners before the war. I assume they've been used to create an Engineering corps of at least 500,000, all with the skills needed to construct and equip the underground shelters required in this war. At a guess, the French mining industry had a workforce of around 100,000 men. We couldn't afford to lose a single one, but we've squandered the lot. What's more, some Engineers officers, and some generals and colonels, happily use tons of men and matériel to build their own Swiss chalets.

A wall in my dug-out collapsed last night. A Boche projectile? No. Just the vibration caused by Dudu [the 90mm gun] over the road.

The colonel, who turned down my request for planks yesterday, has accumulated piles of timber – logs, beams, props, etc. – to construct his own comfortable shelter behind the lines. At Braux, well-appointed chalets have been built from scratch.

Relieved this evening. My replacement is big M.T. from 124th Infantry. Everything is ready. I have to report to Consul before we leave. Shelling Massiges has cut the telephone lines. We let a Boche relief have a few yesterday and now they're returning the compliment.

I stay behind, sending the company on ahead under the command of Bodin, who is senior to Rouzeaud.

At last, via supplies, I manage to get through to Consul.

En route. Ahead, the shells are pounding Massiges. I'm sick with worry. Has the company made it through unscathed?

The crossroads … My orderly is waiting with my horse.

'Have any of the company been hit?'[1]

'No, sir!'

'Off we go then! To Virginy!'

The Germans have raised their sights. The shells are now falling on the Virginy crossroads and, as far as I can see, on the track to Côte 181. Their information is spot on.

We pass through Virginy. The *marmites* have fallen silent. Forward! Try to catch up with the company! The lethal crossroads entering Berzieux – behind us. Our 75mm batteries are behind the ridge. We can breathe again. Through Berzieux and we're pretty well home and dry.

---

1. At every relief, the captain and his runners stayed back to pass on orders before hurrying to catch up with the company.

Crump! *Crump*! Arthur starts to splutter. Just our luck! A salvo! The shots form a single line of fire in advance of Berzieux. If Müller replies, we're cooked. Already we can see the black, shell-pitted walls of Berzieux. A sudden rumble through the air to our left. A shell. Quick, flat in the ditch. A huge explosion. It has to be a 210. It goes off slap in the middle of Berzieux. The horse is spooked and gallops off with my orderly clinging to its neck. *Crump*! Another, then another. We stay down for at least twenty minutes, hoping against hope that Müller keeps his sights lifted.

Fancy picking Berzieux[1] – under constant shellfire – as the battalion assembly point. It's original, to say the least.

Arthur has shut up shop. Müller seems to have quietened down. We clamber from the ditch. Forward! Here's Araja ... At Le Poncelet, the company! Hallelujah!

Can you believe it? Consul has ordered the men to pile arms! On the right-hand side of the road! The verges are a quagmire, so men can no longer pass two abreast. Fortunately, it's 1.00 am. The meal break is over ...

But the best is yet to come. After reaching the Valmy crossroads, Consul is totally lost. Halt. Dismount. Check the map by the light of the electric lamp. He's holding the map upside down. The men roll their eyes. I quietly suggest he turns it the other way up. He looks daggers at me: 'It's fine ...' He orders a man to scale the signpost. Three routes present themselves: one seems excellent; the other two, rather less so. Naturally, Consul chooses one of the latter. After 300 metres the track becomes a morass. Still we march on, up to our calves in a glue that sucks at our boots. Then the morass starts to become a lake. Is there a crossing point? A muddy little track is just about discernible at the top of a talus. We move forward in Indian file, each man clinging to the rifle of the comrade in front. Men get stuck in the mud, they become separated, and soon the entire battalion is squelching around in the dark. We haven't a clue where we are. I'm at the rear of the company with five men. I've no idea what's happened to everyone else. I'm advancing by guesswork alone.

After thirty minutes feeling our way through the darkness over this shifting ground, we spot houses. Valmy. We're there. It's 4.30 am.

With all his years of service, Consul will, I suspect, be nominated for a promotion.[2]

---

1. A crossroads well within range of the enemy guns.
2. No one ever went that far.

Wednesday 1 March
Dismal day in Valmy. The men are harassed and exhausted. They're all in. Their faces are pale and drawn, covered in muck.

Thursday 2 March
On my horse by 8.00 am. Spring weather. The Valmy obelisk stands on a mound south of the village. Before it, an iron post topped by an outline plaque of a windmill marks the site of the famous Valmy mill. The view from here is superb. But where were the troops lined up? I can't remember in enough detail to work it out. A very fine statue of Barrau by Kellermann. Beautiful bronze, well sculpted. Just one fault. It's a bit too like Rude's [Marshal] Ney.

On such a glorious morning I decide to treat myself to a ride across the fields. Sunlight and birdsong fill the valleys. It's mild. The hillsides are bare in this impoverished countryside, the few trees still leafless, but my heart soars at the warmth of approaching spring. I forget all about the war, the horror of bodies rotting before the lines and within the parapets or buried here and there in small groups within our trenches, mangled and disfigured, a pathetic white cross and upturned bottle on a mound often flattened again already …

Amid all the joys of spring, a field covered with blue–tinted crows reminds me of the charnel house to come.

I return via Gizaucourt.

On the road are 6th Hussars. I meet M. d'I. His mount is a magnificent chestnut filly, with fragile, skittish legs, a proud mien and red nostrils. I approach on Entrepôt – just a hack by comparison. The beautiful thoroughbred balks at anything coming too close. She kicks out, happily catching only my stirrup and the sole of my right foot. According to d'I., 6th Hussars have nothing to do but ride around from billet to billet. 'If we didn't ride, we'd be bored to death.'

When I return at 11.00 am, Consul gathers us together. He reads the circulars from beginning to end, including one from a general on the lessons to be drawn from events at Verdun. Top marks.

'Shelters will in future be dug 6 metres deep,' he intones. Fine! But where are we going to get the bradawls, beams, stanchions we require?

'Shelters will be dug 6 metres deep.' *Voilà*! It's as easy as that: danger averted at the stroke of a pen. Our general staff and high command have never solved problems any other way – a strange kind of homage to the master whose name they invoke with such fervour. Napoleon always took infinite care to ensure he had the means to execute his strategies.

Following these helpful instructions, Consul provokes us even more. 'You newly minted officers have everything to learn from we regulars. You can never hope to be our equals.'

I reckon that a very moot point, particularly after he got his battalion lost yesterday.

He 'entertains' us like this until noon, then informs us we'll be leaving at 3.00 pm for Côte 202 and Côte 138. Miserable old bugger! We'll hardly have time to strap on our canteens. He left it as late as possible just to annoy us ...[1]

At 3.00 pm we top up our canteens. A good road, beautiful weather. The men react with admirable stoicism.

The first movement is over.

My company is off to Côte 138. B. definitely gave me his dimmest runner as a guide. You couldn't imagine more of a dolt. To reach our shelters, he made us tramp 800 to 1,000 metres through mud knee deep in places. We arrived in pitch darkness, to be greeted by an Engineers sergeant – Sergeant Marchal – who was expecting us tomorrow. Fortunately he was woken by all the commotion of our arrival and came out of his dug-out. He kindly indulged us and showed us to our shelters – two east-west tunnels, some 50 to 80 metres long and 5 to 8 metres underground. The way he explained things suggested a sharp mind and a rare competence. We started chatting. He's a mining engineer. Consequently, he's now a sergeant in the Engineers. Of course, our gentle regular officers failed to consult such an experienced specialist (he's around 40 or so) before drawing up their plans. Apparently, if we see roof beams supported by double stanchions, it's because the Engineers refuse to use logs. It's against regulations. They square off the timber and weaken it in so doing. The stanchion is the regulation model though.[2] Oh, Doctor Diafoirus!

Having not had any rest, the men were already feeling harassed. Tomorrow they'll be vaccinated and fall ill. Now, because we've turned up unannounced, they're having to sleep in water, on this damp, oozing ground. Marchal did us a favour by bringing up some timber to use as insulation. But it had been standing in water all day. A man has to be pretty tough to survive this kind of treatment.

---

1. He loved to order us around like a sergeant-major. It's hard to believe that men expected to lay down their lives at any moment could be treated like this.
2. The Germans took care to do otherwise.

Friday 3 March

We are messing with Captain M.V., a territorial from 104th Infantry. We found him in the dug-out with a group of other 'terribletorials'. He is 45 years old, but scarcely seems a day over 35, despite the deep creases framing his mouth. He's my height, trim, quiet and mild mannered. He's a solicitor's clerk in Lyon, an unlikely warrior.

Apparently, the 155s in the adjoining ravine are very poorly served because the general staff retains all the good artillery officers for the 75s ... in expectation of a resumption in the war of movement.[1]

Saturday 4 March

My dug-out is a tunnel in the northern flank of the ravine below Côte 138. The ridge facing us blocks the view from the open door. Marshes in the bottoms, a bare slope falling away to the west, grey sky above: like a Pointelin landscape.

Sunday 5 March

I visited Virginy this morning. Weather cool and sunny. I wanted to see the Engineers captain in charge of the stores – a friendly territorial called German, very obliging. We would have talked for longer, but it was 10.00 am already – time for the shelling to resume.

In the afternoon, M.V. and I climbed the hill opposite and went to Côte 202 via the Plateau. The weather was fine, and the cold air made our cheeks glow. We breathed deeply. Nestled in one of the combes in the ravine, we found a shanty town surrounding a battery of 75s. We could see the dug-outs with their wooden roofs, tethered horses, men moving around. We passed the Roman road, the Decauville [railway track], then left the barbed-wire entanglements

---

1. Like General [Dantant] addressing his company commanders on 15 November 1915 on the need to prepare 'for a resumption of normal war'. In March 1917 we listened to another general, a member of the high command. 'The cavalry will have its day,' he claimed. He was envisaging a breakthrough and a Murat-style pursuit! Over three years of war and he'd learned nothing.

   Why did we take so long to develop a modern heavy artillery during the war? Why did 'a lack of trench mortars – the only weapon effective against entrenchments or a line of positions – remain the dominant feature of our artillery throughout the conflict?' (Gascouin, p. 112).

   It took almost three years for our high command to realize that trenches were the product of improved ballistics. They remained preoccupied with a resumption in the war of movement. So why burden ourselves with heavy guns?

and trenches of Ouvrage M to our right. Now we were confronted by a shanty town three or four times bigger – Côte 202. The little black holes and wood or corrugated-iron roofs occupy three of the slopes and the entire rim of a ravine. Life in these camp sites imposed upon us by the Boches is strange indeed. So too is a battlefield you can at times stroll around in the middle of the day – because this is still a battlefield. Batteries lurk everywhere, ready to fire as soon as they get the signal. In the distance, returning via Côte 199, we could see the Chenille and Cernay-en-Dormois,[1] whose houses were shining in the sun.

All is quiet now. The odd burst of gunfire. Yet the broad craters hollowed in the white chalk show the shells are regular visitors. No matter. What a strange war. Apart from the shanty towns clustered like vermin on the slopes, there is not a soul to be seen.

At 7.00 pm, beneath the stars, in the icy dark, we dig trenches at the foot of the pinewoods on Côte 199.

Monday 6 March

Pale sky and white earth this morning. Everything is shrouded with snow.

General T[atin], the provisional divisional commander (since Dantan was sacked), is installing his HQ beside the narrow road that runs along Côte 199. Magnificent view embracing the whole of the frontage held by his division. Two solid timber-clad shafts to serve as observation posts. They couldn't be better sited.

Both artilleries open up at 5.00 pm around Butte-du-Ménil and Maisons-de-Champagne. The din reaches us in our ravine, which is hit by several big *marmites* to remind us we're still in the firing line. It's like a sudden fit of anger on both sides. The two adversaries quarrel violently, utter mutual curses at the point of a gun, spend an hour hurling big lumps of metal at each other, then gradually grow silent.

Night has fallen. Black clouds float immobile in the dark blue sky; the only light, a purple band in the west. The evening star is shining brightly; so too, the silver crescent moon. The last of the light is reflected faintly in the marshy bottoms. In the distance, the rounds begin to tail off, then peace returns.

---

1. They lay within enemy lines.

Monday 6 March
I was woken last night by the thud of the nearby 155s. The sky was full of stars; the moon, a red crescent. The guns were still raging from Mont Têtu to Maisons-de-Champagne.

Tuesday 7 March
Shrove Tuesday. We ate pancakes.

Last night we were working at Point 180, in the cold and dark, by the light of the stars and the crescent moon. Around 10.00 pm furious shelling towards Maisons-de-Champagne. You could see all the action from our vantage point, if you were prepared to brave the shells bursting and whirring like spinning-tops over your head. Over to our left, the red flash of the explosions lit up the darkness completely. You could make out the crackle of rifle fire, the sharp explosion of the grenades. A French counter-attack? It seems likely.

Beautiful weather today. Saw Adjudant Coupry, the Engineer replacing Monsieur Marchal. He's another mining engineer, who says the Boches are turning out 400,000 shells a day to our 250,000.[1] The first figure is no surprise, unlike the second. The Boches are bound to bring up their heavy artillery and reposition it. Then they'll resume firing.

Lovely evening. Fine night. A straightforward relief. I'm replacing Captain Roussel, who relieved me at the Verrue. A fine chap, round as a plum.

Wednesday 8 March
The shelters at the Col des Abeilles are foul. The entrance to my HQ is marked by a mound of filth dating back who-knows-how-long. We need to organize a proper quarters cleaning party. It's amazing how apathy and neglect allow rubbish to accumulate. Without appropriate action, the men will happily moulder amid stale crusts, cheese boxes, all kinds of litter, and worse still. Permanently shrouded in mud, wearing their boots for days and nights on end, they doze in these holes, grimy, filthy, riddled with vermin, slumped on a grating covered in rotten straw, crawling with rats and lice. A brazier at the entrance fills the place with smoke, poisoning them with carbon monoxide.

My response is to get them working. Clean *boyaux*, clean trenches. They've developed a taste for it: they manage to shave and to wipe their faces – I won't say wash because I don't know where we'd find the water. Their captain freshens himself up after the fashion of Louis XIV – with a dab of *eau de cologne*.

---

1. These figures were pretty accurate.

Clear skies and bright sunshine this morning. I reconnoitre the sector through frozen *boyaux* and across a no man's land white with frost.

By 9.00 am the sun is fading. It's starting to look like snow. The white flakes begin to fall. Beneath a bleached sky, the ramps in the ravine, the shell-holes, quickly disappear beneath an immaculate soft white carpet, whose pale glare hurts the eyes.

Thursday 9 March
The snow is still with us, marked today by long dark streaks – the tracks followed by work details and rations parties.

We're spending more and more time as sappers.

Chatted with Y. and [Vinerot]. Both are excellent comrades, but the conversation of some regulars hasn't changed a jot. All they ever talk about is promotion and decorations. Needless to say neither is happy, although both are captains and [Vinerot] already has the Légion d'Honneur. The brave Y. – a very cheerful comrade – believes he hasn't had enough mentions-in-despatches. But he's never seen any action. He served in transport until May 1915 and was in reserve on 25 September. Since then he's been a machine-gun captain – i.e. he signs chits – and he's just been appointed adjutant in 3rd Battalion – i.e. in future he'll spend all his time 'blethering on the phone'. Let's hope he soon has a whole forest of palms, like [Captain] L[etondot], the sight of whose breast turns everyone green with envy.

Saturday 11 March
The shelling begins at 11.00 am, just as the orderlies are returning from their meal. We're worried. The shells start falling on Massiges, then the ravine. Suddenly, 'Quinze-Grammes'[1] appears, head swamped by his oversized helmet. He's so out of breath he can't speak. After a moment he recovers his voice: 'Pigs!'

Sunday 12 March
Sun at last. Bright sunshine, a mild spring morning. A sparkling Sunday, with the promise of a blooming Easter. The shelling starts on the Médius at 10.30 am.

---

1. Surname Guichard. A likely lad from Tours. His slight build earned him the nickname 'Quinze-Grammes'. Very apt. He was buried beneath his pack but carried it regardless. Seldom have I met a braver man.

It gradually grows heavier and by 11.00 am the barrage is infernal. The shells are 105s: the calibre used by the gentle Boches to pound the slopes of Massiges, the Médius, the Ravin and the Annulaire, and, of course, [our positions] on the Col des Abeilles.

An intolerable odour of powder soon penetrates the dug-out, making us cough.

Consul sends a warning order: 'the Boches have fixed bayonets in the trenches opposite'. I order my men to stand to, without making too much fuss, because I think this an odd time to attack and the preparation completely inadequate. Still, I mustn't upset Consul.

An hour passes, then two. No attack.

This evening, the relief. A still, bright night. Return to the Balcon HQ. I wrote recently of the noxious atmosphere in the dug-outs. The air at the Col des Abeilles HQ was of a rare purity compared to here. I wonder how many germs per cubic centimetre would be revealed if it was analyzed. A shaft-like staircase leads to a sort of steamboat cabin, full of mice. Three bunks are covered with straw at least three months old. Four straw-covered planks form another four bunks on the staircase. Worst of all, at the top, by the entrance, is a charcoal stove. The air is quite simply unbreathable. One oddity. The telephonist, who has already spent four days here, has got used to it. He can tolerate this atmosphere! It explains how whole families can survive in hovels, workers in the steamy conditions of a textile mill, etc. The human body adapts.

I'd rather this not happen to my body, so I order the stove to be removed and the staircase cleared of its bunks. That will get the air circulating a little.

Consul summons us for the reading of the orders. Most illuminating.

Sous-lieutenant Clément, temporary CO of 5th Company, is an ex-adjudant, with somewhere between fifteen and eighteen years' service.

'I didn't change a thing, sir! I handed on my orders exactly as received.'

'Excellent,' exclaims Consul.

B[iancardini] (6th Company) reads out his orders. 'I had to amend my orders, sir! We now hold Tranchée du Plateau!'

'You had no right to do that.'

'But, sir! The trench didn't exist when the orders were issued.'

'That doesn't matter. You still had no right.'

B[iancardini] looks down, muttering under his breath. He holds his tongue. There's no point arguing.

I await my turn rather anxiously. I freshened up my orders a little. Anything out of date went straight to the latrines.

Blaise (7th Company) made no changes. Now it's my turn. 'I decided I should revise our orders in case of attack, sir!'

'Why?' bellows Consul, face puce. 'Orders are orders. I pass them on exactly as I receive them. I am a slaaave to my orders.'

'The current orders are a month old, sir!' (And even then were probably a reissue of their predecessors.) 'The redoubt in Tranchée 35 allocated to the platoon in case of attack didn't exist then. I had to issue new ones.'

Consul falls silent for a moment. 'Fine! Let me have a copy.'

Monday 13 March

Bright sunshine.

Did my usual round last night. It takes in all my little world.

My soldiers are a fine bunch of men. They lie prone on the parapet under the clear blue light of the stars, watching and listening, helmets covered in mud to stop them glinting in the moonlight. Fritz isn't far away – behind the bushes and the stagnant pond. Let's hope he keeps quiet. You can sleep soundly in Paris. The poilus are on guard.

And as soon as their watch is over they grab their picks and shovels. They dig and clear trenches, reinforce the walls with iron posts and wire mesh, construct protective berms wherever possible. They create firing steps from all kinds of materials: planks laid lengthwise, supported by stakes, crates, sandbags and wire mesh. Solid splinter-proofs reinforced with wooden stakes 1.5 to 2 metres long and retained by chicken wire present a rounded profile. Meanwhile other men are deepening the saps, positioning props, uprights and caps, erecting timber cladding …

In the soft light of these fine nights, the slopes of the Cratère are bright as day. The sound of distant rifle or artillery fire barely reminds us that over there men are on watch, seeking human targets.

I go to visit Bodin at the old Boche aid post. We've been occupying this sector for six months now without managing to dig the 10 metres of sap required to link this splendid shelter to Tranchée Balcon-Ouest. No man's land is still littered with Boche corpses. One is buried head down, just his legs and stomach showing. He still has all his equipment: solid, supple boots on his feet. Another – he looks huge to me, at least 1.8 metres tall – is still on watch.

Smart remarks abound.

'The corporal of the relief will have him put on a charge …'

'I don't know who's feeding him, but they can't come round often.'

Tuesday 14 March

Glorious morning. Birdsong all around. Nature's joyful reawakening has a strange effect here. It makes you think of life, of beautiful days lost and never to return.

Sunday 19 March

We came out of the line to rest two days ago after twenty-four days in the trenches. Twenty-four days under constant gunfire, without any opportunity to wash or take our boots off.

I was sorry to see [Sergeant] R[enaud][1] get injured on Friday. I had taken a little night tour towards the German lines. In the moonlight, it was bright as day. Escorted by young Rouzeaud, we climbed over the parapet and out into no man's land, where the Boche corpses have been standing eternal guard since 25 September 1915. Beyond the Abris post, [Sergeant] Provent[2] pointed to what looked like a collapsed dug-out. We started digging. I slid through the hole, masked it with a greatcoat and switched on my electric lamp. A load of Boche cartridges, still in their wrappers. In one corner, a metal-covered crate. I opened it: Boche illuminating rockets, dated 13 June 1915, all in perfect condition in their cardboard boxes.

Their waterproof crates do a proper job.

The following day I took receipt of the French equivalent. Pathetic. Cut-down dustbins with lids held down by wing-nuts. No keys to open them, of course. And to top it off, one had a hole in it. 'Rather a disadvantage in a waterproof container,' I commented in my report.

We hung around a while longer looking for buried treasure. Then R[enaud] turned up, clad in a silk balaclava. He immediately started rooting around and soon unearthed a box of detonators. A few rounds greeted us on our return, but not enough to stop us dragging the crate of rockets back to our HQ. I forgot all about the detonators until 10.00am next morning, when I heard that R[enaud] had blown his hand off and hurt his eyes.

---

1. Young, fair haired, delicate.
2. A Paris policeman who had volunteered for the trenches. Excellent fellow. I could never get him to wear a helmet. He said it gave him a headache.

The daft beggar wanted to see inside a detonator. He tried to dismantle one and it exploded. I visited him at the aid post yesterday. He has lost three fingers from his left hand, but I hope that will be all.[1]

I went to Châlons yesterday with D. and the [regimental] paymaster. Arrived at 3.00 pm. The streets were packed. Military types everywhere. I say 'military types', not soldiers, because no one we saw is not serving in the rear. They pack the shops on the Rue de la Marne, romancing the shop-girls with whom they seem well acquainted.

There are certainly some fortunes being made in these small towns in the rear!

The cathedral and the church next door are both very fine. Despite the proximity of war and tragedy, I was the old Delvert once more, seized by tender feelings for these lovingly worked stones.

The indifferent herd walked by, concentrating only on a good dinner ... or more. Instant gratification. The beast within is back. War is definitely not conducive to contemplation. Tramping the streets of these small towns in the rear, clad in their motley uniforms, all these men – worker, bourgeois or peasant farmer – turn into idlers and lowlifes. A pretty poor show. I can't resist drawing comparisons with the past. Strict discipline was enforced even when soldiers were at rest. The words of [Marshal] Soult, describing the men of 1794, often come to mind: 'It was then that I saw the greatest moral goodness in the army.'

In the café, D. introduces us to one of his innumerable friends – a small, trim, lively chap of 60 or so, with a greying goatee beard and a beaky nose. Bright eyes constantly darting from side to side. What does he do? Probably something in intelligence. He claims to be on the editorial staff of *Le Journal*. He jumps up and rushes around, shaking hands and protesting his friendship. His brother is the parliamentary deputy for Constantine [Algeria]. Within the space of five minutes, he has outlined the political allegiance of every Algerian deputy and most of the French ones, too. A real live wire amid the placid northerners surrounding us.

Incidentally, Corsicans are all related to each other. He knows Consul, he knows F. He's delighted to hear of S[ivan]'s promotion. When your superiors are all Corsicans, it's good to hail from 'Little France'.

---

1. He was invalided out – to the enormous delight of his family – after I wrote my official report. He was not awarded a pension.

Monday 20 March

Today we took the Berzieux road and went to reconnoitre the Calvaire sector. We chose a good time: 3.00 am. A good route, too. No shelling at all on the outward trip. Quite extraordinary. But as soon as we arrived we got our fair share.

Met a captain from 104th Infantry, a young man of 29 or 30, confirmed in his new rank after five years as a lieutenant. Excellent going, yet he says 'the war has brought him nothing but wounded pride'.

I suggested that all it's brought me are wounds plain and simple.

'I know what you mean!' he replied.

Some regular officers are splendid, but also very pessimistic. 'We'll never make the breakthrough. I can't see any end to it all.'

'We'll never make the breakthrough!' What does he know? Our concerns were very different a few days ago when we were fretting over the fate of Verdun.

[Hillère] says the Big Spring Push is scheduled for 7 April.

We returned quick sharp across the grey plain, the setting sun kissing the heavy dark clouds scudding across the sky.

A handful of red lights. Braux–Sainte-Cohière, already shrouded in darkness.

Tuesday 21 March

A spring day.

I've been ordered to provide a party of 'at least twenty' men to dig graves in the cemetery. It feels like ordering men condemned to death to dig their own graves. The military authorities bow to no one in brutality. They could just as easily have sent some territorials from the road crews.

Clear skies this afternoon, so I had a trip to Sainte-Ménehould. Nothing but shirkers in these towns in the rear! The main street apart, Sainte-Ménehould is completely dead. Plenty of smoke at the Hôtel Saint-Nicolas, full of uniforms from Supplies.

Wonderful return by road and fields as night fell. The bare branches of the roadside trees formed a web of black against the gold of the setting sun, glimpses of tawny light sparkling from the calm mirror of the ponds. The air was still. Not a breath of wind. All was quiet. No artillery, no machine guns in the distance. The radiant skies were empty but for the two black wings of a bi-plane stationary in the sun.

Wednesday 22 March

The weather has turned cold again. Grey skies, tipping it down. Miserable.

Our next relief is due on Sunday night.

The situation at Verdun seems to be calming down. The Germans won't pull back until they're on their last legs, but that point seems quite close. At all events the dread we felt a month ago has evaporated. Dread? Too strong a word, perhaps. We front-line soldiers have always been confident in our eventual victory.[1]

The Russians will certainly be lending us a hand.[2] They're planning a diversionary action around Riga and Dwinsk to ease the German stranglehold.

T[ramard] is being transferred. Sous-lieutenant Riballier des Isles[3] has arrived to replace him.

Friday 24 March

Grey clouds and rain. [Hillère] and I went to Sainte-Ménehould in the afternoon. It really is a dismal little place.

Lovely ride home on this delightful road. A long chat with [Hillère].

An army is a hive of gossip. [Hillère], I am sure, has never read the military memoirs of the Revolution and the Empire, but everything he says reminds me of the heroes of Thiébault. In the army of 1915, men argue, criticize each other, resent each other, chase promotion or the Légion d'Honneur, just like their forebears in 1808 or 1809.

[Hillère] described a visit made to his sector by the corps commander after the attack of 25 September 1915. The brigade commander, Brigadier T[atin], had just begun to install the 'redoubts' now common all over the front. The corps commander approached Major N[icolas], commanding 2nd Battalion.

'Where's your redoubt?' he asked.

Major N[icolas] didn't know. 'We've received contradictory information,' he replied. 'Some orders say one thing; some another. I can't really tell you.'

'Very well,' said the corps commander.

Two days later a brisk note appeared, instructing brigadiers and colonels to issue orders giving the precise location of all the redoubts in their sector.

Brigadier T[atin] was incensed. 'I'll put that major on a charge!' A few days later he went to inspect the sector and arrived at the major's HQ. 'Where's the major?' he asked.

---

1. No further comment.
2. The Brusilov offensive of the summer of 1916. [Note: launched on 8 June 1916.]
3. A very short-sighted academic. He had been invalided out in peacetime but insisted on volunteering for the duration. In the infantry, too. 'A fine man.' Killed at Cornillet in August 1917.

'Doing his rounds, sir!'

'Fetch him at once.'

Major N[icolas] is found.

He salutes.

Brigadier T[atin] fails to respond. After scarcely 100 metres he halts in front of a machine gun. 'Can't you see this gun has no field of fire, major?'

'There are two machine-gun captains to look after that kind of thing, sir!'

'You really have no idea! If you can't exercise a command, don't take it up in the first place. And stand to attention when I'm talking to you.' (The *boyaux* were full of poilus.) 'Disgraceful!'

According to [Hillère], Brigadier T[atin] even raised his hand.

Then he turned to [Hillère]. 'Show me round the sector, Captain [Hillère].'

The attack of 25 September 1915 was followed by mutual recriminations. Accusations were made of cowardice, of failing to leave the trenches, etc. It is, however, abundantly clear that the survivors (most of whom remained in the shelters) have all done very nicely for themselves: one received a mention in divisional dispatches for following the attack from the colonel's HQ; Captain L[etondot] got a mention in army dispatches, and the Légion d'Honneur, for manning the phones.

Regarding Captain L[etondot], all the witnesses agree. Colonel Destival was due to leave with the third wave; he climbed onto the parapet and suffered a mortal wound. He called for his adjutant, Captain L[etondot]. No sign of him. The colonel was carried, covered in blood, to his HQ.

Captain L[etondot] appeared.

'Where were you?' asked the colonel.

'I'm not feeling too well today, sir. Not well at all.'

'You shouldn't be here,' said the colonel. He pointed to the German trenches. 'Your place is out there.'

The colonel faded rapidly and died that evening. Meanwhile Captain L[etondot] remained at HQ. In his daily report, he coolly announced that he took over command of the regiment, sidestepping the colonel who later succeeded Destival. This colonel nominated Captain L[etondot] for the Légion d'Honneur, argued his case personally, and L[etondot] was duly honoured.

Best of all was [Hillère]'s conclusion. 'There are only two alternatives in cases like this – either decorate the officer or court-martial him.'

I admit the whole thing is beyond me.

Saturday 25 March

The sun has returned but it's still chilly outside.

Went back to Sainte-Ménehould with [Hillère]. He introduced me to Madame M., who owns a haberdashery near the square. On 3 September 1914, the day we left for the battle of the Marne, she had entertained him, along with S. and Colonel Farret.

We embarked at 7.00 pm, if memory serves. Madame M. says the first uhlans appeared at 9.00 am the following day, and by noon the German infantry had occupied the town. The French, in the shape of two cyclists, returned at 7.00 pm on 15 September; the first cavalryman arrived at 9.00 pm, followed by the colonial infantry.

Madame M. had Boche officers billeted with her for ten days. She says they were perfectly correct, kissing her hand and bringing her flowers. The first group of five asked her to cook dinner for them. They brought a decent-sized goose (which they claimed cost 7 francs) and stuffed it with green apples (!), even though some were wormy.

Madame M. roasted the goose and prepared *petits pois*, fried potatoes and a tomato salad. She brought it all to the table and went out for a moment. On her return, she was horrified to find their plates piled high with roast goose, peas, potatoes, tomato salad – the lot. They were diving in with gusto. They washed it all down with fifteen bottles of wine and two of rum. And, says Madame M., they remained perfectly sober throughout. She couldn't believe how much they had eaten and drunk.

Before leaving, one of the Boches told Madame M. that she'd be German in a fortnight. And that he was going to divorce his wife and marry her instead! Another promised to send her a postcard from Paris when they reached the city in six days' time!

Sunday 26 March

It's windy and cold.

Relief this evening.

Dreadful relief. Leave Braux at 4.30 pm. I send the horse back at Courtémont. We continue via the Minaucourt road and the newly installed corduroy track. Awful going for kilometres on end across this strip of logs, slipping and turning your ankle with every step. The recent rain has made a real cesspool of the bottoms, water squelching everywhere. Carrying haversack, blanket, tent section, reserve rations, etc., the men are all in. One faints before we reach Point 180.[1]

---

1. A point on the route used by the reliefs, still with several kilometres to cover.

From the darkness of the verges loom mud-spattered vehicles, mobile cookers and ammunition wagons, men clad in all sorts of nameless garments – real Romany caravans. The long manes of the horses are matted with rain and earth. The horses look just like their masters: a hard life has fashioned both in the same image. The rough carts look about to topple over. Their wheels are hub deep in clay. Is that old rattletrap stuck there? No. With a 'giddy up', and an oath or two, the team pulls together, just like my poor men heaving their packs back on again.

Arrive at 10.00 pm to find the *boyaux* jammed with troops. We climb onto the parapet to make better headway. Even then it takes us until nearly midnight. Our legs are stiff, our joints hurt, my wound feels like it's being probed by a scalpel. I feel a violent loathing for the plump, cosseted bourgeois, briskly discussing military operations in the lamplight, surrounded by his adoring family … Does he feel any gratitude towards the poor souls struggling so painfully into the cannons' mouth? Only if he can understand their suffering. And you can be sure that he doesn't have a clue.

Monday 27 March
At the Verrue HQ.
'It's a miracle! They've built us some shelters!'
'What? They've decided to put in some infantry shelters!'
'Yes! I can't believe it!'
Don't get too excited: the shelters have been constructed in accordance with the *Instruction on Field Works*, 21 December 1915, i.e. a hole has been dug 2.5 metres wide and 3 metres deep, then covered with logs, earth and a layer of girders.[1] That may be protection enough against the 77s. However, these shelters – which in general have to house some fifty men – only have six or eight bunks. Quite hopeless. And most of the shells here are 105s and 210s. As I write, at 5.30 pm, the last of this afternoon's 210s have just stopped rocking my dug-out. Whenever a screaming shell explodes nearby, it sends a not-unpleasant breeze through the place.

Tuesday 28 March
Grey skies. At 7.00 am I went to check the outposts in Tranchée 30. It roused B., who woke in a bad mood! Blaise was also tucked up in bed.[2] So, too, was

---

1. It was pointless removing earth then re-using it to cover beams and girders. The protection offered was no better than earth alone.
2. Some companies were surprised while they were asleep, and the CO taken prisoner in his bed.

[Hillère] when I returned via Tranchée 32. Life in a hole really does make you drowsy. The *boyaux* are packed with all sorts of dubious rubbish, but the birds above are singing to greet the spring. Frankly, if I were a bird, I'd rather be in the Bois de Boulogne.

Wednesday 29 March

Wonderful weather. Inspection from 5.00 am onwards. Beyond the 77[1] in Boyau 31, a pair of feet are sticking out of the parapet ... probably a colonial, definitely French. In the parapet opposite, another foot, also French.

Ran into a number of chaps in the *boyaux* this morning: a staff major from 4th Corps, with a captain; Major Touveray from 44th Artillery, with a lieutenant-colonel.

Life here is not without its charms. It's like camping. I walk through the trenches and *boyaux*; the air is crisp, the sun beaming down. Cheerful clouds scud across the blue sky. Distant gunfire. I walk for two or three hours, then return to the dug-out to work, read or write. That's enough to keep me happy. The temptations of Saint Anthony do not torment me. Yet fleshly lusts do haunt the dug-outs. For proof, I need look no further than the succession of *La Vie parisienne* prints adorning the wood cladding. Of all the illustrated magazines, *La Vie parisienne*, with its Gerda Wegener prints of a tiny female in corset and bloomers, is definitely the most popular. I find it whenever I visit an HQ. Minnies and heavy shells are falling on the Verrue just now, but to my right a voluptuous, saucer-eyed blonde languorously draped over an armchair reminds me that elsewhere life goes on; that incarceration and death are reserved only for the poilu; that 200 kilometres away human beings are enjoying all the pleasures of civilization. We could be living under the Directory.[2]

I have been re-reading *Le Sens de la mort*, having rescued it from [Vinerot]. 'But he was wounded for our transgressions, he was bruised for our iniquities: the chastisement of our peace was upon him; and with his stripes are we healed,' says Isaiah 53:5 (cited on p. 202). 'He' is Ernest Le Gallic, the wounded lieutenant tended by Dr Ortègue. Le Gallic is the hero, the ideal soldier presented as an exemplar by the author. The truth, I can only repeat, is very different. The real hero is the humble poilu, working so tirelessly even when not holding a rifle. By his labour, suffering and death, he is paying for the mistakes of the generation of 1870; for the selfish myopia of the years that followed, when

---

1. A 77, abandoned by the Germans, which became something of a landmark.
2. Translator's note: the government of France from 1795–9, overthrown by Napoleon.

so many felt entitled to pontificate despite having shirked their paramount duty: military service.[1] Such men would argue that they were only taking advantage of the law as it stood at the time. In return, however, it should have disqualified them from any form of comment on national affairs. Yet did you ever see sterner or more fiery prophets?

Bourget's argument irritates me. To him, the true soldier is the Catholic Le Gallic. It is these believers, he states in his novel, 'who are supplying the workers demanded in this hour of peril', whose 'energies chime with the nation's most urgent needs'.

This is utterly unfair to many brave men.

I have commanded two companies in action since 2 August 1914 – one after another. In neither was everyone a practising churchgoer. My present company contains some devout Christians, all excellent soldiers. But they are not alone, and there are other notable names among the bombers: for example, [Corporal] Théart,[2] [Corporal] Maujean,[3] both Toutain boys,[4] Charlot, [Corporal] Delporte,[5] [Corporal] Courtonne,[6] [Corporal] Coutable.[7]

Paul Bourget's premise is simply an arbitrary intellectual construct. It smacks of the past, of the generation of 1880 to 1910, of a civilization quintessentially decadent and refined.[8] True virtue resides in the poilus all around us.[9] They are

---

1. Others followed their example.
2. Class of 1915. Big, tough, broad shouldered. A leader of men. Wounded at Verdun, 19 May 1916.
3. A strapping lad from Nancy. As mild as he was brave. Awarded the Médaille Militaire for his heroism in Champagne (August 1917). Promoted to sergeant soon after. He ended the war as an adjudant.
4. Paul and Alfred. Two gallant soldiers from Dreux.
5. Class of 1908. A gardener. Average height, brown hair, apple cheeks. Always cheerful.
6. Class of 1914. A baker's apprentice. Slightly above average height, slim, ash-blond hair. Solid and imperturbable under fire. Awarded the Médaille Militaire and promoted to sergeant for his heroism in Champagne (August 1917).
7. Corporal. Tall, slightly stooped, red cheeks. Very brave under fire (see 1 June 1916). He died from the effects of gas in 1929.
8. My humble respect and admiration for Paul Bourget's great talent and fine literary career.
9. 'The soldiers (of the First Empire) fought not for the Emperor, but for themselves, to defend their reputation,' claims Blaze (p. 131), because faced with a choice between danger and dishonour Frenchmen never waver. They fought because they could do no other, because they had to fight, and everything combined to uphold this good habit. Show him a Prussian, a Russian, or an Austrian, and whoever his commander – Napoleon, Charles X or Louis-Philippe – the French soldier will be sure to do his duty.' Very apt. The origins of French military courage lie in French pride.

taking a pasting because of their sense of duty; because they can't stand a bully; because they are men who would consider themselves cowards if they flinched; because, paradoxically, they are citizens of a great, free nation that prizes its liberty, best proven by the way they all pulled together at the start of this chapter.

Le Sens de la mort is also full of sophisms: 'anything that influences reality must necessarily be real'. Utter twaddle. History is full of popular movements driven solely by phantoms of the collective imagination: the Great Fear, for example.

Champion has a daughter, Jeannine, born on 26 March.[1]

Thursday 30 March

The sun rose amid a halo of mist promising a beautiful day ahead. Blue sky, bright sunshine, all shrouded in a pink-tinged fog that means we can move through no man's land without problem.

Accordingly Théart and I went for a wander.

In the pale light of dawn we explored the ground between Bastion D and Boyau 31. From the amount of debris – and, alas, bodies – scattered around, the Boches and the colonials must have had a real set-to here. Many bodies are covered by just a thin layer of soil. The feet are sticking out. The shape of the boot and the pattern of the hobnails show if they are friend or foe. Here, a heap of bones – tibias and two skulls, all with the greasy look (fast becoming familiar) produced by slowly decomposing flesh. Both jawbones are pretty well bare. One mandible contains a single badly decayed molar. The scraps of clothing and two pairs of boots identify the bodies as German. I recall the words of a Boche quack seeking to prove the decadence of our race: 'the French have rotten teeth'.

What's this? A formless mass, with barely distinguishable scraps of green jacket and a leather pack bristling with animal hairs. I crouch down and lift the torn, rotted rags. Horrible! It's a human torso. I can see the innards and blanched ribs. It probably matches one of the two skulls I spotted earlier. I can't look. I move away. Particularly as the sun is now peeping over the horizon and the shelling has resumed.

Friday 31 March

'So much blood spilled, so many tears shed. Have they any wider significance? Or is this global conflict simply a frenzied bout of collective insanity, whose

---

1. I gave the new father a special 48-hour leave to see his child.

only result will be the premature return of countless human beings to the physiochemical cycle of decay and rebirth?' (*Le Sens de la mort*, p. 319).

Wider significance? To future French life and thought? It seems highly likely. We are playing but a walk-on role in a vast tragedy that will shake European society to the core. Meanwhile, we can all testify to the number of men doomed to a premature return to the physiochemical cycle of decay and rebirth. A brief trip beyond – or even within – the *boyaux* is enough to convince us. Not very cheerful, admittedly, but it would be stupid to ignore the facts.

Saturday 1 April
Still splendid spring weather. It's light by 4.00am, and the sun is beating down by noon.

On this beautiful, still, pink evening I head to Tranchée 31 and No. 4 Post. A grenade battle took place there yesterday. The wounded have been evacuated. I shudder when I see the red-streaked *boyaux*. Under this lovely tranquil sky, living beings are slaughtering each other. What savages these Boches are!

At 2.30 am heavy shelling on our right, towards the Bois de la Gruerie.

Sunday 2 April
At 1.00 pm I visited the captain commanding 2nd Battalion, 11th Infantry. He used to be with 14th Hussars.

A pleasant fellow. We discussed art. He's a man of the world, well informed. It was marvellous to talk about painting in these circumstances!

Quinze-Grammes is still keeping us entertained. Over dinner just now, I directed some rather off-colour banter at Bodin. Quinze-Grammes, who was helping serve, saw fit to approve. At the same time he shot up the stairs. I've never seen him take the steps so quickly. Mind you, Bodin's boots are a size eleven, with fifty-four hobnails per sole. A couple of minutes later, Quinze-Grammes could be spotted lurking on the dark staircase, forage cap set fore and aft on his head, pipe clamped in the corner of his mouth, beady eyes sizing up the situation.

Monday 3 April
You can get used to anything – even living in holes like cavemen. We never wash, not even hands and face; never take off our boots. Yet the men are still cheerful! A joke is enough to lift their spirits. Any rough treatment, in contrast, and they report in sick. T[ramard] has mellowed a lot, but this is exactly what happened

to him this morning. The men only returned from work at 11.30 pm and he sent them out again at 4.00 am.

There are some daring aviators at Sainte-Ménehould. One flew over the Chenille around 3.00pm, descending to 200 or 300 metres above the Boche lines. The machine guns crackled, the shrapnel shells were bursting all round, yet he coolly completed his mission.

It made a fine sight, this bird flying through the azure.

5.30 pm. Shelling, probably in response to our 240s yesterday morning. Dining at the door of the Verrue HQ, [Hillère] and his two sous-lieutenants were driven into the dug-out. No sooner had they reached safety than their table was shattered by a four-shell salvo.

Relieved at 10.00 pm by 8th Company, 124th Infantry. Quinze-Grammes fell when his legs gave way beneath him.[1]

Tuesday 4 April
We're at Côte 202. Not bad, apart from the incredible number of rats.

The weather has turned. It's raining again.

We seem to be running short of money. Everything is being cut back. You wouldn't believe what our poor soldiers are given to eat: a lump of tough meat, a bit of clear soup, a quarter of a round loaf and three or four biscuits. They don't complain; they accept their lot stoically. At morning briefing, I told them it was a soldier's duty to keep up his morale in the face of such hardships. I heard the sound of clapping. It almost became a round of applause. These brave men are truly splendid.[2]

Wednesday 5 April
Weather still cloudy and rainy. T[ramard] has transferred to 7th Company.

Thursday 6 April
The company is working on the ouvrages at Virginy this evening. Leave at 5.30 pm. Arrive at Côte 138 at 6.10 pm. A sapper comes to take us to the Engineers sergeant in charge. Not a bad dug-out for a sergeant, comfortable and well built. He's the same southerner in charge on our last visit. He and I have an

---

1. Poor man! Boundless courage, not so strength.
2. Conditions for the front-line soldier did not improve until May 1917.

understanding: the men will complete the job as quickly as possible, then I can take them back to get some sleep.

The sergeant describes the task at hand, gesturing expansively. The men remove their equipment, strip off their tunics and away they go. they 'set to' with a will. It surprises me, as well as the sergeant. 'Perhaps it's true what they say about southerners,' he says in his strong Béziers accent. 'You can tell when the 53rd and 142nd are here, and when it's the 101st and 124th. Especially the 142nd (his compatriots)! They're a bunch of idle devils. Always moaning.'

It starts raining at 9.30 pm, but I can see we're nearly done. So soon? It was due to take until 3.00 am. The sergeant gives us the nod. All we have to do now is to get back again. He sends us on an impossible return route, fine for two men, but very different if you're dragging a whole company behind you. I had a nasty fall earlier, hurting my leg when I jumped into the *boyau* leading to a concealed machine gun and misjudged the depth. Now, in the rain and the gluey mud, another slip compounds the damage. I come back leaning on Branchard.

Bodin had already left us at Côte 138, suffering from dizzy spells. We're a real set of crocks, the officers at least.

Friday 7 April
[Vinerot] took me to La Charmeraie this afternoon. A pleasant enough route, especially beyond Courtémont. Rolling countryside with a scattering of trees. No doubt very cool and restful in summer. The château chosen by General T[atin] for his HQ is charming. Lovely house, beautiful shady grounds.[1] Somewhere he can take a break from the cares of command and enjoy a little vital relaxation. Thank goodness our leaders can enjoy such comfort if the war is to go on indefinitely. How could we possibly hold on otherwise?

At La Charmeraie we meet Captain D.,[2] Captain J., Major F. and several sous-lieutenants. The place is delightful, full of trees and greenery. The dug-outs are picturesque and comfortable. Such a contrast between this life and our own. The people here are pleasant enough, with an eloquence reminiscent of my scientific classmates at the École [Normale Supérieure]. They are quite sharp with each other, another reminder of our discussions in the Rue d'Ulm. But their obsession with promotion shows that they are soldiers, too. [Captain] D. graduated from the Polytechnique in 1899 and feels very bitter. The latest

---

1. This explains why many generals found it so hard to comprehend the realities of war.
2. From the Engineers staff. 'The life of an Engineers officer is worth more than that of an infantry officer,' he told me icily. 'He takes longer to train.'

list of promotions was issued today, with no fourth stripe for him. Alas, not enough captains and majors have been killed!

Saturday 8 April

We are relieving 315th Infantry at the Calvaire, in front of Ville-sur-Tourbe. [Hillère] and I are leaving ahead of the companies to pick up our orders.

Grey skies. A light mist. We'll be able to use the Araja-Berzieux road safe from any risk of shelling.

I am relieving B Company (the worst sector), commanded by Lieutenant R. As soon as the CO of 315th Infantry revealed this sector is the most heavily shelled, [Hillère] asked to relieve A Company. His men will be paddling, but he'll be in no danger. Charming! He'll see the end of the war.

Lieutenant R. is tall and strong, with brown hair and a black beard. He looks like a businessman or a politician. A businessman, as it turns out. He gives me a tour of the place. The *boyaux* are composed of a mixture of mud and filth, with duckboards in the bottom to save you having to swim. The sector runs between the Verger and the road from Ville-sur-Tourbe to Cernay-en-Dormois and Vouziers. It is bisected by a track called the Chemin du Calvaire, which climbs to a cross still standing between the lines, where Christ extends his crucified arms towards our trenches.

Immortal and immutable, the cross offers a gesture of peace towards our posts. 'Come,' it seems to say. 'Come, fulfil the age-old dream! Drive out the hordes that assail me, that already threaten to overwhelm me, to topple this cross from which I make the ultimate appeal of wounded humanity to the Great Redeemer!' And, at night, when the moon is up and bathes the killing fields in its white light, two black arms lie open to receive us.

Our dead are here, the dead from the attack of 25 September. They are lined up, still in combat pose, deployed in open order. Death halted them in mid-bound towards the rusty-red barbed wire, still unbreached – apart from one spot marked by a pile of bodies.[1] Two riflemen sought cover behind a hummock, only for machine-gun fire to lay them low for all eternity. We can see their blue greatcoats. Their helmets have rolled alongside them. Some men are lying on their backs, faces towards the sky. Others are bent and twisted, a line of small

---

1. The high command and their staff would have found this a useful tour of inspection, demonstrating as clearly as possible the futility of pitting men, however brave, against barbed-wire entanglements. It took a further bloody reverse in 16 April 1917 to force an end to these tactics.

cairns before the trenches of the Germans who abandoned them there: an awful warning to all who would follow.

We return to HQ. [Lieutenant] R. was educated by the Jesuits and is effusive in his praise. 'They're excellent. And the best thing about them is that they always keep in touch with their former pupils. They have contacts everywhere!'

Physically and psychologically, he reminds me of D., the Freemason. They think alike. Their main concern is to join the group that offers the greatest number of contacts, the most assistance to smooth their path through life. He lists several examples of the help provided by the Jesuits. Choosing a regiment, for example: they got him a transfer from [137th Infantry] in Fontenay-le-Comte to 31st Infantry in Melun. When he went into business ...

'What business is that?'

'Anything that makes money ...'

... they provided the best contacts.

Seizing the moment, he asks me to keep in touch. 'Is that all right with you?'

'Perfectly, dear sir!'

Here's one man at least giving some thought to life after the war. He certainly doesn't devote much to the war itself. His files are a complete mess. And he knows precious little about his sector. It doesn't take a genius to see that he's done nothing while he's been here.

Sunday 9 April

Still bright sunshine. The birds are singing loudly.

Last night I replaced Bodin on watch in the trenches. He seems a little shaky at the moment.

We were planning to send up some illuminating rockets. Young Rouzeaud snatched the rifle while I positioned myself in our best observation post ... the officers' latrine. The night was fine – clear and full of stars.

'The maréchal des logis in command of the 75[1] (who was in our trench) requests you to illuminate Point 473, sir.'

'Perfect timing. I was just going to send up some rockets. Wait. Stay where you are. You can observe as well.'

Rouzeaud took up station in Tranchée Balcon, which lies below the observation post.

---

1. This shows when artillery NCOs were first sent to liaise with the front-line infantry: early April 1916. But it didn't happen everywhere. I never saw an artillery NCO in the front line at Verdun.

'Are you there, sir?'

'Yes! Go!'

Bang. The rocket climbed into the sky, a red streak in the darkness. It exploded. Magnificent, but the strong north-westerly wind was against us. Far from lighting up the Boches, the rocket illuminated us instead. Amid roars of laughter, a volley of rifle fire sent us diving for the trench.

Rouzeaud was vexed by our failure. He sent up another rocket. Same result, same volley of rifle fire, same dive for the parapet, same chorus of laughter.

We experimented with a few flares, but they're a dead loss.

'Could be the Fourteenth of July,' said one comedian.

I spend the night inspecting the outposts and trenches between Tranchée Balcon and Tranchée Vix. My staunch little bantams are watching at every loophole. They didn't get much to eat this evening. It was 10.00 pm by the time the grub reached us, and it was burnt. No complaints. They know times are hard.

'Everything is so expensive these days, sir!'

My mind turns to Villars and his troops on the eve of Malplaquet. 'You have to suffer a little,' they told their old marshal.

My men are suffering a lot. They spend their nights on watch. At least the weather is fine. The French peasant virtues survive intact, the eternal guarantor of the nation's security.

I return to the dug-out at midnight.

I come across an article by Lieutenant E.R. His pieces are normally pretty good, but this one is right on the money. 'Nothing comes closer to universal significance than that which is profoundly personal.' And this: 'This is a time of national rebirth. Authors will in future have something to say ...' (Yes, those who played an active part in the struggle.) 'putting an end to the mannerism, endless description and idle repartee that purportedly compensate for lack of subject matter and so outlandishly influence literary style. The new style will be plain, raw and vigorous – I might even suggest military.'

Yes, indeed! Simple, lively language! Seeking 'the state of the soul' has led modern authors in completely the wrong direction.

I set off again at 2.00 am.[1] I can't comment on the state of their souls, but the state of my men at the parapet, rifle at hand, is perfectly satisfactory.

---

1. So the captain returned to his dug-out at midnight, then left again at 2.00 am to inspect his trenches and posts. This was the hardest time of night for sentries, the hour when they were most likely to be found asleep. A quick shove, and they woke shamefaced,

Monday 10 April
Still bright sunshine.

As I made my rounds last night I could hear the Boches hammering in some new barbed-wire entanglements. Today, we've asked the guns to shell their handiwork. Aspirant Elloel – tall, fair and handsome – has arrived to that end, accompanied by Sous-lieutenant Dumas, a native of Toulouse.

Tuesday 11 April
Target practice on a new Boche loophole between Points 469 and 470.

'Arthur' hits the spot but the loophole is still intact. Constructed at 1.00 pm, pounded at 3.00 pm. The Boches opposite by now must have realized that they have new neighbours. Our comrades in [315 Infantry] didn't give a damn: they kept their heads down so the Germans would leave them in peace.

That is no longer the case.

We won't give the enemy an inch. With Charlot at the loophole, every flat-cap is good for a D-bullet. Nor is Charlot the only one. There are plenty like him in the company. And the Germans opposite are remarkably casual. They retaliate with ferocious shelling like today's bombardment. It won't make any difference. That lump of 105mm shell Dubuc has just brought into the dug-out is pretty impressive though.

Wednesday 12 April
Bright sunshine in the morning, the odd downpour.

At 9.00 pm Bodin and I went out into no man's land. A darkish night despite the stars. We left via Sape II. This bit of the line has no barbed wire at all. [Corporal] Théart was there with his men: four stooped shadows working quietly in the darkness, fixing smooth wire round the pickets. We threaded our way along a faint trail marked where the pickets are fewest, constantly bumping into each other.

We entered [Tranchée] Doerflinger and reached No. 10 Post.

'Evening, sir!'

'Evening, lad. Keeping your eyes open?'

'Yes, sir. Pretty quiet over there. I spotted one and took a shot. They didn't even fire back.'

---

babbling excuses. You could be confident they wouldn't nod off again that night. As the diary shows, I never punished anyone for this – or any other reason.

'Keep going! Goodnight, son.'

'Goodnight, sir!'

Then we slipped off to No. 9 post, and from there to No. 8 and No. 7. Every man was at his loophole, swathed in his tent section, rifle to hand.

Friday 14 April

Had a letter from Monsieur Pfister.[1] He says that Parisians wait at dawn and 4.00 pm for the latest news, and that 'communiqué fever' is as strong now as at the start of the war. Trust me, we don't suffer from that here. We're holding Fritz under rifle, machine-gun and artillery fire, offering him no leeway at all. On Sunday, Monday and Tuesday we heard gunfire over towards Verdun. It's quietened down now. We're not too worried. We imagine our pals are doing exactly the same as us.

Saturday 15 April

Damp, gloomy weather. Wrapped in their tent sections, the sentries pace up and down Tranchée Balcon. This war has done away with any romantic notions of battle. I can't repeat this too often. The sight of filthy, mud-covered men, watching at the loopholes, yellow canvas tent sections draped over stained, discoloured, washed-out greatcoats, can't help but make you reflect how far we have travelled from the brightly uniformed cavalcade of childhood imagination.

Sunday 16 April

A big to-do this morning. At 1.00 am the Boches planted a flag in front of our barbed wire, right of No. 2 Post.

This evening a patrol (a corporal and four men) went to retrieve it. Bright moonlight. We were following the manoeuvre, but we lost them as soon as they hit the barbed wire.

When they returned with the flag, we found there was wording on it: 'The English will fight until the last Frenchman. Is that your motto, too?' Attached was an old issue of *Simplicissimus*. It was purely and simply an invitation to surrender!

---

1. My old teacher in the Rue d'Ulm [the École Normale Supérieure]. He died as rector of Strasbourg University – his lifelong dream.

Monday 17 April
We are billeted in La Neuville[-au-Pont]. Pretty church, probably begun in the late fifteenth century. It still has a finely detailed portal, set on a plinth of good stone, most likely quarried elsewhere. A vine runs along one archivolt, with birds and bunches of grapes among the stylized leaves fashionable at the time. Bas-reliefs decorate the transoms in the Italianate style popular in the late fifteenth and early sixteenth centuries. A portal on the north side of the building offers two medallions in similar style. Work began in the reign of Louis XII, a period of short-lived prosperity clearly interrupted just after Francis I's salamander device was carved at first-floor level. Were donors less generous after 1520, hit hard by taxes raised due to the Crown's financial difficulties?[1] Highly likely, because work then continued piecemeal; consolidated in 1730, reads one inscription on a buttress on the south wall; and again in 1782, according to a second on the adjoining buttress. The stone is the rough local marl. The golden age of the 'Father of the People', once believed permanent, had vanished. And that's how a humble church presents a history in shorthand of three centuries of life in this little town.

Tuesday 18 April
Our reinforcements have arrived from the class of 1916. They look the part. They've brought some flags with them. They seem solid and cheerful enough.
    General Tatin came to inspect them.

Wednesday 19 April
At 10.30 am Consul summoned all his officers to his dining-room. Squalid: greasy newspapers, crusts of bread, coffee-stains on the table.
    Young Rouzeaud was tapping out *La Marseillaise* on the piano in the corner, when Consul stormed in. 'I've invited you here to discuss military matters, gentlemen. Not to attend a theatrical performance. I'm sorry I have to raise the matter. I never indulged in such behaviour when visiting a senior officer.'
    Miserable old fuss-pot!

Thursday 20 April
Six days' leave from 21st April. The colonel asks where I'm planning to go.

---

1. This was the start of the struggle against [Emperor] Charles V. The war, which twice brought the enemy close to Paris, involved huge expenditure.

Friday 21 April

[Vinerot] and I left La Neuville-au-Pont at 1.30 pm. Arrived at Sainte-Ménehould. No train until 8.00 pm. We were planning to catch the 3.30 pm to Revigny but it no longer exists. [Vinerot] grumbled away. Of course, he blamed me. I didn't let it bother me. I left him chuntering while I went in search of a lift to Châlons. He chaffed me about it, but I wanted to get to Paris tonight.

Eventually we found an aviator going to Vitry-le-François. Just the ticket! Off we went, top speed across country.

Arrived at Vitry-le-François at 6.10 pm. Luckily, the Nancy-Paris express was running late.

It felt odd being on a railway platform after six months in the trenches. Lots of men going on leave. A few civilians, who seemed quite extraordinary to me. Women in mourning. The train was literally taken by storm. We shared our compartment with an aviator, bemedalled and beribboned. It was [Charles] Nungesser. Small, slim, long fair hair. His mouth is twisted by a wound that has also left him with a hare-lip. He showed us an issue of *Le Monde sportif* that contains an article, with photograph, celebrating his deeds. He also showed us his jaw, which is held together with gold wire, visible in places. He limps heavily too.

He's staying in Paris until Monday. The life suits him. He's married, although still only 23.

'She's a pal, not a woman. We go out on the razzle together. All airmen are roisterers. I climb into a fighter aircraft, chase a Boche, or perhaps fly a mission (no more special missions for me, by the way, they're too dangerous). I come back, then it's off to Paris for forty-eight hours. That's all there is to it.'

He's also extremely elegant: a black tunic, cinched at the waist by a tan leather belt; the salmon-pink breeches with sky-blue piping of an ex-light cavalryman; kepi with red top and sky-blue sides; hands manicured and beringed. But at heart he remains the simple mechanic he was before becoming an aviator – a nice chap, easy to talk to.

Saturday 22 April

Spent the day in Paris.

The city is delightful. The trees are green, the sun shining on boulevards as lively as ever.

I can't help but think of the desolation I've just left behind me in Champagne; of the houses reduced to a few scraps of wall; of the vast wastes laid bare of almost all vegetation – just a few pines reduced to pickets by the shells, or the odd blade of sparse grass forcing its way between the shell-holes that pockmark the greenish-white earth.

Here, it's business as usual. The Avenue de l'Opéra, Boulevard des Capucines, Boulevard de la Madeleine, Rue Royale and Place de la Concorde all look no different. A few soldiers on crutches pass me on the Champs-Elysées, probably from the convalescent hospital at the Grand Palais. Yet the lawns are green, the flower baskets bright with colour, the trees in new leaf. Light silver clouds scud across the sparkling blue sky. It feels good to be alive. No wonder those in the rear can resign themselves to the war.

I catch the 9.50 pm train to Bordeaux, packed with holidaymakers.

I console myself with the thought that if I do end up hanging on the barbed wire, the world certainly won't feel too much of a loss.

Sunday 23 April
Woke at Coutras. Lovely countryside, green and smiling. The crops seem well tended, the ranks of staked vines hoed as carefully as a garden.

Beautiful country. Beautiful sky. White houses, almost flat roofs. The sun makes it feel like a totally different climate. It's the Midi.

Arrived at the Gare du Midi at 7.30 am. Lot's of people around, plenty of coming and going. Only the gendarmes and the information post betray that we're at war.

Bordeaux is a beautiful city, which I rushed to explore. The Cours Saint-Jean leads straight into the centre. The market was teeming with shoppers and stallholders.

'Where's the Rue Sainte-Catherine?' I asked a policeman.

'Carry on up the Cours Saint-Jean to a big square. You can see the trees ahead. Look for a monumental gate. That's the start of the Rue Sainte-Catherine. Just look for the gate.'

He pronounced 'monumintal' in a most peculiar way, with a gravity worthy of the Sublime Porte.

I decided to walk through the market and look around Saint-Michel. The market was a hive of activity. The girls are very pretty: dark hair, arched backs, clear skin, red lips, long-lashed dark eyes.

Saint-Michel is a fine church. Like Saint-André, it dates from the late fifteenth century – a time of prosperity in Bordeaux, as was the late twelfth century (see Sainte-Croix). Following the marriage of Eleanor of Aquitaine [to Henry II], the town became a stronghold of the dukes of Normandy, then kings of England. This also may be when the English developed the love of 'claret' that has so enriched the region's merchants and wine-growers. Bordeaux experienced another era of prosperity during the eighteenth century. The Louis XV mansions of the Place Gambetta, the sumptuous Notre-Dame, the Grand-Théatre and the Place des Quinconces display it to perfection. The Quinconces is a grand square reminiscent in style of the Place de la Concorde, bounded on one side by the Monument aux Girondins, a fine example of modern sculpture, and on the other by the Garonne.

The quaysides were lively. The owner of one three-master said that Senegalese troops are arriving just now. He seemed happy with the war. Freight has never been so profitable.

The Café de Bordeaux was packed. I met an old quartermaster of mine from early in the war, now transferred to aviation for pilot training. I'm not sure what they're teaching him at the airfield, but he and his chums seem to know plenty about the local girls.

Here, too, the war felt very far away.

Monday 24 April

I went to see the beautiful Romanesque church of Sainte-Croix.

One last tour of the town, then back to the station for 11.00 am. My pass was checked. It's Easter Monday and the station was crowded with holidaymakers.

'Are people really still going on holiday?' I asked a dapper, greying man of 50 or so.

'Yes, thank goodness!'

What a reply! Here's a man who believes every word churned out by hacks desperately trying to justify the blind indifference of certain elements of the population amid this cataclysm. Poor comrades lying dead before the barbed wire at the Calvaire ... You will not be long mourned. If, indeed, you ever were.

Bordeaux is surrounded by beautiful countryside. A medieval castle looms over a village tiered up a hillside: Montmaure. An artillery captain joins the train at Poitiers. He's just been awarded the Croix de Guerre – with palm, of course. We pass through Tours, then race along the valley of the lovely Loire, its still waters reflecting the white houses on its banks and the fluffy clouds above. Vouvray, Amboise, Limeray – the very names of the stations evoke a life of ease and joy.

Then comes the château of Blois, with its lofty white towers. The artillery captain engages me in conversation. He tries to persuade me that if the 75 so often imperils the infantry the fault is ours. Naturally! He also reckons that the further the gunners are sited from the front line, the more accurate their fire.[1] This doesn't convince me, either.

In Paris, dinner at the Café de la Paix. Full to bursting, packed with pretty women and their beaux.

Tuesday 25 April

Bright blue skies. Back in the Parc Monceau, the Place de l'Étoile, the Avenue du Bois [de Boulogne] and the Sentier de la Vertu. It made my heart sing. The Sentier de la Vertu really was excelling itself. The women were wearing short, ruffled dresses, Second Empire style. They've decided hips are back in fashion. It won't be long before they deign to stop flattening their bosoms.

The Bois was very lively. How did it differ from peacetime? Fewer cars. Fewer soldiers. All airmen, or officers in Administration or Supplies. How nice 'to enter the trenches' in the [Avenue des] Acacias.

Wednesday 26 April

I visited the [Théatre du] Gymnase this evening to see [Édouard Boudet's] *Le Rubicon*. Wartime prices, but that was no hardship. A marvellous little play. [Madeleine] Lély is a very intelligent artist. Full house.

Thursday 27 April

Enjoyed a boat trip this afternoon on the lake in the Bois de Boulogne. Perfect weather. Very crowded. It could have been a holiday or race day at Longchamp. The nation is supposedly suffering, straining every sinew to ensure our eventual victory. Yet none of this effort reduces the number of strollers.

Friday 28 April

Lunch at the Restaurant Weber; dinner at the Boeuf à la Mode. Crowds everywhere. If, as seems likely, the war continues, the smart restaurants will make a fortune.

Sunday 30 April

Crowded boulevards. Not a seat at the Café de la Paix at aperitif time. Still glorious weather.

---

1. General Gascouin (p. 249) disagrees: 'There is an optimum distance for effective liaison between infantry and support artillery that should not be, but often was, exceeded.'

Monday 1 May
(Lunched with Pfister and Lévy.)

Returning to the front this evening.

I met up with [Vinerot] again. All the men returning from leave were nodding off on the train. He chatted to a comrade travelling with us. 'I've lost interest in the war,' he said, for the umpteenth time. 'I've got my third stripe and the Légion d'Honneur. I'm not ashamed to say that all I want now is to shirk. I've had enough of the war. It's gone on too long.'

Once Napoleon's officers had become marshals or divisional commanders, i.e. once they had fulfilled their military ambitions, they were tired too.

Monday 8 May
En route from Argers ...

At Belval. Played bridge at 8.00 pm with the brigade commander and two officers from 8th Chasseurs [à cheval]: a major, and Lieutenant de P. Both are sound fellows. Young Lieutenant de P. speaks softly but plays with great boldness. Both he and the colonel are Bretons and it's interesting to hear them talk family. They each have a gaggle of cousins of both sexes. And of course they discover that they're related by marriage because 'your Cousin X. is married to my Cousin Y.'.

The major could be 52 or so. Tall, trim, beaky nose, sharp eyes. An impression of rare intelligence. Meanwhile the colonel dabbles in Breton philology, although I rather doubted his linking of 'Plou' to [the Latin] *plebs* or *populus*.[1]

Tuesday 9 May
Leave Belval at 7.00 am, after Consul's normal orders and counter-orders.

While waiting for the whistle, B[iancardini] has fun trying to make his horse Saïd follow him by calling him like a dog. The animal meekly obeys. The men chat behind their piled weapons or rush to buy some last-minute supplies. Sous-lieutenant Tournery, who commands the neighbouring company, tells me his dreams for the future. He's a handsome young man. Class of 1913. Tall, blond, smartly turned out, intelligent, energetic, very military bearing. He was a teacher in some godforsaken commune in the Jura. He has taken very well to military life and looks good on horseback, with his long greatcoat, and his forage cap pulled down over one ear.

---

1. I may have been mistaken. The words may share the same root.

He's just received a commission in the regulars.

A sous-lieutenant at just 23. Watch out. He could go far.

His deputy Bétron is a farmer from the Beauce. Twenty-five years old, medium height, brown hair covering a rather shallow forehead. 'Turned out nice again, sir!' he says hoarsely. 'A good day to be in the fields with your dog beside you, seeing if the wheat is coming through.'

His eyes smile. He gestures as if encouraging his beloved wheat to grow.

'Do you know what the cavalry call the road we'll be following, sir?' asks Clerc, one of my runners. A good lad, round face, clean shaven, class of 1915.

'No. What?'

'Le Chemin de la Mort [Death Road].'

The whole company is decked in lily-of-the-valley. I've been draped in it too. [My horse] Zidor has a white bouquet behind each ear. He looks like he belongs in a wedding procession.

[Major] de Benoit[1] is just passing. 'The company of flowers,' he remarks.

We cross the Forêt de Belnoue. Glorious. Ponds, stands of beech, cool depths. The forest is truly nature's most sumptuous creation.

All is well. No heat. From the quiet underbrush, constant birdsong. The road runs straight ahead, clean and neat, like a promenade between the lofty, leafy depths.

The men start to sing – marching along to the popular *marche italienne*. In the crisp air, the flower-capped barrels of the rifles sway in time to the music.

The sky is in festive mood; our spirits, too.

Beyond Laheycourt the march becomes a struggle. The packs carried by the men are very heavy, with blanket and tent section, as well as all the linen and bits and bobs they've gathered over the winter. Consul is on horseback, directing affairs, pompous as ever. He couldn't be making a bigger hash of it.

Zidor becomes a beast of burden. I take the packs from the five weariest men and strap them across his back, carefully balancing the weight.

We reach Laimont, in full sun, at the top of a dreadful hill.

The men have marched for an hour without a rest. Calté's [Third] Battalion reached Laimont ahead of us. Rightly enough, Calté didn't whistle a halt with just a few hundred metres to go. Meanwhile our battalion was still at the foot of the Côte de Laimont, with another 2 kilometres to cover in full sun. But Consul

---

1. A cavalry major recently named as the colonel's second-in-command. Pleasant, courteous, a splendid soldier.

followed his 'leader', refusing to assume the onerous responsibility of whistling a halt for his men.

He's a man who follows orders to the letter.

We're billeted in Neuville-sur-Ornain. This little village was destroyed during the battle of the Marne, mainly by the incendiaries fired by [our own] 75s, according to the old lady providing our billets. Leaning on her stick, waxen face framed by a halo of wavy white hair, she greets us warmly. So too does her daughter – a kind, capable, bustling lady of 35 to 40. The house is a single block, and these excellent ladies keep the best room for an officer from the units constantly passing through the village en route to Verdun. On the left of the courtyard are two barns where the men are sleeping. Beyond is a lovely garden, all green, surrounded by flowering blackthorn. The grass is full of buttercups, stems glowing in the sunlight, alive with thousands of tiny insects.

I'm staying in a decent house over the crossroads. It's owned by a reservist from the class of 1891, recalled to serve with the motor transport. His wife seems a bit of a slut. They have a very pretty daughter in her early twenties. Another daughter is in Bar-le-Duc, apparently taking care of the result of the over-zealous suit of a passing officer.

My room is very pleasant, with something of a view, which I particularly like.

Wednesday 10 May

We will probably be leaving for Verdun tomorrow.

[Hillère] invited Lévy[1] and me to a musical evening: *Tosca*, *La Bohème*, a ballad from *Le Roi d'Ys*, the waltz from *The Merry Widow*, even the andante from the Fifth Symphony.

We sang until 11.00 pm. That's how you prepare for battle.

But the men of Colonel Carlier's 90th Infantry coming out of the trenches at Mort-Homme and Côte 304 say the fighting is horrific. [The division] has apparently lost 50 per cent of its strength, with three of the four colonels killed.[2]

Thursday 11 May

We left at 7.00 am. A misty morning. We retraced our steps through Laimont and Louppey-le-Château, but continued via Rembercourt-aux-Pots instead of Laheycourt. A remarkable church, even more astonishing given the size of the town. A monumental façade, apparently Renaissance. The main body of

---

1. A violinist and one of our bandsmen.
2. At this date a division still consisted of four regiments.

the church dates from various periods, thirteenth to fifteenth century at first glance. Here we find troops from XVIII Corps, en route to Verdun like us. A captain from 34th Infantry says that they're due in the lines between Vaux and Douaumont by 15 May. Most of the village, and sadly the church, has been destroyed. Everywhere fragments of wall marking the site of houses. The ruins of Pompeii.

After a long halt we reach Beauzée-sur-Aire at 4.00 pm. This village looks just like Rembercourt. Here too a fine late fifteenth-century church has been ravaged by the shells. It breaks my heart to see such beauty so irredeemably destroyed. Our poor villages have taken such a pounding at the hands of these savages. I tell my men how the church used to look. We are all determined to have our revenge.

A good journey before we go to form up in advance of Verdun.

Friday 12 May
Still at Beauzée.

A note has arrived requesting the colonel to nominate captains for promotion to the rank of temporary major. But all nominees must have been captains since 1911 or earlier.[1] Only one officer in the regiment fulfils this qualification: a captain in Supplies with scarcely two months' front-line experience.

Brilliant!

The latest from Consul. Top of the list yesterday was deciding whether the men should complete the next stage in helmets or in forage caps. He made them take off their forage caps. Then, seeing how tired they were, he insisted they put them on again … And we're heading for Mort-Homme or Douaumont.

Saturday 13 May
Grey skies. I rode over to Rembercourt-aux-Pots to revisit the church this morning. It has a huge fourteenth- and fifteenth-century nave, while the west wall bears evidence of a narthex from the same period. In a lofty triangular tympanum, the tracery of the rose window is clearly visible. The vault is of astonishing height and beauty, flanked right and left by double side-aisles. The choir is formed by a circular apse, whose tall bays are separated by elegant, slender jambs. The vault with its lattice of painted and gilded ribs is late

---

1. Only those with experience of front-line combat can fully appreciate the absurdity of this note. The lieutenant promoted to captain in the field because of his leadership qualities could progress no further. In other words, the best candidates were ignored.

fifteenth or early sixteenth century. Beautiful carvings on the choir stalls and other woodwork. Lovely, gentle faces, confidently handled; garlands of flowers; ornate frames made to appear like incised metal. The padre of 34th Infantry dated the work to the reign of Henry IV. I wasn't going to argue, but I reckon Louis XIII.

The side-aisles contain faint traces of wall paintings. The fifteenth-century narthex has disappeared, replaced by a west front completely at odds with the rest of the church. The padre showed me a guidebook written by a teacher. According to the author, Duke René II of Lorraine acquired the seigneurie of Rembercourt around 1501, and the façade was built on his orders between then and 1508. Whatever, it's definitely sixteenth-century Italianate work. Although unfinished, the upper storey is still very beautiful, festooned with swags of fruit and foliage, medallions enclosing busts in bas-relief, light ornament, delicately carved little angels in the spandrels. Lacy stone pedestals adorn the archivolt of the central portal; they support small groups of figures in very high relief, unfortunately mutilated – probably scenes from the Old and New Testaments. Six male busts with their attributes decorate the lower storey, with more busts on the buttresses. In each of the two flanking bays, two male busts frame that of a bare-breasted woman. In the left-hand group, one of the men offers an apple to the woman, who is brazenly flaunting her bosom. Perhaps the seven deadly sins?

In short only the roof has been damaged.

A storm was threatening as I rode back. In the afternoon it poured with the rain. [Vinerot] and I stayed indoors. How could we keep ourselves occupied? The cavalry liaison maréchal des logis in Third Battalion has advertised for a penfriend[1] in *La Vie parisienne*, and [Vinerot] sent a man to fetch the replies. He returned with two big packages: 254 letters. We worked our way through them. All kinds of women have replied – from the batty society lady to the chambermaid in the Latin Quarter. Most describe themselves as romantic ... and unhappy. All are in search of care and affection. Relatively few demi-mondaines in pursuit of a meal ticket. No surprise there: the advertiser is [only] a maréchal des logis. Two madams bluntly offered their services; one simply sent her card. Some of the letters were charming, really quite touching, enclosing sprigs of lily-of-the-valley or tricolour ribbons. And the fiend has been very crafty: 'Looks and personality not important. You and I will hit it off. De Maurec, maréchal des logis de liaison, 101st Infantry.' Modest, a cavalryman, a member of the old

---

1. This was the start of the penfriend craze. Everybody had one.

Breton nobility. All that's needed to stir the romantic imagination. Today's post produced another nine letters, swelling the number of females to 263.

Too many!

Sunday 14 May

It's been raining since this morning. It rained all night, too.

Officers and NCOs were summoned for the reading of our secret instructions from Second Army Staff. The usual phrases, technical terms in profusion. These gentlemen really do love their fine words, dishing them out in abundance!

Still, we did obtain some useful information. [Enemy] documents, which must remain secret, show that – unlike us in Champagne – the Germans [at Verdun] did not use departure trenches.[1] The two fronts were between 600 and 800 metres apart, allowing the enemy to destroy the French front lines with their heavy shells without risk of hitting their own. Meanwhile their infantry were gathered in secure underground mustering stations, emerging as soon as our barrage ended. The Germans then raised their sights, some batteries firing barrages in advance of our second lines, while others targeted our guns.

Such method, such genuine care for the lives of their men can only be applauded. Our high command compensates for its errors and shortcomings with our blood, as it has since the start of the war, truth be told.[2] And, despite the nonsense that GQG feeds to the press, the documents confirm the Germans attacked in small groups or by infiltration, not in columns of four as legend has it.

[Vinerot] and I are sharing a billet. He's tired of the war. He's had enough. He never shuts up about it. Verdun doesn't appeal at all. The giant is a coward at heart. That's what Major N[icolas] said, and he was right. After twenty-one months of fighting [Vinerot] does have some excuse, though. He seems to have been particularly affected by the attacks at Perthes [25 February 1915]. He says his four runners were hit as soon as they left the departure trench, while he only just managed to jump back in.

It remains his worst experience of the campaign.

---

1. We used departure trenches during the Champagne offensive of 25 September 1915, thus warning the Germans of the time and location of our impending attack, as well as the departure point of the assault waves. I leave the reader to imagine the slaughter inflicted by the enemy guns on the infantry in the departure trenches. Why did we use them? In homage to Sebastopol?
2. General Gascouin (p. 143) listened to a general lecturing at Nancy in 1913. 'At Nancy,' states Gascouin, 'the army was not afraid of heavy losses.'

Monday 15 May

Leave for Landrecourt at 5.30 am, via Ippécourt. Finally arrive at 1.00 pm. Bucketing down throughout.

At Ippécourt we pass lines-of-communication troops from 38th (Moroccan) Division. We're crossing rolling countryside, dotted with woods. The fields are green and full of buttercups. The gentle russet of English oaks and poplars, not yet in full leaf, adds an autumnal note to the woodland. Yet my mind absorbs little of the scenery, turning inevitably to our destination, Douaumont.

Thoughts of mortality and of Verdun are clearly oppressing the entire column and making the men more irritable. At Landrecourt, I am the only captain in the battalion sleeping on straw. [Hillère] is a regular so he gets a bed. No comment. He has more years' service than I do, though not in the front line. But, for some, that kind of seniority doesn't count.

Our mess is in premises owned by a nice woman of 50, who lives with a chap of 92. He was a police officer in Lyon, so he's been receiving a pension from the city for almost forty years. He's still fit and active. He was a soldier in 1848 and remembers the June revolution. He smokes his pipe contentedly by the fireside and for exercise goes to split a log or two.

His vigour rather rankles with the woman: '"Move in with him," they said. "He can't last much longer." He's still here though, *monsieur*. Fit as a flea. He'll see me out.'

She pushes her glasses up her nose and goes back to her mending: the 'old man's' corduroy breeches. Inside, the house is clean and rather smart. A big carved oak cabinet, probably Louis XV. A writing-desk and mirror, both Empire. A vase of lily-of-the-valley on a shiny, polished table. But for the incessant gunfire, we could be miles from any war.

The woman grumbles about our current woes, high prices, supply difficulties. 'Things will be even worse next year. We're all going to starve to death.'

On the way we came across two naval 100mm batteries. Everyone was travelling by car or lorry: nobody on foot. The officers even had their own comfortable little motor. I asked an NCO if his battery had suffered much by way of losses.

'Not many.'

Such was his surprise, I reckon 'not many' is really 'none at all'.

I watch my poor men slogging miserably along the road, doubled beneath the weight of their packs, water streaming down their faces – all to be blown to bits in a muddy trench. The hardships of this war are unequally divided between the various front-line combatants, not to mention those in the rear.

At Landrecourt, infantry officers marching to their deaths are less comfortably billeted than sergeants in 3rd Engineers.

Tuesday 16 May

Today's paper includes a very timely article by Lieutenant E.R. – 'Notes from a soldier on leave' – commenting on the widening gulf between front and rear. The people we're defending haven't got a clue. I'm particularly sensitive to this today. My old wound is playing up after yesterday's downpour and I've had to take some aspirin.

E.R. repeats the fatuous remark that greets us in Paris: 'You look well, considering.'

Cordier, his orderly, says everyone there is enjoying life. The cafés are full, as are the theatres and music halls. 'If the war goes on much longer, people will get used to us being in the trenches.'

I can perfectly well imagine it. Those still at home are the old and the young, the times of life when man is at his most self centred.

E.R. protests, but only for form's sake.

Behind him someone, probably Cordier, considers the relative dangers: 'Anybody who has someone in Supplies – one of those cushy numbers with a 5 per cent chance of dying in the field, not 95 per cent like us – will be happy to wait it out. Their lives, as you say, will carry on as normal; a small donation to the Red Cross and they'll think they've done their bit. As for us, my God! We sacrifice our time, our hides and our happiness; we wallow in mud, at constant risk of being wounded by a bullet, blown up by a shell, buried by a mine, forced to cough up our lungs by chlorine gas. There's no comparison!'

Quite right, too.

People in the rear take indifference to the giddy limit. My correspondents want me to entertain them with tales from the front! Pure *Gaspard*! Our job is to provide empty boasts for armchair warriors so they can wallow in a hackneyed heroism, while we endure the mud, the blood and the horror so those in the rear can relax and enjoy themselves.

'[The soldier] must never feel others are profiting from his suffering.'

They rush us 1 franc 30 centimes for a litre of lousy wine.

'Nor must those in the rear believe that their normal efforts will be enough to see us through. They must work until they drop. On this condition alone will they be pardoned their absence from the killing zone.'

The sun is shining. We'll have good weather for today's march to the Bois de la Caillette.

Leaving Landrecourt at 6.00 pm. Said farewell to our hostess, and to Mlle Georgette, a teacher I met yesterday – a pale, gentle, thoughtful woman in her early twenties. She told me about the problems she has with her pupils. All they think about is the war. Never addition, subtraction, multiplication and division. 'Can you believe it, *monsieur*! Thirteen-year-old boys unable to do long division.' I sympathized, but I can see why older boys might find Vaux or Douaumont more interesting than their times tables.

We leave at 6.45 pm. The evening mist is beginning to envelop the woods, the meadows, and the blue hills on the horizon that house the fort at Dugny and conceal Verdun from view.

An infinite sadness descends upon the twilit countryside.

We cross the Meuse right of Dugny and continue to Haudainville on the road alongside the canal. By the last light of day, the stagnant water is a dull mirror tinged with green; the reflection of the moored barges creates a black pattern, sharp as a silhouette in Indian ink.

To the east, the moon has risen broad and brilliant in the clear sky.

We start to hear the whine of the shells.

It's nearly 10.00 pm by the time we reach our billets in Belrupt. The quartermaster takes me to the two barns set aside for the men. Squalid beyond description: the straw is a vile powder, full of rags, refuse and broken glass. I have it all swept out, raising a cloud of stifling dust. My quarters present a rather different picture. All the cupboards have been ransacked, their contents heaped on the floor – corsets, women's hats, postcards. In the room next door, the drawers of the tallboy have been turned upside down. It's all such a mess that the comrade supposed to be occupying this billet has refused it.[1] I've never seen an apartment after a burglary, but it can't be any worse than this. Everything has been pawed and probed. If French soldiers were let off the leash, would they turn into brigands?

Wednesday 17 May

[Vinerot] is as glum as ever. The weary giant is starting to get on my nerves.

Belrupt makes an interesting spectacle. Men from all arms of service are milling around, the infantryman's horizon blue mixing strangely with the khaki of the neighbouring Moroccans. The Moroccans look very fine. They are muscular, with a distinctive, hip-swaying gait; wiry legs, thin arms, coat-hanger

---

1. Captain Biancardini, CO of 6th Company.

shoulders, heads shaven apart from the single lock that will permit them to join Allah. With their tanned skin, thick lips and flat noses, they look more Negro than Arab. They also include a few genuine Negroes with wiry hair and very dark skin.

Beautiful weather.

Leave at 6.00 pm to reconnoitre the sector. Taken by lorry as far as the Ferme du Cabaret, where we wait for our guides, who fail to turn up. At 7.15 pm Consul decides to follow the *boyau* wending its way to the front line. We speak to a rations party who offer to show us to the Digue. Night falls. The valley is full of shadows, the grass dotted with huge shell-holes. Suddenly our guides tell us to hurry: a bad spot. A shell explodes 50 metres away. Consul hits the ground. His need to explain this – perfectly natural – reaction shows how nervous he is.

We are marching through the bottoms, where it's now fully dark. Silently, we make our way through the woods, chilled by the sight of the enormous shell-holes that punctuate our route. All I can hear is the sound of birdsong, of gas-mask cases hitting the branches, of shell-bursts rocking the ground, shaking us from top to toe, making our ears ring.

Again, at the double. We enter a tunnel.[1] Some 1500 metres long apparently. It shelters several companies from front-line regiments. The dark vault runs with water. Beneath all is hustle and bustle; voices call out, working parties cross, men march past, weapons slung, probably part of a relief. Electric bulbs shine feebly through the heavy, reeking atmosphere. A stench of men, sweat and latrines that catches you by the throat.

Several small corrugated-iron dug-outs have been erected. In one, we are welcomed by the commander of 42nd Infantry, Major L[avalette-Coëtlosquet] Around 50, tall, thin and clean shaven. Something of a thespian.[2] Eyes sparkling with intelligence. Lip curled in a wry smile. He greets us warmly and – much to Consul's disgust – offers us a Picon [aperitif].

He starts chatting to Consul.

'We're heading for the Digue,'[3] says Consul. 'Is there much shelling?'

'Good heavens, yes,' replies the major phlegmatically. 'One of my officers counted on average four shells a minute throughout the day in his sector.'

Consul pulls a face.

'And the battalion CO. What is his HQ like?'

---

1. The Tavannes tunnel.
2. With all due respect.
3. The mill dam of the Étang de Vaux.

'It's solid enough, but you can't go outside. It opens into a ravine under constant shelling.' (He pointed to it on a map.)

'Which direction do the shells arrive from?'

'North, west and east. Not usually from the south. Except when our 155s are firing short.'

Consul's face is a picture. The major can't resist an extra dig. 'Then, of course, there are the beasties,' he drawls. 'They get everywhere.'

'Beasties?' gulps Consul.

'Of course,' smiles the major. 'Lice!'

'Uugh!' says Consul, grimacing again.

We leave the tunnel by the way we came in. There are two ways in and out. The one used for an exit is more clearly marked but a sergeant was decapitated there a few hours earlier.

There is only one *boyau* leading to the Ravin des Fontaines, no deeper than 60 to 80 centimetres for most of its length. The landscape grows increasingly poignant in its desolation. The trees are just pickets. Shell-holes everywhere. Worst of all, the *boyau* becomes a canal in places, with 40 to 50 centimetres of water. Although Consul is wearing galoshes, he has to resort to gymnastics to avoid getting his feet wet. He never looks round to see if he's delaying our little group too much. He doesn't want damp socks.

The hail of shells begins, arriving as promised from all directions. Our guns respond. Then another farce ensues. Every time a shell falls or a gun fires, Consul crouches in the bottom of the *boyau*. The guide announces another bad spot. He speeds up.

Consul gets down.

'Better keep moving forward, sir,' [I say.]

'We've got to get over the road,' he croaks.

(It's in the open.)

We cross at speed and slip back into the *boyau*.

The shells all around are deafening, a cloud of acrid black smoke billowing out with each explosion. We must hurry, and we must make Consul hurry too.

Catastrophe! A relieving company from 124th Infantry is blocking the *boyau*. Then a company from 35th Infantry appears from the opposite direction, coming out of the line.

'Company relieved,' calls the CO, in a voice that betrays all his joy at escaping from hell.

We force our way single file through a tangle of helmets, rifles and mess-tins gleaming in the white light of the full moon. The skies are clear, and the Boches are flying their reconnaissance missions as if it was daylight. The line of mess-tins in the *boyau* are as bright as the opening day of the war. They're impossible to miss. When will Supplies understand that they must be dulled?

The consequences soon make themselves felt.

The Boche batteries pepper us, front and rear, the shell-bursts shaking us to the core, the shrapnel whistling over our heads. We can't move in either direction. At last, the *boyau* starts to clear. The column from 124th Infantry turns right, while we go left into a *boyau* leading into a ravine. That's where it gives out. We walk on bare earth pitted with shell-holes. The trees, cropped to trunks 1.5 to 2 metres high, cast long shadows in the moonlight.

This gloomy ravine, echoing with shell-bursts, was once refreshingly named the 'Ravin des Fontaines'. More accurately, the men call it the 'Ravin de la Mort'.

Brief halt with Major P., a pleasant southerner, whose words Consul finds ever more disconcerting.

Final stop with the CO of 35th Infantry [Lieutenant-Colonel Roland]. Aged 50 to 55, tall, bald, very pale complexion, red veined. The glazed expression and jumpy eyes of a hunted animal. He launches into some long-winded explanation. He looks frightened to death.

[Hillère] and I are given a guide.

We go outside.

'Watch out! Bad spot.'

The shells pour down.

Here, not a single tree. Everything razed to the ground.

'At the double, sir!

And the guide – a Parisian by his accent – sets the example.

I stumble. A body. Puttees neatly wound, limbs not yet stiff. They were talking at battalion HQ about a man in a working party killed here an hour ago.

We hurry along.

'Faster, sir,' shouts the Parisian.

I'm out of breath, I've got a stitch. My map-case is banging against my legs, my field glasses bouncing on my chest, my pince-nez slipping down my nose with sweat. A 150 explodes on the spur to our right. Black smoke gushes out. Shrapnel whistles in all directions.

We speed past the huts. At last, the Étang [de Vaux].

The Digue. We've made it. That's it for me. I'm beat.

Thursday 18 May
I am replacing Captain Allemand [of 35th Infantry]. He shows me the countryside.

My Tranchée de la Voie Ferrée[1] overlooks the Ravin de Vaux, which is marked like a slotted spoon with shell-holes great and small, all full of water. Ahead is a ruined house, 50 to 80 metres from Vaux village – the house west of Vaux as described by the official communiqués.

The village proper is now just a heap of rubble, flattened by our 155s.

Facing my HQ is Fort Vaux. Boche trenches surround it to the north and east, advancing along a double spur on the opposite side of the ravine. This is Point 246.

To our right, across the Digue, is the Bois Fumin (Retranchements R.2 and R.3).[2] Behind, beyond the Ravin de la Mort, lies a wood: Retranchement R.4.

To the north, the Ravin du Bazil runs between this wood and the Bois de La Caillette, separated from us to the rear by the Ravin de la Fausse-Côte. Overlooking the trench is the edge of the Hardaumont plateau.

Nothing can convey the desolation of this landscape.

Now (at 7.00 pm) it is bathed in the warm pink light of the setting sun. The hilltops seem stripped bare, not a blade of grass. The Bois Fumin is reduced to a few pickets bristling across the hilltop, like the Bois Chausson we nicknamed the Caterpillar [La Chenille].

So churned up is the ground by the shelling that the earth is loose as sand, making the shell-holes look like dunes. Suddenly the gunfire, which had slackened off a little, begins to rage again. I count eight Boche shells whistling over our heads in the space of a minute.[3] On top of the hill, pink with the setting sun, clouds of black smoke from our 155s rise on all sides, turning the blue sky dark.

Captain Allemand gives me a guided tour. The *boyau* connecting my forward trench with the trench below – in reality an 8-metre long sandbag barricade – is only 40 to 50 centimetres deep.

There is no shelter for the defenders.

---

1. Our initial destination was therefore not Retranchement R.1 as claimed in several accounts.
2. These were the redoubts situated north-west of Fort Vaux, on the slope descending to the Étang de Vaux.
3. This rate was often surpassed.

The captain's lodging is a shell-hole covered by some beams and a bit of earth. Beneath the ground are bodies, perhaps those buried by the shell. A few sandbags are lying around. You sleep on them, resting your head on the bag.

The men are crammed into niches that offer no protection, not even from the rain.

The staff and the generals write wordy notes ordering shelters to be 'dug 5 metres below ground'. But what about tools and supplies? No one takes care of that. There's nothing here: no logs, no planks, not even enough picks and shovels – just fifteen for the entire unit. We had a feeling this would be the case, but it's incredible to find it confirmed. Not even a *boyau* to access the front line. Some poor soul will be put before a firing squad for nodding off at his post, despite all kinds of extenuating circumstances – like lack of food and sleep.[1] But what will happen to General Herr, who has so many human lives on his conscience?[2]

Bodin arrived at 11.00 pm, winded, completely done in. Once he'd got his breath back, he gave me the big news of the day. The major running the billets

---

1. I am aware of no one executed on these grounds. But some unfortunate platoon commanders were put before a firing squad without hesitation.
2. 'I can state without fear of contradiction that the battlefield of Verdun contained not a single *boyau*, trench, barbed-wire entanglement or buried cable,' writes Colonel Mélot (*La Vérité sur la guerre*). 'Meanwhile grotesque defensive networks were constructed around the ramparts of the town itself. Why? Because that's where we took visitors from the rear. They were told the whole zone bristled with similar arrangements and could then go home and report on the succession of formidable defences established north of Verdun. In fact, there was just one – the complex adjoining Vauban's [seventeenth-century] walls.'

   General Gallieni, then minister of war, told General Joffre on 16 December that Verdun's defences were inadequate. Joffre retorted that the sectors mentioned in Gallieni's dispatch contained 'three or four defensive rings, completed or under construction. ... Your fears are completely baseless.'

   Gallieni offered his resignation. (Gallieni, p. 234*ff*)

   'Joffre's reply should be framed and displayed in the offices of bureaucrats worldwide,' claims Captain Liddell Hart, and rightly so.

   After replacing General Coutanceau as commander of the Verdun Fortified Region in August 1915, General Herr had enjoyed six months of total calm to repair the neglect of his predecessor. What most annoys former front-line commanders is his failure to organize his sector during that time. GQG did believe, however, that 'Verdun will not be the objective of an attack' (Gallieni, p. 233).

at Landrecourt has put in a complaint about us, and Consul is under threat of very severe punishment. This major was shocked to receive a memo on 15 May making him responsible for the state of the billets. Until then all he'd thought about was smoking his cigarettes and collecting his major's pay, and to cover his back he has picked on the first regiment passing through.

The complaint took forty-eight hours to travel from Army, to corps, to division, to regiment. It will take me much longer to get a response to my request for tools.

Friday 19 May

The shelling continues night and day. It's deafening. I'm punch drunk.

The formidable artillery duel never lets up for a second. The slopes of Vaux have been disappearing beneath our shells since 6.00 pm. From our positions, we could see them hitting the white lines in the ground formed by the Boche trenches and *boyaux*. But at night, under the stars, green rockets climb into the sky from our own front lines in the ravine. 'Raise your sights! Raise your sights!' is the desperate cry. Our poor comrades are taking a pounding from our own 155s. More rockets appear on all sides. Red rockets on the Hardaumont plateau: 'We're under attack! Fire! Fire! Block the road ahead of our trenches!' Red rockets in advance of Fort Vaux, red rockets in the distance behind Fumin. So many desperate cries in the dark! Others soar from the Boche lines, illuminating rockets this time, emerging in a constant stream to stop the intended victims of the enemy shells turning a single spadeful of earth.

With the whistle of projectiles criss-crossing over our heads, it's like being by the sea, ears ringing as heavy waves pound the shore, except the shell-bursts punctuate the storm with lightning strikes that crash together in one continuous roll of thunder.

Saturday 20 May

The talus below my trench contains a shell-hole around 5 metres deep by 7 or 8 metres wide. I think we could sound the Last Post if the lump which did that was to hit us.

11.00 pm. The Étang extends its dark waters towards the three hills closing the horizon. The silver moonlight bathes the hills as they fade into points of deeper blackness. Below my trenches, it flickers on the marshy bottom of the ravine, like a blinding wave amid the ripples. To my right, a funereal column of shadows slips silently across the mill–dam. The relief is passing. Seamlessly, in one continuous movement, it marches towards the Hardaumont plateau, where our shells are falling, where sprays of white, red or green climb incessantly into the sky – a firework display for those who are about to die.

Beneath the tranquil gaze of the firmament, a thousand unseen trolls unleash a deafening thunder on this underworld. Whistling shells criss-cross the air, the din of their explosions rocking earth and skies ...

Captain Dupont[1] of 124th Infantry arrives to discuss Monday's relief. He looks marvellously young and fit. A sound chap.

Sunday 21 May
The fine weather continues. So, too, the guns.

Midnight. The Germans sent over some tear gas at dusk. Thoroughly unpleasant. Your eyes sting, your head grows heavy; you cry and gasp for breath. Torture! It has only just started to disperse.

The guns are raging. The shells pound the ravine and the slopes. We're in a wonderful position here. Between the French 155s and the Boche shells, we cop it from both sides.

The men of 124th Infantry have orders to attack the slopes of [Fort] Vaux, in front of Retranchement R.1. I'm off to check that my men are all in their combat positions. The Vaux ridge stretches dark beneath a crescent moon reflected immobile in the ravine below. A silver mist shrouds the whole of the horizon – the fort, the ravine and the distant heights masking the [plain of the] Woëvre.

Right and left, the helmets of my troops rise above the trench, glinting dully in the gloom. I recall the sentries on the Elsener platform, relieving each other throughout the night. My sentries do not relieve each other. Beneath each helmet, a pair of eyes keeps watch, scouring the ravine, the slopes, the railway

---

1. A postman. A magnificent soldier, 25 years old. He would have made an excellent major, but he wasn't a regular! He died of Spanish flu in 1919. One of his sous-lieutenants was living in Argentina on the outbreak of war and took the first boat home to answer the nation's call. He carried a light cavalry sabre – originally his father's, I believe. I remarked on it because no trench infantryman had carried a sabre for months. He was a young man of average height – neat, brown hair, sharp profile – energetic and brave. The captain and the sous-lieutenant were real kindred spirits. The sous-lieutenant got hold of a Chauchat machine-gun and operated it alone (this weapon was still very new). He was killed a few days later, using the gun to fight off a German attack.

track. All around, the red flashes of the shell-bursts. A noisy hail of shrapnel falls in the marsh; more arrives with the whirr of a spinning-top, burying itself in the trench wall.

Rockets leave the German lines. They climb like shooting stars, describe a graceful arc and fall gently to earth.

The ghostly battle continues in the darkness. At 1.50 am the gunfire intensifies. Rifles and machine guns crackle. The sounds of a free-for-all echo through the valley. Red rockets climb from the German trenches. From our parapet we witness a mysterious struggle. Dumb with horror, we can hear the melee without seeing it. A stream of green rockets rises from our lines: 'Raise your sights!' An enemy machine gun enters the action: yet another missed by our artillery preparation. An opaque cloud of dust and smoke fills the valley, blocking everything from view.

Dawn is breaking over the Hardaumont plateau. Yet, in mist streaked by rockets and the red flashes of the shell-bursts, the battle rages more fiercely than ever. Bullets are whistling all around. For the babes of the class of 1916, this is their baptism of fire. They huddle in the lee of parapet. They don't dare to look up. I approach one and grab his rifle. Poor babes! I've never seen them look so young.

Sergeant Branchard – small, thickset, warm blue eyes, long, fair moustache – has been involved from the start. Coolly, he hands me the rounds one at a time. Every now and then he removes the long pipe clamped between his teeth and shouts to the babes. 'You see, we're not in danger. The captain here is fine! So am I!'

Suitably reassured, the youngsters give the Boches a sustained and well-aimed volley of fire. I stand them down before it gets light.[1]

Incredible, the zeal for action of my grand old veterans. Courtonne mans the barricades, sleeves rolled up, dashing from loophole to loophole to find a better angle of fire – quite literally on 'piecework'. The imposing figure of Mouquet stoops, takes his shot, then slowly stands. A calm peasant hunter. To my right, Génin[2] – usually shy and stuttering – is lost to the world, wholly absorbed in his task.

In the first light of day, we see the Germans flooding down the slopes below the fort. Every man has done his duty.

3.30 am. The rifles have stopped. The guns are still firing. I don't care. I'm going to lie down.

---

1. To their shelters in the lee of the parapet. This was enough to start with. They needed some rest.
2. Killed on 2 June 1916.

Monday 22 May

I slept very well. Suddenly I was woken by earth hitting me in the face.

At the same instant: 'Sir! Sir! I'm wounded, sir!

It's my orderly, Charpentier.

He drags himself to the entrance of the dug-out.

'Where's the damage?'

'My leg, sir!'

He looks drip white. I try to get up and help him. There's a shell case beside me. I can't resist touching it. It's red hot. It ricocheted off Charpentier's leg and landed right next to my head. It's a 130mm, weighing at least 12 to 15 kilos. It would definitely have straightened my nose out.

I make Charpentier lie down, then give him some of the sloe brandy A[ubry] brought me last night. He begins to come round a little. Lévêque arrives.[1] We cut away Charpentier's trousers. Three deep gashes in the knee. He's bleeding heavily. It doesn't look too serious.

11.00 am. Small groups of Boches are crossing the slopes below Fort Vaux. Here's one about thirty strong, moving quickly.

'Branchard, pass me a rifle.'

'Here, sir!'

He's holding a box of rounds. He opens it and hands them to me as I fire. The Boches dive for the ground then get going again. One stays down. He must be hit. They're brave soldiers, these lads! On the sides of the ravine, the Boches are counter-attacking with grenades. Devastating fire hits the Bois Fumin, from where reinforcements will be (or perhaps already are) appearing.

The stretcher-bearers report that in the Ravin des Fontaines 7th and 5th Companies are under incessant fire from 210s. Losses are heavy.

Today's Boche counter-attack has virtually wiped out 3rd Battalion, 124th Infantry. Colette says the dead are piled parapet high in the (one) *boyau* our reinforcements could use.

On our left, we retook Douaumont this morning.[2]

---

1. A stretcher-bearer. Small, skinny, grey eyes, ginger moustache. Something of a veteran. Exemplary devotion to duty.
2. It was recaptured by III Corps under General Mangin, but the Germans retook it almost at once.

Wednesday 24 May

1.00 am. Now we really are in hell. The night is black as ink; the ravine, a gigantic chasm; the surrounding hills, fantastic masses of dark shadow. In the depths of the abyss, the marshy pools gleam mysteriously in the dark. With a terrifying din, dark clouds of vapour climb relentlessly into the sky; red and white lights criss-cross; the mountains of shadow appear suddenly, briefly haloed with light, before returning to the gloom. Invisible objects slice through air heavy with dust and smoke. It's horrific, an unremitting maelstrom of roaring and crackling, followed by spurts of flame.

Is this the Twilight of the Gods? The *Götterdämmerung* that haunted the lofty imagination of their barbarous giant [Richard Wagner]?[1] A rent in the earth and the collapse into the fiery abyss of this savage world whose monstrous pride has all but consumed the human race. No, it's just one episode in this war. The German attack on the trenches around Fort Vaux. No more than a line in the official communiqué.

I drop into the *boyau*.

'Right, anyone for *pinard*!

'Watch out, twerp. You're spilling it. And there wasn't much to start off with.'

'For God's sake! The monkey's going on the ground. Put it in here!'

Right at the climax of the drama, the rations party has arrived.

Mother of God! It was a close call, crossing the ravine.

A few men have dropped into the *boyau* to carry the food back to the dug-outs. Everyone else is at the parapet, wholly concentrated on the fight.

8.00 am. The slopes of Fort Vaux seem barer, grimmer and more churned up than ever.

All along the German trench are blue-clad bodies, helmets, black streaks. In places the earth looks scorched. One man has been stripped of his greatcoat. His naked back is visible in the sun. In the ravine, the main street (?) of Vaux is a heap of rubble and charred beams, with the odd low fragment of wall. Nestling in a valley surrounded by woods and meadows, with a tree-girded pond to the rear, this little village must once have been quite delightful. Now look what's left of it: a jumble of ruins full of rotting corpses.

The Pan-Germanists and their delusions of grandeur truly are costing us dear.

---

1. The hidden meaning of the Ring Cycle has been revealed only since Hitler's triumph (5 March 1933) and his subsequent racist excesses.

Visitors are few in Tranchée de la Voie Ferrée. At the Calvaire, we saw up to the rank of artillery colonel. Here, not even a corporal.[1] Needless to say, we've seen no sign of Consul's crimson face.

On our left, a cavalryman from the chasseurs à cheval has been sentenced to a month with 3rd Battalion as punishment.

Enough said.

8.00 pm. Tear gas.

11.00 pm. The relief.

I am with 1st Platoon, who assemble in front of [Sergeant] Colombani's shelters.

The only way across the chute is a narrow plank, 2.5 metres long and 15 centimetres wide. Men laden with pack, rifle and equipment have to use it. The path then meanders between shell-holes where we stumble at every step. The Germans are sending up a stream of illuminating rockets, forcing the men to crouch. The stench of death and sulphur catches us by the throat. Shells are falling right, left and ahead of us. This is the Ravin de la Mort.

We pass through at top speed. Exhausted, we finally reach battalion HQ. The entrance is blocked by the wounded, bleeding and moaning. By the dim light of a candle I spot the stretchers: shattered human beings, the white marks of bandages, and against them, fresh red blood.

Major Letondot, CO of the relief battalion, is downhearted. Yesterday's disaster, no doubt. He gives me the details. Two companies of 124th Infantry attacked the Boche trenches and entered them without firing a shot. But no one had thought to issue extra grenades (three per rifleman, four per bomber). The Boches counter-attacked with grenades and annihilated the two defenceless companies. When 3rd Battalion went to the rescue, the Boche artillery blew them to bits in the *boyaux*. All in all, nearly 500 men were lost – for nothing.

It's enough to make you weep.

---

1. This was an exposed position – part of the outer defences of Fort Vaux – in immediate contact with the enemy. Indeed, it was first to fall to the attack of 1 June. At least one NCO runner should have been available to liaise with the artillery batteries. But not even Retranchement R.1 – of prime importance as Fort Vaux's last line of defence in the direction of the Étang de Vaux – had such a runner. During the major attack of 1 June, the absence of runners in this sector would have tragic consequences. Our infantrymen were annihilated by our own artillery.

We set off again. My stomach is in turmoil. Gut-wrenching cramps. Diarrhoea, brought on by the gas. We take Boyau de l'Étang. It's a metre deep – but not uniformly – and we're soon forced into the open. We cross the Plateau de Souville like this, then back into the *boyau* to cross the wooded ravine that will take us to the tunnel.

The cramps are so violent that I have to stop beyond the parapet, a few steps off the path leading to the *boyau*. I relieve myself. A 77 explodes on the path, the flash blinding me. Some poor devil is writhing in pain.

'Here, sir! I've broken my leg! Don't leave me!'

No one goes to his assistance. The men are dead to everything but fear of losing contact, of lingering too long in such lethal surroundings.

Eventually we go to collect him.

Arrive at the [Tavannes] tunnel. No preparations have been made for our arrival. After all our toing and froing, the men are bedded down on the railway tracks. The earth is damp, covered in debris. The tunnel is almost 1500 metres long, but nothing has been done to convert it. No ventilation. One shaft is under construction, but work only started a few days ago.

The front-line troops feel like beasts driven blindly to the slaughter. The general has a billet. His cooks lounge around on bunks. The men, however, are shoved into a corner amid the shit and the ordure. At some point, when there is a gap to be filled, they'll be ordered to their feet and thrown to the mercy of the bullet that wounds, the shell that destroys, the excruciating gas that burns the lungs. If they are wounded, how will they be succoured? No one cares. No evacuation trench; no battlefield shelters.

The newspapers describe in moving detail the pains taken by the General Staff to 'conserve'[1] the lives of our men! The truth must be shouted from the rooftops. In the Verdun sector, which suffered no attack for fifteen months, there is nothing, nothing at all. No trenches! No *boyaux*! No shelters! No telephone wires! No searchlights! No reserves of ammunition! Nothing! Sweet F.A![2]

---

1. Letters arrived from the rear devoted exclusively to the presumed benevolence of our leaders. 'Joffre should be sacked,' said one. 'His attitude is far too paternal.' The poor sap who spouted this drivel had no idea of the truth – that no general in history has sacrificed the lives of his men with quite such indifference as the so-called Grandfather. 'It was their duty,' he said, when learning of the losses incurred during a failed attack. When my informant (an officer present at the time) wrote to me in December 1916, the French army under General Joffre's command had already lost over a million dead.
2. Cf. Mélot, 18 May.

And now digging a *boyau* under shellfire, or bringing up materials and supplies, are extremely perilous tasks.[1]

Wednesday 24 May

The air in this tunnel is noxious.

The worst part of yesterday's relief were the gas shells fired by the Minnies. The explosion produces a phosphorescent layer which releases lung-burning gases. 5th Company was particularly badly affected. [Hillère] is sick and one of his men is dead. The characteristic of these gases is that their effects persist long after inhalation.[2] Bodin fell sick this afternoon and had to be evacuated. The colonel and L[etondot] needed oxygen, as did I. (The oxygen, by the way, has only just arrived. One man died while we waited.)

What a ghastly existence!

Inevitably, my mind returns to the bumf churned out by our leaders: 'Shelters are to be dug 5 metres deep; supplementary defences are to be placed nearby, etc.' In reality: not a beam, or a picket, or a shelter in a sector that for fifteen months had nothing to do but prepare.

If the generals suffered like the men, the war would have ended long ago.

Thursday 25 May

This tunnel. What a dreadful place to be! Perfectly befitting the sector.

A high vault blackened by smoke from the trains; bays 100 to 150 metres wide, each with three tiers of bunks; and, between them, gaps where the men have only the rails and sleepers to rest upon. Amid the gaps are the latrines, noisome pools of urine and excrement. The air is foetid, heavy with the nauseating stench of sweat and shit. After spending the night there, the men are pale and drawn, struggling to stand.

Fifty-three men reported sick this morning, a huge number. I threaten with court-martial any man failing to answer his name. Poor devils. In truth, the whole company is sick.

The attacks on Douaumont and Vaux show the Germans have spotted the chink in our armour. If they can break through here, what is to stop them

---

1. This explains why the Germans persisted for so long with their attack on Verdun. We could only undertake large-scale defensive work at night; and the nights were getting shorter.
2. This is an understatement. I suffered from the effects of gas inhalation for many years after the war – and do so to the present day.

reaching Verdun? Nothing! Nothing at all! Not a line! Not a trench! No barbed wire! Nothing! Bringing up their Minnies and using gas to block access to the Ravin de la Mort shows how determined they are to break through in the Douaumont-Vaux salient.[1]

We have reached crisis point.

Here, panic reigns. The men have been given no rest, they've not eaten, they're living in a dark, airless tomb. In the evening, it's one work detail after another.

The colonel offers cold comfort.

'We're all going to snuff it here,' he says amiably.

Major de Benoit says a grenade store went up on Tuesday, taking some of the colonel's runners with it. 'A mutilated figure came and collapsed at my feet. Men were writhing in the flames. I was only 3 metres away but there was nothing I could do. Arms and legs were flying through the air, grenades going off everywhere. It was like the Bazar de la Charité.'

Friday 26 May

In Napoleon's day, when armies were small and each sought the other out to destroy it, the cavalry was indispensable. With the continuous front lines of today, however, the cavalry no longer has a role. Yet we've continued to teach sabre fencing, the charge, etc. – and probably still do in the depots – while infantry combat is ignored.

What a bizarre military education our army has received.

I'm dazed by the noise, by lack of air and sleep. My head is in a vice. I feel sluggish, incapable of the slightest effort. Will my energy come back with the light? And if we had to return to the front line right now, would we have the stamina to do so?

Endless work details, ferrying matériel to the front line, or other heavy labour. Clearly, it's the only way we will come through this. I just hope we still have the time.

'Anyone for seconds!'

The shit is oozing down the corridor.

'Grab those mess-tins. The coffee's going everywhere.'

There's always one joker!

Most frequent, however, is a jubilant cry of 'Watch out, shit!'

And the shit passes.

---

1. Hence the subsequent German attack on 1 June 1916.

Saturday 27 May

Complete mayhem in the tunnel throughout the night. No chance to get any sleep.

Consul is back. He stayed in the shadows while we were in the front line. Now he's making up for lost time. He sports a smile and a calabash pipe. He sits enthroned, striving for a suitably dignified pose. Bolt upright, head tilted regally backwards, he puffs away solemnly: a great Huron chief smoking the pipe of peace. Now and then he launches into some confused adage, spits a long stream of yellowish phlegm on the ground or cleans his pipe. Claiming to honour us by dining at our humble table, he makes us endure this compelling spectacle until midnight.

Four of us are sleeping in the billet, a wooden hut covered in tarred canvas. A stable lamp casts a feeble yellow glow. And always from the corridor: 'Watch out, shit!'

My poor men. Two more killed and five wounded last night: twenty-five lost in a week. They went to take grenades to Retranchement R.1 around 8.00 or 9.00 pm.[1] A shell fell in the trench opposite the Souville batteries and blew them sky high.

Another working party this evening. How many more will die, wielding a pick or shovel?

Some of the regular officers are particularly despondent. One has been dining with us for the past few days. He's finished. Everything is hopeless. He's sick of it all. Understandably so. A cavalry officer leading our sort of life! He didn't sign up for this at Saumur. Another huge mistake was to appoint a lot of older captains, like Consul, as battalion commanders. Also, once confirmed in his rank and given a decoration, a captain has nothing more to gain from the war. The fighting is horrific,[2] so his ambitions are consequently twofold: shirk or be evacuated.

'Watch out, shit!'

Sunday 28 May

Defeatism is rife. Everyone is demoralized; spirits are at rock bottom.

'We'll never 'ave 'em,' says one poor comrade. 'Better make up and have done with it.' He turns to us with his big cow's eyes. His huge frame (he's 1.86 metres

---

1. Retranchement R.1 at Fort Vaux, which we would be defending five days later.
2. See 1 May 1916.

tall and must weigh over 200 kilos) has lost all its 'go'. 'We've been tricked. The Boches are much stronger than we were told.'

'Not at all, my dear friend. They started the war with 22 million tonnes of iron in stock. Their metallurgical industry produced four times more than ours. And they captured most of our plant. It was common knowledge.'

'Why did no one ever say?'

'It's all in Birot's *Statistique annuelle* [*de géographie comparée*]. Only 19 sous, published by Hachette.'

'Birot? Who's Birot?'

My excellent comrade – and [Hillère], who is listening in – have obviously never heard of him.

Our beloved Consul is taking some bold initiatives. B., V., Bétron and I are summoned to the presence.

'I'm the ranking officer here. I see you've been issuing orders without my leave. Who's fetching your food tonight?'

'?'

'Don't worry. I've sorted it out. I'm astonished that *amateurs like you* (*sic*) would take decisions without consulting me first. I am the CO.

'What's your plan, sir?!'

'To send 7th Company!' (The one that never lifts a finger.)

A touch of military genius! It's impossible not to admire such insight. No less to explain his need to prove it by upbraiding four of his company commanders. When we have to name a rations party, he's in commmand; but when it comes to defending the outworks of Fort Vaux, he leaves it to the 'amateurs'.

We're leaving on relief at 9.15 pm. At the last minute we notice we have no reserve rations.

'I'll go to brigade HQ!' says Consul with a rush of blood to the head.

I hurry after him. (You never know with a madman!)

I reach the colonel's dug-out and peer round the door. No Consul. However, the lieutenant colonel and the adjutant are deep in a rubber of bridge, the brigadier's slim figure stooping over them, following the game. We're about to be blown to perdition, but nothing will divert the brigadier from his game of cards. He still hasn't set foot in his sector. He won't come out of the tunnel at any time. All he's done so far is to issue a threatening note demanding silence 'between 10.00 pm and 7.00 am'.

'Watch out, shit!'

We leave the tunnel via the ramp and enter the *boyau*. The whole of 3rd Battalion is working there! On the night of the relief! Surely they could have set off an hour later? Could they, hell! It's more important for the brigadier not to miss his bridge evening. I will always be able to picture his long, thin form and shining face, in that shadowy hut, leaning over the table where L[etondot], in the light, holds his cards like Christ holding the bread in Rembrandt's *Supper at Emmaüs*. Meanwhile in the sole *boyau* leading to the front line, the battalion is getting entangled with a second despatched there through culpable negligence.

Our men run into each other, trip over the picks and shovels. They push through the working party, struggling by in a *boyau* no wider than our packs.

We're opposite the Souville batteries. If the Boches start shelling, they'll make mincemeat of us.

They are shelling!

The working party, previously such an obstacle, are now crouched in the bottom of the *boyau*. We trample them underfoot, but they say nothing. Despite our troubles, the men are following. The fresh air has revived them. Shells or no shells, the paralyzing fear we felt on emerging from the tunnel has evaporated.

Monday 29 May

In the Ravin des Abris, as in the Tranchée de la Voie Ferrée, my hole contains a body, now lying beneath my feet rather than my head.

I think back to our last dinner in the tunnel, shared with the [Alsatian] businessman who views the war in commercial terms. He does his duty, full stop. Sadly, this dreadful war requires much more than that. He tells us what he saw of the Boche counter-attack against 124th Infantry. A German unit came out of the trenches, with an officer in command.

'He was a big beggar. He marched bolt upright. The bullets were hitting right and left, raising little puffs of dust. He never flinched. He gave his orders calmly, gesturing to indicate which direction to follow, which position to occupy. The bullets never touched him.'

Who was this colossus? Probably some Prussian Junker. As far as we know, we have III Corps opposite us.

Meanwhile our Alsatian kept his head down. He never fired a shot.

'It was better to stay hidden. Give them no sign of my existence.'

It would certainly have been 'a poor deal'.

8.40 pm. We are providing a working party of fifty-four men tonight to work on the *boyau* between the Digue and Retranchement R.1. The orders are given: the working party is assembled in the quarry above my HQ.

Scarcely am I back in my dug-out, when it's rocked by a huge explosion.

Dubuc comes hurtling in.

'Sir! Sir!'

Shouting and moaning from outside: 'Here! Help me!'

Dubuc has got back his breath. 'The working party's just been hit. It's ghastly. I'll send men to recover the wounded.'

He stands! So does Rouzeaud, the officer of the day. I feel like I've been hit on the head by a hammer. I reach the left-hand exit, a couple of paces away, to the rear of my HQ. The night is so black that I hardly dare put one foot in front of another. An illuminating rocket casts a sudden brilliant light. There, by the tree trunk, a pile of bodies. Not moving. How many are there? I go towards them. A huge explosion. A jet of red flame hits me in the eye. Another shell falls, shaking me to the core. The smoke catches my throat. Shrapnel and earth rains around me. From the darkness I hear cries and groans. Dubuc and R[iballier] were ahead of me! In a daze, I return to the dug-out. Dubuc appears and slumps down on the bunk, face distraught.

'More casualties, sir!'

Only three stretchers can be found at the aid post. The shirking bandsmen cowering there refuse to collect the wounded, arguing that as divisional stretcher-bearers their only role is to carry the wounded to Tavannes. The aid post was designed for six to eight men at most. But the wounded are flooding in: first my men, then those from the front line. It's utter carnage, all blood and moans. Bloody red streaks on white flesh, haggard faces, scraps of cloth with strips of flesh attached. A nauseating stench. At the rear, by the light of a single candle, the medical officer and the padre, hands drenched in blood, bandage non-stop. And around us in the shadows, shells continue to explode, finishing off the wounded left outside.

Consul initially orders the working party to go ahead. Too bad if half the company's out of action. But after a visit to the charnel house,[1] and when I press the point in writing, he gives way.

Nine or ten dead, twelve seriously wounded, a dozen or so with minor wounds or shock.

The Boches continue pounding the ravine throughout the night.

---

1. I took him there myself.

Tuesday 30 May
This morning I visited the scene of the massacre.

A long, sticky pool of crimson blood is clotting by the tree. Helmets full of blood, packs ripped apart, shovels, blood-streaked rifles. From a heap of debris pokes a white shirt, sickeningly gory. Near the tree, a head awaits recovery. Probably poor little Deline, who has been reported missing.

A cloud of bluebottles gorged with blood buzzes around the slaughterhouse.

Summoned to meet Consul at 8.30 pm.

We leave to reconnoitre the positions currently occupied by 53rd Infantry. At [the 101st's] Fumin HQ, no guide has arrived from the 53rd. We enter Boyau Sundgau in the pitch dark. It disappears after scarcely 100 metres and turns into a succession of shell-holes, any track very hard to identify in the blackness. We're following the edge of a wood, stumbling over tree-stumps with every step.

The shells are falling all around us, luckily fired too long to affect our little group.

Suddenly the *boyau* runs out. We all crouch down to dodge the shrapnel. Blum,[1] a sergeant from 7th Company, is sent on ahead to reconnoitre.

'Lord above!' wails Consul. 'What a life! Death hanging over our heads like the sword of Damocles.'

The shells *are* falling heavily round here. The German 77s are pounding the rear of Fort Vaux. The shells arrive with astonishing speed. They burst almost as soon as you hear them whistle.

'And my only protection is this tree in front of me,' yells Consul. 'I've got to keep it there. If it takes a direct hit, I'm done for! Finished!

Silence. We all studiously ignore this invitation to offer up our spot.

Blum returns. He's found some men from 53rd Infantry. We carry on across the shell-holes. A light! At last, we're at the Batterie HQ – a rectangular concrete box. Shells are bursting right by the entrance. A lieutenant is there to greet us.

'Where's the major?' asks Consul.

'At Fort Vaux.'

'Oh!'

Consul slumps down, dejected. With good reason. It's 11.15 pm, and we've spent over two hours running the gauntlet for nothing.

'But he was meant to be here.'

'No! He realized it wouldn't do. No telephone lines and not enough room for the runners.'

---

1. Killed on 2 June. Remarkably cool and brave.

Consul presents our orders: Tournery is going to Tranchée Vaux-Ouest, [Hillère] is going to the Courtine, I am heading to Retranchement R.1, while Biancardini remains at the Batterie in support.

We passed the *boyau* leading to Retranchement R.1 an hour and a half ago. I asked Consul if I could go straight there.

'No,' he replied. 'We all have to report to battalion HQ. Those are my orders.'[1]

The company commander from 53rd Infantry – a southerner, tall, brown hair, an ex-NCO in the tirailleurs – knows nothing, and I mean nothing, about the sector.

'Sorry, I'm not familiar with R.1.'

'The Courtine? What's that?'

[Hillère] explains, pointing to it on the map. 'Ah, yes! That's our centre company. I send a patrol there each evening. They navigate by compass. There aren't any *boyaux*, not even a path.'

Charming!

After wasting half an hour there, the company commander, [Vinerot] and I head off to 53rd Infantry's HQ. This is on my return route, thence if possible via Boyau Sundgau.

Once again we pick our way across the shell-holes and arrive at 53rd Infantry's HQ, which is situated in a sort of big dug-out called the Dépôt. It opens onto a huge trench at least 10 metres deep. The trench walls have no steps cut into them and are under fire from large-calibre shells.

Deep underground, at a table lit by an acetylene lamp, is the colonel of the 53rd. A gaunt old man, with a white moustache, and a glass eye. They know no more here than at the Batterie. It's obvious all they're thinking about is the next relief – happy to leave their successors to muddle through as best they can.

That's what happens in a gerontocracy. Napoleon chose colonels with rather more go. Here is a typical example. At this regimental HQ, they don't know who's on the right or who's on the left.

'Just give me a guide to show me into Boyau Sundgau. That'll take me in the direction of Fumin HQ.'

No one can be found. I know the entrance to Boyau Sundgau must be close by. I'll have to chance it, picking my way through the shell-holes in the dark. I square my shoulders and set off, followed by my adjutant.[2] What a journey! In

---

1. This was incorrect as will be revealed below.
2. The excellent Dubuc.

the dark, blinded by red flashes from shell-bursts, tripping over tree-stumps, falling into shell-holes, surrounded by a hail of shrapnel.

By 1.30 am I'm back at Fumin HQ, my mission to reconnoitre Retranchement R.1 still unaccomplished. If I try again, it will now have to be in daylight, via a *boyau* I know to be under shell and machine-gun fire. Undertaken at the proper time, I would have completed my mission two hours ago – in favourable conditions, too. Could there be a crueller way of falling victim to an imbecile?

I have a word with the colonel.

'Do I have to reconnoitre R.1.?'

'No. It's not worth it. Someone will guide you from here this evening.'

'But why did I have to go haring after the colonel of 53rd Infantry? The major refused to let me go straight to R.1. He said he was following your orders.'

'I ordered no such thing!'

Charming!

Wednesday 31 May

Off to relieve [the company occupying Retranchement R.1].[1] Sous-lieutenant Riballier des Isles will remain in the shelters to pass on orders. The usual dreadful barrage at 8.00 pm. It's still going strong at 10.00 pm but we have to go.

The shells are pounding the Ravin des Abris.

I order the company to assemble in the *boyau*. They will be slightly more sheltered there. The *boyau* is heavily shelled, but it's nothing by comparison with the *boyau* leading to R.1. That's just a succession of shell-holes.

---

1. The Germans attacked at 8.00 am the following day. It was an effort very like that of 21 February, targeting the same point on the Verdun front: the Vaux-Douaumont sector. The Germans already held Fort Douaumont. Now they were hoping to overwhelm Fort Vaux before pressing on, through a sector they knew to be only lightly defended, to the citadel of Verdun. They wanted to end matters here before the launch of the joint Franco-British offensive then in preparation on the Somme. (It started on 1 July.) The attacking force consisted of three elite corps – from left to right, I Bavarian Corps, X Reserve Corps (recruited from the Guards depots) and XV (Strasbourg) Corps – supported by a thousand guns, mainly heavy and semi-heavy artillery, with a high proportion of rapid-firing 210s. Facing the brunt of the attack on 1 June 1916, between the Étang de Vaux and the battery at Damloup, south-east of the fort, were just five front-line battalions: two from 101st Infantry, two from the 53rd, and one from the 142nd. Our artillery consisted of five groups of 75s (sixty guns) positioned behind Souville, plus a number of batteries of Bange 155 longs, which fired an excellent shell – but slowly. We had not yet received our new heavy artillery. Writing just after the armistice, thus not long after the event, Louis Madelin (*Le Chemin de la victoire*, p. 180) states: 'From 31 May to 5 June, the Vaux massif was the target of perhaps the most formidable attack of the entire battle of Verdun'.

A harrowing night march, bent double throughout, ready to dive for cover. In the darkness, some kind of white structure: the Redoute.[1] Then a high talus overlooking the *boyau*: Retranchement R.1.

From the middle of the *boyau* come the cries of the wounded. The men of 7th Company have been hit by a shell en route to Vaux-Ouest. 5th Company (heading for the Courtine) are blocking our passage. Understandably, the men begin to fret. At last! After a half-hour halt we reach our position, and S. hands over my orders. He shows me round my HQ: a niche below the remains of a reinforced concrete wall destroyed by a 380. During an earlier relief, a sous-lieutenant was killed here by [one of our] 75[s]. Most reassuring. S. has lost fifteen men over the last four days, all to the 75s. He says that yesterday our gunners fired a destructive barrage for him! Quite literally so for this bit of trench.

The artillery refuse to send a single extra corporal to spot for the front-line trenches.

[General] Tatin has written to [Hillère], ordering him back to the regiment.[2]

Thursday 1 June

The Ravin de la Mort is lost. This valley of delights has fallen to the Boches.

At 8.00 am we watched the German infantry swarm down the slopes of the Hardaumont plateau ahead of us,[3] like ants after someone has kicked over an anthill. Without a shot from our gunners,[4] they flowed towards our Tranchée du Saillant.[5] Our troops hurriedly abandoned the trenches and fled in confusion for the Ravin de la Fausse-Côte. We fired on the attackers with no obvious impact.[6]

---

1. A small concrete cube used as an aid post.
2. He had gone down to Belrupt. Tired as we were, we worked through the night to finish the sandbag parados begun by S. It overlooked the *boyau*, which formed a ravine below and to the rear of the talus, itself the last vestige of Retranchement R.1. We finished shortly before the Germans launched their attack at 8.00 am the following day. The parados protected us very effectively from shrapnel and in short enabled us to hold out in the terrible circumstances described below.
3. The village of Vaux was situated in the bottom of the ravine, next to the Étang. Retranchement R.1 overlooked the slopes leading from the village to the fort. It gave us a balcony view of the action.
4. To my right, in the observation post at Fort Vaux, Major Raynal had noticed this too. To his bitter regret, his two 75s had been removed from the gun turrets following the decree of 15 August 1915 that disarmed the Verdun forts. Only the firing tables remained! He maintains quite plausibly that he could have stopped the enemy in their tracks.
5. At the far end of the Hardaumont plateau, almost opposite Tranchée de la Voie Ferrée. The trench ran alongside the Étang de Vaux, immediately below the edge of the plateau.
6. This does not mean we had no effect at all.

The Germans jumped into the trench. The puffs of white smoke told us they were armed with grenades.

Then all went quiet.

Further off, masses of blue greatcoats tried to work their way back up the slopes of the Bois de la Caillette, already in full sun, but they soon fled back in disorder towards the Ravin de la Fausse-Côte. Shells were exploding in their midst but from here it didn't look as if anyone had been hit. The Boches slipped in single file along the railway line. Then we saw a line of blue greatcoats making its way, without weapons, back up to Hardaumont. Prisoners, sixty to eighty.

I order my men to fire at the advancing Boches. I hit a few myself.

S. rushes like a madman from the shelter: 'Don't shoot! Don't shoot! They're ours!'

'No, no! They're Boches. You can tell.'

'Hang on to your ammo.'

But I have 23,000 rounds! To hold a trench that, 60 metres[1] at most from the Germans opposite, can only be defended with grenades! Still the same old bad habits. 'They're too far away![2] Don't waste your bullets!'

When we have bullets kicking around all over the trench!

In [Tranchée] Sarajevo opposite, a grey helmet occasionally pops above the parapet. Every time a head appears, we fire. A battle to excite us. Lauraire, a lad from the class of 1916, slumps beside me. His helmet is holed. It falls off. A gaping hole disfigures his skull. His head falls to his chest, blood gushing like a fountain from the wound.

Men streaming with blood pass constantly through the trench, heading for the aid post in the Redoute. And opposite our elevated position, we can see the Boches move along the railway line and across the Digue, all without a shot from our artillery!

1. The Germans were 60 metres away on one side; 20 metres on the other. S. had been relieved. Unsurprisingly I told him to shut up and carried on firing. The German trench was called Sarajevo. It saw plenty of action.
2. They were around 800 metres away, while our rifles had a range of 3 kilometres! From long experience I knew that the only troops who never hit anyone were those who didn't fire (see 19 September 1914). And I never saw troops run short of ammunition.

Twelve noon. The Boche are approaching Retranchement R.2[1] Heavy gunfire. We're retaliating at last. There to greet them is our 3rd Company.[2] I go down to the Redoute, which overlooks the ravine separating R.1 from the Bois Fumin (and ahead of it R.2). From the Redoute, and from the left of R.1, machine gunners and infantrymen are firing at any grey grub scrambling up the slopes of the Fumin.

2.30 pm. The [Germans] have taken R.2 and are threatening to turn our left. We see blue greatcoats lift their arms in surrender and trail away, surrounded by grey tunics.

As soon as R.2 was taken, the Boches started digging a trench in front of it,[3] to the amazement of my men. Now only the ravine separates us from the enemy. Are we going to be caught here like mice in a trap? I have two machine guns raking the ravine.[4] In front of their field of fire, groups of grey-clad bodies lie sprawled on the ground.

The trench is a ghastly spectacle. Red spatters the stones. In places, pools of blood. On the parados and in the *boyau*, dead bodies lie covered by tent sections. One has a gaping wound in the thigh.[5] Already rotting in the hot sun, the flesh has burst through the material and is swarming with bluebottles. Right and left, the ground is strewn with unidentifiable debris: empty tins, packs ripped open, helmets holed, rifles broken; everything splashed with blood. An intolerable stench poisons the air. Then, to render it completely unbreathable, the Boches send over some tear-gas. Meanwhile the heavy shells continue to pound down non-stop around us.[6]

---

1. Moving uphill from the Étang de Vaux, the Germans had first taken Tranchée de la Digue (1st Company, Lieutenant Abram), then two of the line of entrenchments halfway up the slope: Retranchement R.4, at the tip of Vaux-Chapitre, and R.3 on the slopes of the Bois Fumin. They were now closing in on R.2, before finally attacking R.1, which blocked the way into the fort.
2. Under the command of Lieutenant Goutal – a proud Auvergnat, vigorous, apple cheeks, a splendid soldier. He defended his position heroically but sadly was hit in the stomach. Taken prisoner, he was cared for and later recovered. After the armistice he returned to his architect's practice.
3. Stripping to their shirt sleeves to wield pick and shovel.
4. I placed them in a kind of col leading to the Bois Fumin, from where they overlooked, and could cover, both flanks of the ravine climbing to our left.
5. Young Aumont, from the class of 1916.
6. So, by 2.30 pm, after six and a half hours of fighting, the Germans controlled all the external entrenchments on the north-west flank of Fort Vaux, R.1 excepted. R.1 was now

Friday 2 June

A harrowing night, always on the alert.[1] No rations reached us yesterday. We desperately need something to drink. The hard tack is disgusting. A shell has just made my pen slip. It didn't fall far away. It hit the dug-out right next to me, where Cosset, my poor sergeant-quartermaster, was sleeping. Everything shook. I was covered with earth but otherwise emerged unscathed!

To judge from the direction, it was a 75. A poorly calibrated piece firing too short. I send up an illuminating rocket and a green rocket to ask the gunners to raise their sights. I could have spared myself the trouble. Waste of time. They carry on.

'A piece of shrapnel set off a red rocket,' shouts Clerc.

'That'll be it. Our gunners are shelling ... us.'[2]

I order the signal to be repeated: illuminating and green. At last! They decide to raise their sights.

'Chevaillot is dead, sir!'

My other quartermaster! A strapping lad, class of 1915, so innocently recounting his amorous adventures just moments ago.

Coutable goes past, face covered in blood: I'll never forget that head disfigured by streams of crimson.

1.30 pm. I immediately despatch a runner to take my report to the colonel. Young Clerc has volunteered.

'Give it here, sir! I'm not scared of dying ... We've got to save our chums.'

---

the last remaining barrier to the fort from this direction. '[It] is the fort's only safeguard against encirclement and right in the front line,' notes the diary of a reliable, high-ranking eyewitness. He also states the generals had no idea what was happening in the front line 'because bad weather is stopping the planes from flying'. By bad weather he must mean turbulence. The day itself was fine and warm.

1. Major de Benoist despatched a constant stream of notes on the colonel's behalf, advising me that the enemy was determined to take R.1 at all costs – in truth, I rather doubted this, as R.1 was the only external entrenchment still in our hands – enjoining me to greater vigilance, or announcing a relieving counter-attack. By chance, I still have one: '11.50 am. Colonel to Captain Delvert. Second Brigade (on our left) will counter-attack via the Ravin des Fontaines. Continue covering the ravine leading from Vaux to prevent infiltration. Step up your watch this evening.'

2. This was not the case at all, as will be revealed below.

Bloody gunners! If only they'd deign to reconnoitre the front-line trenches, we could avoid these dreadful mix-ups. A pounding from the German artillery is quite enough, without our own guns joining in too.[1]

8.00 pm. The Boches opposite are leaving their trenches. We're all at the parapet. I've ordered grenades distributed all round. Rifles are useless at this distance.

Here they are! Let's go! Sortais[2] cuts the strings and we despatch the grenades. The rifle grenades they send in reply pass over our heads.

'Send up a red rocket!'

Surprised by our grenades, the Boches rush back to their trenches. Behind me, a sudden burst of flame, accompanied by torrents of black and white smoke. These are proper jets of flame. The Germans must have broken through on our right. They have to be targeting us with flamethrowers. But from the heart of the blaze, green and red flames are soaring skywards. I realize what's happened. My rockets are alight. At a time like this! Thank goodness we've driven off the Germans.

Some wretches appear from our right. 'Every man for himself!' they cry. Some men near me start to panic and step down from the parapet.

'Back to your posts, for God's sake. As for you, dolts! You're scarpering because a couple of rockets are on fire!'

Order is restored immediately, but it shows how easily panic can take hold. Over nothing, when the real danger is past. The fire crackles away amid the darkness and the shells. A constant succession of fresh rockets send out their jets of flame. The fire is soon licking around my HQ. My first priority is to save the grenades stored nearby. A bag of ammunition remains within the inferno: we can hear it going off. Even worse, the sandbag-walls are feeding the flames. Meanwhile the shells are still falling, the bullets whining.

At last, all the cases of grenades are moved clear.[3] Clods of earth are falling on the fire, which is starting to die down.

---

1. The eyewitness cited previously explains the tragic mix-up. It had nothing to do with a 'poorly calibrated 75 firing too short' or a 'dreadful misunderstanding', but a barrage deliberately ordered on the basis of dud information. Retranchement R.1 had been reported lost. The report was inaccurate and an odious slander on the captain in command. So odious, indeed, that the general initially vowed to have him put before a firing squad – only to decorate him for valour on later receiving an accurate account of events. Who started the rumour? Who was to blame for the insult?
2. Dubuc's runner.
3. Only just in time. The last box was completely charred down one side.

Champion was the unwitting author of the disaster. The red rocket he lit on my orders flew backwards instead of forwards!

Ah, we lack for nothing here in the front line! Nothing but the best for us.

Fortunately, the Boches were quietened by our grenades. But we'll need more if we're to hold off another attack.

10.00 pm. A man arrives from Fumin HQ with five 2-litre water bottles – one empty – to be shared by the entire company. That's eight litres, as near as damn it, to be divided between sixty men, eight sergeants and three officers.

The water smells of dead bodies. With scrupulous care, the adjutant doles it out in front of me.

Saturday 3 June

I haven't eaten for nearly seventy-two hours.

In the small hours (2.30 am) the Boches attack again. Distribute more grenades.

We went through twenty boxes yesterday.[1] We'll have to watch it.

'Steady, lads! Wait until they're out of the trench. We've got to go carefully. At twenty-five paces! Hit them in the gob! On my orders. Now!'

A volley of explosions. Bravo! Black smoke appears. Groups of Boches whirl and fall to the ground. One or two men get to their knees and crawl back towards the trench. Another man rolls into it in his haste. Yet a few continue to advance, while the machine gunners and those still in the trench riddle us with bullets. One Boche even manages to crawl as far as my barbed-wire entanglement. Bamboula gives him a spoon grenade flush on the head.

By 3.30 am they've had enough. They return to their hole. A song comes to my lips.

'You're cheerful,' says Corporal Lecomte.

Obviously. We've won the day.

6.00 am. The German stretcher-bearers arrive to collect their wounded. I order my men to hold fire.

7th Company has lost its CO, Tournery, killed; his only sous-lieutenant, the brave Bétron, also killed. 6th Company,[2] Lieutenant Biancardini, killed; Sous-lieutenant Leroy, killed; Sous-lieutenant Tétard, captured at the Digue.

---

1. Just ten boxes were left at my HQ and we still had another three days to hold out.
2. Our reserve company.

With an endless stream of Germans crossing the Digue, and R.2 in enemy hands, we're threatened on all sides. Our situation is critical. Fear tightens its grip.[1]

And still our 75s are shooting us in the back! At 2.00 pm they destroyed two of my machine guns, buried all my munitions, made mincemeat of a gunner and wounded two others. At 5.15 pm they started up again.

Just one thing left for us to do: prepare to die!

One machine gun[2] is enfilading the narrow ramp that descends to the Redoute, while another threatens the passage in front of my HQ.

Tremendous Boche artillery preparation this evening. They will definitely attack again. I order the machine-gun platform to be rebuilt,[3] reinforcing the battery with a second gun that we've managed to repair.

It's raining, so the men are setting out bottles and tent sections to try to catch something to drink.

At 8.30 pm the gentlemen opposite leave [Tranchée] Sarajevo.

The poilus are confident.

'My round, sir!' shouts Rouzeaud from his combat position.[4]

The Boches are greeted at 15 metres by such a barrage of grenades and machine-gun fire that they decide not to press the point. The attack is stopped dead in its tracks.

At 10.00 pm Lieutenant (Brunet) appears in the dug-out. He says he's brought reinforcements: a company from 124th Infantry. We count them: eighteen men in all. An hour later Lieutenant (Claude) arrives from 298th Infantry.

'I've brought you a company as reinforcements.'

'Another one? Where am I going to put them? How many in total?'

'170.'

'And with you right now?'

We count again. There are twenty-five!

---

1. Could we hold out for another two or three days? Another worry on top of that caused by the horror of our situation.
2. A German machine gun sited in the north-west corner of the fort's superstructure, by then in enemy hands.
3. By Sergeant Machine-gunner Rigallot and Machine-gunner Sauviat. These two heroes coolly dismantled, cleaned and reassembled the guns under fire, as if they were in a workshop. I pay tribute here to these two wonderfully courageous men.
4. I can see him still, cheerfully balancing his grenade at arm's length. Poor lad!

The others never made it! They must have got lost out there in no man's land!

I position the men from 298th Infantry in the Redoute, then divide up the group from 124th Infantry. Half go left of the crossroads (to Colombani), the other half go right (to 5th Company).

[Hillère] grabs the opportunity to recover his men,[1] just leaving me his bombers.

Exhausted men crowd the *boyau*, blocking it completely. Let's hope the Boches don't start shelling! We can't even light a candle. The merest glimmer of light will attract the shells. I write my daily report crouched in a corner, under cover, resting the paper on the ground.

As for catching a moment's rest, that's out of the question. The shelling never stops. Besides, we're so riddled with lice that we're scratching as if we have scabies.

Sunday 4 June

'Those Boches aren't having much luck with R.1.,' shouts Frémont[2] as he waddles past.

I'm at the Redoute arranging liaison with my left.

'I understand it was all go this time yesterday,' says [Lieutenant] Perrin.[3]

'Yes, but you saw what kind of welcome they got from our grenades.'

Just then, a significant stream of explosions: the grenade battle starting up again.

I hurry up the ramp to the centre of my line. It's a glorious day. The crack of grenades all round. A bombing contest is a beautiful thing to behold. Feet firmly planted behind the parapet, the bomber throws his grenade with the action of a pelota player.

Crouched among the boxes, Sortais cuts the protective string around each grenade and hands them over ready primed. Black smoke climbs into the sky in front of the trench.

By 4.00 am it's all over. The Boches have hurried home again. A few rifle shots still crackle; the final sobs that follow the crescendo. After yesterday's rain, the sun is shining, making the desolation in this ravine even more poignant.

---

1. He could see [the troops in] R.1 were exhausted. 'It didn't look promising,' as we say. He wanted as little as possible to do with us. Always keen to cover his back, as he made perfectly clear the following day (see below).
2. One of my poilus. From Mortagne. As good as he was brave, killed in Champagne on 27 May 1917.
3. A machine-gunner, killed at Cornillet in August 1917.

The wounded pass covered in blood. We bring back two dead: Pingault and Bamboula. Poor Bamboula stood on the parapet to bag a Boche officer and was shot in the head. Two Boches who penetrated the end of the trench held by 5th Company's bombers and the ten men from 124th Infantry were shot to ribbons.

A Boche prisoner appears. Clean shaven, eyes haggard.

'Kamerad!' he shouts, lifting his bloody hands.

Our men hurry him to the aid post. I follow. His wounds are being dressed. He thought he was about to be shot. He's laughing and crying, grateful for the care he's receiving. He's a cobbler from Essen, 19 years old.

We have another prisoner in the Courtine, class of 1915. And a 24-year-old NCO, an architect, a refined sort of chap.

The aid post is bleak. Men lie moaning in the candlelit gloom. They recognize me and cry out. One has been calling for me for some time[1]; he wants me to contact his brother.[2] Another asks me to write to his parents. Poor Corporal Champ, death writ large on his face, brings tears to my eyes with his farewells. All are in agony, burning with fever, not a drop of water to slake their thirst.

At 5.00 am Riballier enters my HQ. 'Sir, Captain [Hillère] has just said to me:[3] "The reinforcements from 124th Infantry – it's been agreed that Captain Delvert and I are sharing command. I have those right of the Courtine; Captain Delvert has those in R.1." That's right. Why did he bring it up?'

'I'd better have a chat with him.'

I go looking for [Hillère]. After a little hemming and hawing, he finally comes clean. 'Sous-lieutenant Riballier's post is on your side [of the Courtine],[4] so I think it would be best for you to take command of all the men from the 124th.'

---

1. Corporal Paul Toutain. A model of conscientiousness, who by some miracle escaped this inferno. He was evacuated to a hospital in Lyon and recovered.
2. Alfred. Two years older than Paul.
3. It was 5.00 am. We had just repelled the fifth German assault on Retranchement R.1. It must have worried my neighbour, who was eager to disclaim all responsibility for defending the ouvrage. It reminds me of Louis XV's navy and the '*officiers rouges*' who watched impassively while the '*officiers bleus*' were overwhelmed. [Note: the '*officiers rouges*' were aristocrats; the '*officiers bleus*', more recently commissioned commoners.]
4. This post was officially under [Captain Hillère's] command – a disposition adopted by the generals so Retranchement R.1 could be assisted by troops positioned between it and the fort. Captain [Hillère] hereby managed to evade all responsibility for R.1, and I knew I would receive no help from that quarter.

'That's all right with me. The whole of R.1 and all the men from the 124th are now under my orders.'

'Fine. And once we've sent Fritz packing, I'll hand over the post for good.'

2.30 pm. Under fire from the heavy artillery since noon. The ground is shaking, the dug-out is full of grit. They really have it in for this trench. My ears are ringing. It's a torrent of iron!

A 'field-grey' bursts into my HQ escorted by one of my men. It's the [German] NCO taken prisoner this morning. He wants to shelter with me. All I can offer is moral support. His face is drawn. He's shaking like a leaf. I've never seen a Frenchman in quite such a panic.

'It's awful,' he stammers. 'Quite, quite mad.'

'They're your guns,' I reply coolly. 'This is nothing.'

I send him back to the Redoute.

The shelling stopped at 3.30 pm. Casualties: two men wounded! But in the rear, at the Batterie,[1] where 6th Company was held in reserve, things were very different. Consul had ordered a trench to be dug in advance of this position. He had already sent Lieutenant Biancardini and Sous-lieutenant Leroy to their deaths here, and his latest brainwave was to bring 6th Company out of their concrete shelters and line them up in the trench. What was he thinking? Poor 6th Company was in reserve, its task to provide a second line of defence in case of attack. With a jot of common sense, Consul would have realized that an attack is never launched while a position is being shelled. It follows once the guns have raised their sights.

The losses were appalling. A company that should have got off lightly has been reduced to just twenty-two men, commanded by a sergeant!

News arrives that Charlot has been buried. He's occupying the post closest to the Germans, 5 or 6 metres ahead and to the right of R.1. I go to investigate. A 210 has gouged a shell-hole bang in the middle. Charlot is nearby, still on watch, deathly pale, dusted with earth from top to toe.

'Trying their damnedest to bury you eh, Charlot?'

'It's nothing, sir,' he says, calmly. He smiles his bashful smile.

'Nothing broken?'

'No, sir! My time wasn't up yet. They've just had another go, but I've already seen them off with my grenades.'

---

1. A small fortification approximately 200 metres to our rear, used as a shelter.

6.30 am. The Germans are still climbing the slopes of the Bois Fumin, still untroubled by our guns!

I rush to position a machine gun in the flanking trench above the Redoute, overlooking the Ravin, and tell [Sergeant] Choplain[1] to take eight men. They do what they can, but it's heartbreaking to watch the Boches bringing up reinforcements in broad daylight while our artillery sits on its hands.

In the *boyau* I find Courtonne. He's created his own little sandbag bastion to give himself a better shot at the Boches. Excellent position; splendid field of fire. The bullets, however, whine continually round your ears, like a swarm of wasps. One goes clean through his left forearm. He has the wound dressed, then calmly returns to his bastion.

The Boches are advancing with terrifying speed. The machine gunners, 5th Company – men are reporting in panic from all sides. Alas, I can see it only too well! What now? Send a runner to the colonel? A suicide mission! And the colonel must know what's happening: the attack is taking place right before his eyes.

I decide to send poor Clerc with my report.

Will I ever see him again?

'Don't start back until it's dark.'

That's the only thing I can do for him.

5.00 pm. A note arrives from [Hillère]. 'Literally flattened by heavy shells. Only one platoon commander left. Send me the men from 298th Infantry, all the reinforcements you can.'[2]

The men from 298th Infantry!

These poor lads are like hunted animals. A few more have turned up. Lieutenant [Claude] now has forty-three men. Out of 170! It could be worse though. He only had twenty-five yesterday.

6.00 pm. The shelling starts up again. Our guns are firing at last ... but on our own trenches. Destructive fire. Twice in a day, it's too much. This is even worse than before.

'Launch the green rockets. One illuminating, one green!'

---

1. Small, brown hair, 23 years old. He was promoted sous-lieutenant in 6th Company in June 1916 and killed in the final battles in Champagne (May 1917). Engaged to be married, he was often teased about his sweetheart. A brave soldier, incomparably staunch under fire.
2. He wanted my help, having refused it to me. And mine was the front under attack, not his!

Up go the rockets. The shelling continues.

'Another green rocket.'

'We've run out, sir!'

No more green rockets.

The sharp, fierce crack of our shells is very distinctive, terrifying and demoralizing the men. The shells fall more heavily than ever. The section of trench right of the R.1/Courtine crossroads is completely flattened; every man killed or wounded. Nothing but moans, stretcher-bearers running hither and thither, overwhelmed despite their dedication.

Lévêque appears, gasping, resting briefly against the wall of my HQ. A courageous, decent man. His face is hollow. His eyes, ringed with shadow, are popping from his head. 'That's it, sir! I can't do any more. We only have three stretcher-bearers left: the rest are dead or wounded. I haven't eaten, drunk or had a shit for three days.'

He's so skinny, he can't weigh any more than 50 kilos. I don't know where he gets his energy. People constantly talk about heroes. Here is one. A genuine hero too. He has no Croix de Guerre. He's modest and brave, performs his duty unto death, ignoring the bullets and shells. A hero, all right. But he'll never have gold on his kepi, never give himself airs. Take your hat off to him!

The dreadful shelling continues. Our gunners are bang on target. They're hitting our trench now and I'm out of green rockets. Not one, despite my repeated requests for more. Beneath a low, wooden, sandbag-covered lean-to, Dubuc, Riballier des Isles and I wait for the shell that will finish us off. Our faces are sombre, our guts knotted with fear.

8.00 pm. We're relieved! It's such wonderful news, I refuse to believe it.

Who by? These 'chaps'? They've never thrown a grenade.

'We don't know how. Our corporal does though. He'll show us!'

8.30 pm. Clerc is back from Fumin HQ. One less weight off my shoulders. He looks terrible – scrawny, beard scorched by the fire the other evening.

'It was me who raised the alarm at HQ, sir!'

'Oh!'

'I got there along with the Boches.'[1]

No comment.

---

1. The Boches continued their advance towards the regiment's Fumin HQ (see above).

At 9.30 pm we start the relief, with Lieutenant Claude, CO of 28th Company.

A quiet night. Just a few shells.

11.00 pm. A runner arrives from the colonel: 'Under present circumstances 101st Infantry cannot be relieved.'

Thanks for nothing.

What a let-down for my poor men. Lieutenant Claude is in awe of them. Rightly so. Only thirty-nine remain: but such courage!

A further note is attached: 'Do you still occupy R.1? Do we still occupy the Courtine?'[1]

A momentary lapse amid the most appalling hardships will see an unlucky poilu court-martialled for a bagatelle. But what will happen to commanders who make no effort to reconnoitre their own lines, whose senile funk and criminal apathy condemn their men to the slaughter? They'll be promoted in the Légion d'Honneur.[2]

Monday 5 June

I'd be happy to rest for a while but the lice will have none of it.

The order cancelling the relief means the company still has no water. I despatched a rations party as soon as I received the counter-order, but it isn't back yet. It must have been caught by the daylight. It will still be at Tavannes or in the tunnel.

Luckily it's raining. The men are going to spread out a few tent sections and catch some water.

The terrible thirst is making my throat dry. I'm hungry.[3] Eating monkey and hard tack will only make me thirstier.

'Coffee, sir!'

It's Champion, grasping a steaming mess–tin in both hands. It's coffee right enough. I can't believe my eyes.

---

1. 'Miserable devils!' reads my diary. 'They thought we had surrendered and turned the guns on us.' I later had second thoughts and erased these words. However, my hypothesis was correct. A. notes the comments made by one general on 6 June: "'So be it," he replied, to my objection that our shells might hit our own infantry. "Kill a hundred telephonists a day," he claimed when told we had lost contact with the front lines. "That's the way to maintain communications."'
2. This was indeed what happened.
3. It was four days since I last ate.

'I found some coffee tablets, sir! Just the job, I thought. I'll make some coffee. If I could offer you the first cup.'

Good lads! Again I'm speechless. 'But what about you, my friend? And your chums?'

'There's more where that came from!'

'I can't have a whole cup. A gulp, perhaps.'

'No, no, sir! It's all for you. Here, Vatin,[1] pass me some tin cups. I need this mess-tin.'

I follow orders. I carefully set the cup to one side. It will allow me to eat some hard tack.

'We heated up some monkey, sir! I'd have brought you some but I was worried you'd say no. You told me off this morning.'

It's true. I did reprimand him. He inadvertently started the fire which destroyed our rockets. So when the French guns fired on us this morning – accidentally or otherwise – we had none left. He was in tears, poor lad. But after all!

'I'll make you some tonight! With butter. We found a tin.'

Good lads! Good lads!

The Boches are quieter today. They can afford it. They've made good progress – advancing up to a kilometre in places – and, I must emphasize, without any losses. We watched them calmly descend from the Hardaumont plateau, cross the railway line and the dam, then disappear into the Ravin de la Mort – previously so deadly for us – all without a shot from our guns.

Constant movement up and down Tranchée Sarajevo, parallel to us. They must have deepened the trench to almost 2 metres – the communications *boyau* at least. And what artillery preparation! On their side, science and attention to detail. On ours, the apathy and ignorance of our generals! Not a shot fired by the French guns during the German attack! The reason is plain: no front-line artillery spotters. Half my losses were down to the French artillery, the 'glorious' 75. Bravo!

'The artillery will as ever provide a model of self-sacrifice!' Signed: Nivelle. That isn't what we ask of them. All we want is for them to do their duty and send spotters to the front line as well as to the quiet sectors.[2]

The Germans are settling into the captured positions. We can see them methodically digging in and moving up reinforcements. Meanwhile GQG,

---

1. Drummer.
2. This degree of liaison was regulation after May 1917. General Pétain insisted on it.

which controls the press, has reports printed daily that the German general staff cares nothing for human life. We know whose generals murder their men, and whose spare their troops while sharing none of the danger or fatigue. GQG's communiqué should read: 'The Germans attacked in the Vaux sector. They managed to penetrate one of our forward trenches, suffering huge losses in the process, but were halted by the volume of our fire.'

The relief has been ordered for this evening. I just hope it goes ahead this time.

5.30 pm. Our guns are shelling Retranchements R.2 and R.3.

We will leave our dead in the trench as a reminder. There they are, stiff in their blood-soaked tent sections. I recognize them still: Cosset, in his corduroy trousers; Aumont, poor soul; Delahaye, the red-haired "Bamboula", who extends a waxy hand, so wonderfully adept at grenade-throwing; and many more – fierce, sombre guardians of this corner of French soil, seemingly eager, even in death, to bar it to the enemy.

Holding the trenches west of Fort Vaux is not our only problem. Now we have to get out of here.

The relief to end all reliefs. Departed at 9.00 pm. We couldn't go earlier. First our successors hadn't put enough men at the loopholes, then it was still too light. The narrow track passing in front of the Redoute is covered by the [enemy] machine guns in Retranchement R.2 and we would be silhouetted too clearly in the twilight.

A terrifying march through the darkness to Fumin HQ. Clerc is ahead of me, picking his way from shell-hole to shell-hole. The *boyau* disappears, leaving us to stumble through a no man's land full of shell-holes and dead bodies. It's a nerve-wracking race through the inky blackness, broken by rifle fire, lit only by the rockets that send us ducking for cover and the red flash of the shell-bursts. These gentlemen would happily block our passage. But I'm in no mood for a trip to Baden-Baden.

As my orderly (Laporte) is still not back from battalion HQ, I'm carrying my own pack. I'm out of training. I'm tense with my efforts not to drop it. Fumin HQ has been flattened by the shells, around it a scene of utter carnage. Bodies everywhere, one every five or six paces in Boyau de l'Étang. We march, and march again, colliding with the silent men moving up to the line.

In front of me R[iballier des Isles] is desperate to reach our destination.

'For God's sake get a move on!'

The Boche guns are terrifyingly accurate: a 77 bursts straight ahead of us. Clerc turns round.

'That's what's waiting for us, sir!' he croaks.

We can't see above two paces.

'Good job we've the light from the guns, sir!' shouts one comic.

Now we're bang opposite the French batteries. A succession of deafening claps of thunder and blinding bolts of lightning in the dark. Jumping on top of the parapet, we go down through the wood to the tunnel.

At last! Inside the tunnel. We can breathe again. Alongside me are R[iballier des Isles] and seven men!

Only when saying: 'Captain, 8th Company, Retranchement R.1', do I grasp the full horror of our previous situation.

We're greeted as survivors. We're offered something to drink. The brigadier gets up and walks towards me, escorted by Consul and [Vinerot]. His long face is strained. He stammers out some confused apologies. He's been stuck in the tunnel for the past three weeks. I can't decide what worried him more: his fate or our own. I reckon his greatest fear was that one fine day the flat-hats would appear at both ends of the tunnel.

We set off again in the darkness, following the railway line. The woods here are intact, so branches are brushing us in the face, but we can stop worrying about the shells and chatter can once more be heard.

'How about you, Delvert?' asks Consul. 'Were you hit by our 75s?'

'I came under heavy French fire on Sunday evening, sir! You'd have thought R.1 was in enemy hands.'

'If you *had* surrendered R.1,[1] I'd have had you court-martialled,' he snapped back. 'I would have broken you.'

Poor fellow! He's already forgotten his own criminal panic, his total ignorance of his sector. He's forgotten that I never clapped eyes on him at R.1 or Les Fontaines. He's forgotten the blood on his hands: Biancardini,[2] Leroy, the brave men of 6th Company – their deaths all his fearful responsibility.

Our guide loses us crossing the wooded slopes that separate us from Belrupt. At last we spot Chevert Barracks and the road. We've arrived. Our suffering is over. Dawn is breaking.

---

1. As had been suggested by the inaccurate report of 2 June.
2. 'It was me who got Biancardini killed,' he kept saying as we came out of the lines. 'It was me.'

Tuesday 6 June

Consul never shuts up about the horror of the Batterie; his HQ crammed with the wounded, full of blood; he and [Vinerot] huddled in a corner, unable to stretch out their legs, receiving reports and 'giving orders' amid the moans and groans. What orders? I certainly never received any. The wounded were jamming his HQ? But who caused the massacre, put 6th Company so gratuitously through the mincer?

Now his sole concern is to sing his own praises to ensure he receives the rosette of an officer of the Légion d'Honneur!

At Belrupt, we're greeted as survivors by the colonel and his staff. Hugs and congratulations all round.[1]

We're exhausted. So what is our accommodation like? The men are parked on rotten straw. Absolutely foul. The bed found for me has broken springs that dig me in the ribs. Sleeping on the ground is marginally more comfortable.

At Belrupt men march by all day – zouaves, tirailleurs, colonials – all worse for drink, all talking about fighting to the finish. Poor lads! I wonder how many will be dead within the next few hours? It's endless bloody madness, an incessant stream of human fodder tossed into the maw of the guns. GQG knows of nothing else. And yet the instruction of 15 January 1916 solemnly decrees: 'Men should never be pitted against matériel.'[2]

Wednesday 7 June

A comic interlude.

[Hillère], who was CO at the Courtine, who had to be dragged by the ear to provide an outpost beyond the R.1/Courtine crossroads, and did so only on the express orders of [Captain] Susini, now claims to have played an equal part in defending Retranchement R.1.[3]

That sums up the attitude of some soldiers. When it's time to stand up and be counted, some officers disappear. If an affair succeeds beyond all expectations, even the most ... cautious claim to have participated.

'I held the eastern end of R.1, sir! Delvert occupied the west!'

---

1. 'Good to see you, R.1,' said General T[atin]. 'The eyes of the world have been upon you over the last five days ... You have been awarded the Légion d'Honneur.' This took me by surprise. Of course I had no idea of the award made on 2 June.
2. Especially men who are drunk.
3. In the heat of battle, rather than offer assistance as military duty demands, he had shamelessly disclaimed all responsibility for the defence of R.1 (see above).

I was completely dumbfounded. What a cheek! Still, I think General T[atin] saw through it.[1]

The best was yet to come.

At 2.00 pm [Vinerot] turned up. He'd come to write a report on the conduct of the battalion. Consul is eager for the battalion to take centre stage, so [Vinerot] will produce a short fiction that earns the CO his rosette. It's as simple as that.

Quite nauseating, these battlefield vampires.

Thursday 8 June

At 3.00 am, Major Fralon, S. and I leave to reconnoitre a trench we're planning to dig tonight south of Tavannes.

The water in the only *boyau* leading to Tavannes is 50 centimetres deep in places. We complete our reconnaissance and set off back, passing before the batteries left of Chevert Barracks, then up the hill – a green lane awash in buttercups and wild mustard. The countryside is lovely hereabouts: rolling hills covered in woods, villages nestling in the valley bottoms, clustered around their church tower like sheep around their shepherd.

The continual thunder of the guns brings us down to earth.

7.00 pm. The working party leaves in torrential rain.

The men do splendidly.

They dig the trench in two hours flat. Ten men from the so-called Engineers turn up to fix some barbed wire. They disappear somewhere to have a lie-down. When we leave, still no barbed wire. We're not surprised. We've seen no officer there to supervise.

Setting off this morning to reconnoitre for tonight's working party, I saw a superb *boyau* marked on the map. Two clear red lines.

'Where's this *boyau*, corporal?'

'It starts higher up, sir. This last section only exists on paper.'

We struggle back in the early hours, in the rain, across slopes slick with mud. Two steps forward, one step back. We reach Belrupt at 3.30 am. [Châtenet], the sergeant-clerk, appears.[2] The regiment has moved overnight. It's gone to Haudainville!

---

1. The general sent him packing.
2. A model of the type.

Come on! We'll have to wait. It's teeming down. And Zidore has a friction burn. He'd get me there, but it really is too much. My poor men have spent three weeks in the front line. They still haven't been given an hour's rest. They've had enough.

Friday 9 June

The zouaves and the colonials aren't up to much. Quite a few dropped out even before reaching the front lines. We passed some as we headed towards Boyau Altkirch yesterday. They weren't wounded: they had left their companies and were ambling back. On their first day in the sector!

Here at Haudainville they are all over the place already.

'Well, if it isn't the man who defended R.1,' says General Tatin. 'You're the talk of the corps.'

Saturday 10 June

Returning to work this evening, under the orders of Major de Benoit. I needed 2,000 sandbags, but the Engineers only brought me 1,000! They're white, too! White as snow! I've done what I can to camouflage them with soil. But honestly it's enough to try the patience of a saint.

Three ne'er-do-wells were loitering in the *boyau*, hands in pockets.

'What are you lot up to?

'We're from Nth Engineers.'

'Ah! And what are you doing here?'

'Putting in stakes,' said their spokesman, in a heavy southern accent.

'Putting in stakes? In the trench?'

'In front of it. But there are shells falling.'

True enough, I suppose, though they are 200 or 300 metres away. There'll be no more barbed wire fixed today than before.

Major de Benoit is a splendid fellow. We came back at 4.00 am for a bit of a rest. He talked interestingly and eruditely about Reims cathedral and the role of the cavalry at different points in military history; none of which detracts from his merits as a soldier.

Sunday 11 June

According to [Hillère], the battery of 75s near where we've been working has been destroyed. The lieutenant in command also says that his requirement is in raptures over one sous-lieutenant daring to spend four days ... at Fumin HQ! We still have no spotters in the front line! We send up signal rockets, but the battery CO lacks the authority to order a barrage. He has to await orders from his group commander, who takes his orders from regimental HQ, where the signallers observing the rockets are based. Using their information, orders are passed to the group CO, who gives orders to the battery CO, who gives orders to the individual guns.

Furthermore, none of the batteries has a dedicated sector. They fire in all directions.

After all that, is it any surprise that our 75s pose more of a threat to the French infantry than to the Germans?

The Russians seem to be advancing in Galicia.[1] Will their offensive be a success? And apparently the English fleet has trounced the Germans.[2] If the Allies are to have good conditions to conduct their offensives, we must hold on to Verdun at any price.

This is the critical moment of the war.[3]

Monday 12 June

My men were at work again last night. We rounded everyone up – orderlies and stretcher-bearers included – leaving behind just three cooks per company. Even then I could only scrape together ... thirty-seven men! They're all I have left.

We really are at the end of our tether. A rest! A rest!

The weather has turned colder, with endless downpours. Verdant countryside here alongside the Canal de la Meuse. But for the leprous barracks dotting the greenery, it would all be quite charming.

I feel dazed by our recent experiences. My brain is numb. I can't think. A lead weight is pressing down on me. Apparently we're going to the Haute-Marne, south of Saint-Dizier. A land of forests and greenery. I hope we'll be left in peace for at least a week.

While I was out riding this evening I bumped into old S. This decent man was still tipsy. Until now, he's probably been a model husband and father, but the war is turning him into a boozer. He needs his 'better half' to keep an eye on him. Without her, he's going off the rails.

Tuesday 13 June

Battles as long and as terrible as this definitely take their toll on the nerves. I'm still finding it hard to sleep, for example.

1. The Brusilov offensive.
2. The battle of Jutland.
3. Correct. Sadly, the Russians imploded in 1917.

The weather is awful. It's raining. The men are wallowing in mud. It's depressing. We wait impatiently for the lorries to take us away.

The Germans launched their latest attack at Verdun at the perfect time of year. The nights are at their shortest, leaving us with the least amount of time to do the work required. They're practical men, our opponents. Not dreamers!

The weather is grey and miserable. It's been raining since this morning. The first letters have arrived from the mothers of my dear departed. Oh, the sorrow contained in these clumsily penned sheets! To improve her chance of a reply, one mother includes some writing paper and an envelope. Another commends her letter, and her son, to God. I can see him in the front line, near the crossroads, covered in blood, forehead holed by a bullet, turning blue already. Poor woman! What savages are these Boches with their cult of war! Like Wagner, who has erected so 'colossal' a shrine in its honour. If they're that keen to enter Valhalla, let them fight between themselves.

Today I re-read Albert Samain's poem, *In the Garden of the Infanta*. Re-read? It's so long since I first came across it that it seems quite fresh to me. Dreamy, voluptuous, languid verse. The verse of a lost age, two decades past, of a generation that basked in its gentle, amorous, enigmatic ambience – occasionally a little too subtle, but rare and full of charm. How distant it all seems! How dated! But it prompts all kinds of unsettling memories. The happiness of early youth, the confused hopes of adolescence, much-cherished landscapes – the banks of the Seine as I walk home in the evening from the Hôtel de Ville, the river gilded by the setting sun, the tall towers of the old cathedral enveloped in the gentle purple dusk. The beautiful dreams of far-off days also return to me, like white-draped muses bathed in golden mist. Dreams that echo harmoniously in:

> ... *Ce coeur d'ombre chaste embaumé de mystère* / ... This pure shadowed heart in mystery shrouded
> *Où veille comme le rubis d'un lampadaire,* / Where burns night and day
> *Nuit et jour, un amour mystique et solitaire.* / The forlorn red flame of love.

A turbulent world, which I believed dead and buried, in fact lay dormant deep within my soul.

Wednesday 14 June
Rain, mud. The sky is grey and cold.

Troops are still passing, poured as if by a giant hand into a pitiless machine that kills, wounds, mutilates and grinds, reducing their bodies to an anonymous heap of mud and gore.

Monsieur Aulard continues to grace the *Journal* with his historical essays. Today he expounds on coalitions: disagreements among the enemies of Frederick II led to their defeat in the Seven Years' War, while the harmony that reigned among Napoleon's opponents resulted in their triumph. Let us therefore emulate the latter.

Exactly what you would expect from a good pupil who pays attention to his learned master!

I suspect that every Ally, without exception, would prefer the means to acquire a heavy field artillery equal in number and mobility to the Boche 105s, 150s and 210s. The 210s in particular. These basic truths are rather out of fashion at the moment. Yet, however united the Allies may be, they will never defeat the Germans without a gun to match the 210.

And what about this gem regarding Fort Vaux? 'Official sources state that communication between Retranchement [R.1.] and the rear was prevented by a lack of *boyaux*. This is not the case. On the contrary, there were lots of *boyaux*, but they had been destroyed by the terrible shelling.'

The 'terrible shelling' had no trouble flattening *boyaux* that did not exist.

Thursday 15 June
I'm sharing a room with Rouzeaud and Cardin. [Corporal] Hubert Walter came in around midnight. I won't say he woke us because nobody is sleeping too well.

We're leaving at 8.00 am tomorrow. The baggage will go at 5.00 am.

Great sorrows are silent. Great joys too.

We burrow under the covers to try to enjoy our last few hours of rest, but I'm pretty sure none of us slept. We're all up and doing by 4.00 am. Our windows look down on the barn occupied by the men, and when I pull back the curtain I can see they're ready too.

Depart at 8.00 am. As a final precaution, the companies leave 200 metres apart.

The weather is overcast. We leave Verdun in mist and rain, the companies reduced to a mere handful of men.

Major de Benoit rides beside me for a while. He visited his family home in Verdun three days ago. It was evacuated on 21 February 1916. Since then it has been ransacked from top to bottom, drawers overturned, cupboards emptied, no lock left unforced.

It reminds me of our billet in Belrupt.

As looters, French troops bow to no one.

We push on to Lempire and arrive around noon. The vehicles are waiting. Already it feels like the rear. 'Things are going to change at Verdun,' says a transport officer, clean shaven in the English fashion, sporting a gold-rimmed monocle. 'Dumesnil, the deputy, is back at the front. We drove him there. He's been away for the past few months, but now he's back as a sous-lieutenant commanding a platoon. Joffre could be for the chop.'

I find it hard to see what difference Monsieur Dumesnil's presence will make. A spell in Tranchée Fumin or Boyau Sundgau would be most informative, though. He could give the Chamber precise details of the set-up in the Verdun sector.

With the lieutenant at the wheel, S. and I zoom along the main road.

Bar-le-Duc. What a feeling to see a town again – pavements, civilians, women! I feel drunk with it all. I clearly need time for my nerves to recover.

We arrive at our billet in Fontaine-sur-Marne around 5.00 pm. A pretty village, built around a square, in a valley circled by wooded hills. My men are billeted in three barns at a mill some distance away. Running water nearby. Meadows to lie down in. All green. My poor men will have the chance for a proper rest here.

'No soldier who comes here ever wants to leave,' says the woman who welcomes me.

I'm billeted with a spinster of 50 or so. A lovely house with a garden in front. My pretty first-floor room gets the morning sun. The wallpaper is fresh and bright. And when I return from settling my men, a good fairy has made the bed with crisp white sheets. I can't believe my eyes. After so much hardship, I can't describe how I feel when I see this charming, private guest room, where wooden floor, cupboard and chairs all shine. Let fate lead us where it will. Everything comes to he who waits.

Friday 16 June.
This area is truly delightful. We're in the upper Marne valley, between Wassy and Saint-Dizier. Pasture, wheatfields and gardens, all set amid wooded hills. A rolling, varied landscape, cool and fresh.

The weather is fine once again. I walk through Sommeville and Rachecourt, where a pile of steel cubes in the factory yard waits to be turned into shells. Then I climb the hill overlooking the village from the west. The road climbs between dense copses, treetops gilded by the sun and pierced by the azure blue of the sky. The light slips between the branches, caressing blades of grass that sparkle with the dew. All around me is the sound of birdsong.

Côte de Souville and Côte de l'Étang de Vaux must have looked like this before their fauna and flora were blighted for ever. And the hilltops, desolate and bare, their once-luxuriant mantle of trees reduced to a few black pickets and stumps, the bodies, the overlapping shell-holes return to me in all their horror.

The brutes! The brutes!

Say that mankind is suffering the tyranny of its lowest elements, of those whose animal instincts have remained the most stubborn, whose souls, tormented centuries long, may never achieve salvation.

Ariel and Caliban.

Behold the games of Caliban. He is happy now, his heart must swell with joy. He has done good work. Where creation once ushered in all the splendour of spring, joyously clothing Mother Earth with trees, their supple branches and rich canopy of leaves reaching for the light, with brambles, flowers and grasses, where Ariel taught the birds their gladdest song and men their sweetest harmonies, Caliban has despatched – with perfect aim, I must own – hellish weapons of every calibre.

He has created a desert – a horrible, bloody desert. He is content.

The trees sway gently in the breeze. Between them red roofs are visible, a bright note amid the foliage. The village seems to huddle around its church, nestling in the greenery.

Sunday 18 June

Ride to Joinville. A very pleasant road along the river between high, wooded hills.

The fields are green. A poppy. In my mind I see Coutable rushing to the aid post, head streaming with blood.

Joinville is a pretty place. Undoubtedly prosperous. Lots of women in mourning dress.

Tuesday 20 June

A medals ceremony.

Splendid weather, cool and sunny.

The faded old greatcoats are a stirring sight. As are the soldiers within, stepping out, helmets tilted to one side, rifles on their shoulders, bayonets glinting.

An unforgettable impression of force.

Wednesday 21 June

At Cousances-aux-Forges.

Bombing course until Saturday 24 June. Met my monocled major again.

Sunday 25 June

Returned by night to Dommartin-sur-Yèvre.[1] The company has been disbanded.

From Dommartin to Varimont.

Tuesday 27 June

Left on horseback at 4.30 pm. Arrived at Givry at 5.00 pm. Reached Revigny at 6.00 pm. Left at 11.00 pm. Paris until Sunday 2 July.

---

1. Each infantry battalion had just been cut from four companies to three. My company was to be disbanded and its remaining men distributed between the rest. The news reached my poor soldiers just as the food arrived. No one could eat. Many were crying. Combatants within a given unit developed very strong bonds. But our good colonel allowed me to take my brave handful of survivors – Charlot, Clerc, Mouquet, etc. – into my new 1st Company, along with my two excellent sous-lieutenants, Riballier des Isles and Rouzeaud, who sadly were later both killed on the same day at Moronvilliers in August 1917. We also rejoiced in a new battalion CO. 'I don't think you'll miss the one you're leaving behind,' said the colonel, who shared my low opinion of [Consul]. The old misery had caused him endless trouble over the previous few days, disrupting the entire barracks. The brave Major Fralon, CO of 1st Battalion – who I will mention again – was a perfect gentleman and a remarkable officer.

Book Three

In a Quiet Sector

Monday 3 July
Ville-sur-Tourbe.

I returned from leave this evening. We're back in Champagne and our old stamping ground at Braux-Sainte-Cohière. It's hard returning to duty after a few days in Paris, especially with the rats rampaging night and day through the two big cupboards at the rear of my quarters – formerly occupied by the officers of 8th Company.

The countryside is green right now. The corn is high, but most of the land lies fallow.

It bucketed down all day. The billets are disgusting. The hussars next door are as slovenly as the gunners. And for exactly the same reason – their officers are lax.

I spent all day writing to the relatives of the dead, wounded and missing from 8th Company. What sorrow!

Still, I see from the citation (18 June) in the letter book that Consul has been appointed an officer of the Légion d'Honneur.[1]

Tuesday 4 July
I couldn't sleep a wink last night for the rats.

Still pouring with rain.

Relieved this evening.

We leave at 8.30 pm. An interminable trek through the darkness via Côte 181. We march nose to tail through clinging mud for five long hours, slipping with each step, sometimes going in up to our knees. No marked path, fatigue compounded by uncertainty. Endless halts because the men have stopped following. Unsure where we are putting our feet. Unable to see beyond 5 metres. The shells start bursting all around us. After almost a month away I'd grown used to their absence. A rude reawakening. To compound matters I'm out on my feet.

---

1. As expected. 'I love honours,' he would say.

I think of life in Paris, of a pal of mine, in blooming good health, quietly earning his 7½ francs a day, making ... and grumbling. If he had to spend all night ploughing through mud, his moans would be audible from here.

Arrived at 1.45 am.

Wednesday 5 July

Our Verdun sector was completely bare – not a blade of grass. Here, the vegetation is lush. Tall grasses and golden yellow flowers tumble into the *boyaux*. A complete change of decor.

My company is occupying Sector A of the Ouvrage Pruneau, left of the Vouziers road, where the trees are in full leaf.

Obviously, we're not at Verdun.

I have five outposts, including three in mine craters. The largest of the craters is perhaps 35 to 40 metres wide, and each contains a pool of stagnant water in the bottom. Two or three metres below the northern rim runs a path with niches for a couple of sentries.

Ahead we have barbed wire.

Rendering a position impregnable, barbed wire is the key factor in this war. A single sniper behind an intact, or virtually intact, entanglement can stop a half-platoon. And to think how little we knew about this type of defence before the war. No one ever mentioned it during the famous September manoeuvres, such a waste of time and money. Foolishly, we relied upon the bluster of First Empire veterans who had forgotten over time that terror is the dominant emotion on the battlefield. The better that men are protected, the better they fight.[1] Adhering to this maxim is what has allowed the Germans to retain the advantage for so long.

At 5.00 pm our 75s shell the trench opposite. The Germans reply with their *Minenwerfer*. These Minnies, or mortar bombs, arrive in pairs, with a terrifying crack. The shock wave hits us in the shelters, extinguishing all the candles. A perfect reintroduction to the German artillery. The men call them 'slop buckets' due to their size. They zoom over with a much louder crack than the 210. They

---

1. Vauban had already spotted this, even though contemporary firearms were much less powerful than their modern equivalents: 'A man in a trench is worth six fighting in the open'.

don't penetrate too deeply, but one explosion can destroy a 10- or 15-metre stretch of trench or *boyau*.

The [Somme] offensive is under way and the early signs look promising. But it's clear the British aren't advancing as quickly as we are. Will it get as far as Péronne?

Thursday 6 July

Spend the night patrolling the *boyaux*, checking that everyone is on the alert. No. 5 Post is just 7 or 8 metres from Fritz. Some of the *boyaux* are canals. Most are full of mud. 'Slap, slap,' go your footsteps, and the normally peaceable Fritz grabs the chance to lob across a few wicked rifle grenades.

The lack of sleep is awful. My head feels like lead, as if in a vice. My nerves are on edge. There's nothing worse. I'm starting to understand why sleep deprivation is such an exquisite form of torture. And that's what we're subject to here.

I was counting on a nap this morning. Instead, a constant stream of visitors and telephone calls. I had to resign myself to it. As the sun was peeping through, I thought a couple of songs might help cheer me up a bit – to the bemusement of two telephonists unaccustomed to hearing their CO break into a snatch of Puccini or Saint-Saëns.

Bombardment at 6.30 pm. Dreadful reply from the Minnies. It's routine.

It's raining again, just for a change.

Inspecting the posts at night is no picnic. The mud is deep enough in places for a spade to go in up to the handle, forcing you into a balancing act, legs akimbo, along the parapet.[1]

It's pouring down. The sodden grass dangling into the *boyaux* whips you in the face. You slither through a mudbath, while Fritz sends over rifle grenades that explode with an evil whine.

And sleep is impossible.

Back in the dug-out, life is an interminable round of fatigues, telephone calls, the runner from the right, from Susini[2] on the left. A report to finish, then at midnight a shell. You must be ready for any alert. The candle stays lit. You yawn blearily. You can't sleep or gather your wits. What a life!

---

1. To avoid sinking in.
2. The captain in command of 2nd Company.

Friday 7 July
Rained all day. Gloomy grey skies. I toured the *boyaux*. Nothing to bail out the water.

5.00 pm. R[iballier] des Isles walks solemnly into my dug-out. The daily bombardment is about to begin. Our 75s start things off. The Boches respond with their 'slop buckets'. Not the prettiest of expressions but it gives a fair idea of their size. Our 75s are hammering on the door opposite. A great roar fills the air. 'Crrack!' comes the reply. The noise is terrific – as bad as a 280. The dug-out rocks, fills with smoke. The shock wave hits me and puts out the candle. That'll save a franc or two! I shift the table closer to the door, not to climb out but to be nearer the light.

The explosions continue. The Boches must have it in for every *boyau* and trench in this part of the sector. We're all getting our fair share.

And unfortunately I'm starving.

It's exactly 6.20 pm, the time when the orderlies normally bring up our food. They must have sought shelter. Anyone in their shoes would do the same. What time will we end up eating? We might as well have stayed at Verdun … Bloody Fritz! Two crates of grenades for him in the morning, at least. A cold dinner for us, a cooked breakfast for him. And a lump of sugar in his coffee[1] …

Eh? What? Who's this on the steps?

Heavens! It's Mouquet.

'Mouquet! Is that you?'[2]

'Yes, sir.'

'Didn't you take cover while they were shelling?'

'From the rain, perhaps. Not the Minnies.'

'Where were they falling?'

'Fifty or sixty metres away. I wasn't in any danger.'

It would be poor form to press the point.

Grope around in the inky blackness. A 20-metre stretch of Tranchée 22 has been completely flattened. Boyau Blanc, the same, just beyond [Riballier's] dug-out. And the surviving stretch of Tranchée 21 is now just a memory.

---

1. This was how we kept the Boches quiet in a sector. Effectively, too.
2. One of my orderlies. Extremely brave (see above). I had made him my orderly after Verdun. The orderly in wartime is nothing like his peacetime equivalent. He is your right-hand man, someone to be trusted with the most delicate of tasks.

They do good work, these Minnies.

Excellent tactics, too. We have to work all night repairing the damage inflicted during the day. It's the ideal way to stop us making any improvements in the sector.

Saturday 8 July.

Still raining. Tired as ever. Our task here is very tough on the men. My sector runs in a semi-circle from the Vouziers road to D.14 – in other words, I have around 100 rifles to defend 500 metres of front line.

We are struggling to bear the burden inflicted on us by the failings of our leaders, military and political. On every front – Ethe, the Marne, Perthes and Verdun – they have squandered human lives, using men to replace the matériel denied us by their ignorance and greed.[1]

And now we're running out of men.

The way the regiment has been rebuilt after the carnage of Verdun is very shabby. One company per battalion has been disbanded and its men divided among those remaining. A neat way of providing reinforcements! Men have arrived from the class of 1916 – 100 for the whole regiment! Finally, more men have been dispatched from the depot – perhaps 150 at most, including NCOs! And this handful includes plenty of scrapings from the bottom of the barrel: the dozen or so who have joined my company include a man from the class of 1900, wounded three times already, one from the class of 1896, and six fine black Martiniquais, here to shiver in our trenches. Poor beggars!

We're clearly on our last legs. So the Germans must be really surprised by our magnificent performance on the Somme. They would never have thought us capable of such vigorous action after the slaughter at Verdun. How did the general staff contrive this miracle? Quite simply by treating all sixty divisions transferred from Verdun exactly like our own. In other words, allowing them no rest whatsoever, returning them straight to the front line, and despatching one meagre regiment to occupy the frontage of a division. The contemporary French army reminds me of the fading beauty heading for a night on the town: 'What matter if I die tomorrow as long as I look beautiful tonight.'

We must at all costs hold on for another six to eight months. If the men grumble about fatigue and lack of sleep, hard luck.

---

1. 'The greed of our leaders' is a little unfair. It was the Artillery Staff that rejected the idea of heavy guns, but we didn't know it at the time.

On the needless waste of human life, I have some choice information from our new sous-lieutenant, Bouillet. He was at Perthes and has told us what went on there.

On 25 February [1915], the regiment went into the trenches after three months at rest. They knew their objective – a line of trenches 15 to 20 metres from our own. The companies were at full strength and morale was good. All the men were singing as they left Suippes. The attack was ordered for noon. Artillery preparation was limited to some twenty rounds from the 120s and a few salvos from the 75s ... which landed in our trenches. Consequently there was only one breach in the enemy barbed wire. Yet at noon every member of Adjudant Bouillet's company left the trench magnificently.

The major rushed up in a panic. 'Stop! Stop!' he shouted. 'The attack has been put back by an hour.'

Exactly 127 men had already fallen, including 70 dead.

The survivors then received orders to attack again! On four subsequent occasions!

On 28 February came a new order to attack: 'The 101st will not be relieved until the trench is taken. Signed: J.-B. Dumas.'[1]

---

1. Dubbed 'the Butcher of Perthes'. Colonel Lebaud dates the first attack to 26 February, not 25 February. The regiment paraded past him, then he galloped the full length of the column to take his place at its head. 'I heard the kind of dry soldiers' wit that gave me the most positive impression of morale among these brave men. And all the regiments in IV Corps were certainly the equal of the 101st. With such splendid troops, great deeds were possible!' (Lebaud, p. 165.) The colonel's diary reveals another minor error in Sous-lieutenant Bouillet's account: the attack took place at 1.00 pm, not noon. Complete agreement on morale among the troops. The colonel's detailed description of the preparation prior to the attack is enough to make you blench. Just one machine gun was used to cut the enemy wire! Were the generals really so ignorant of trenches? And what about using 'scaling ladders' as at Zaragoza? Imagine those poor souls dragging their ladders across no man's land under machine-gun fire. These magnificent troops (all the survivors say the regiment had never looked as fine) were needlessly killed. Can it really be true that not one general had ever set foot in the front line here – flouting their most elementary military duty? And that not one of the guilty men was ever court-martialled and shot? The colonel also confirms the episode of the company slaughtered before the counter-order arrived. Like the attacks of December 1914, and those at Vauquois and Les Éparges, Perthes (25/26/28 February 1915) must rank among the offensives so aptly characterized as 'unforgivable' by Jean Bernier (*La Percée*).

Et voilà! That's all there is to it. The art of war reduced to the bayonet charge. 'Rosalie' is surely *the* French weapon. Its praises sung in all the café-concert nonsense.

Methodical artillery preparation, my eye!

'The 101st will not be relieved until the trench is taken!'

'At bayonet-point, sir!'

That's much more straightforward. Perhaps rather too much so.

Sunday, 9 July

Glorious sunshine.

A beautiful summer morning. The birds are singing and so too the shells. The gunners are firing too short, just as they did at Verdun.

General Tatin has prescribed that, 'in compliance with repeated orders', the fall of shells in the front line should be observed by both an infantry officer *and* an artillery officer.

Bombardment at 6.00 pm. No sign of an artillery officer.

9.00 pm. Hit by a rifle grenade at No. 2 HQ. Wounded in my right hand and near my eye.[1]

Monday 10 July

This evening the Germans minnied No. 4 and No. 5 Posts, the two closest to them. Colossal impact.

In fading light I go to check.

Tranchée 22 has collapsed in three places. I'm walking in the open. I pass the crossroads [and] the *boyau* leading to No. 5 Post. No one around; completely deserted. The Ravin des Tombes, where the colonials are buried, is empty too. I enter the *boyau*. Within scarcely 20 metres what a sight! Everything has fallen in. And the Germans here are only 10 metres away. The outpost – two separate bays linked by an open passage – has gone. All that remains is a patch of ravaged earth. They certainly know how to use matériel! How many Minnies did they need? Five or six at most.

I move forward. In a surviving stub of *boyau* leading to the right-hand bay, I find Sergeant Pelletier and Corporal Bourdeau. Pelletier has apparently been

---

1. I had the shrapnel removed and carried on.

knocked out. Bourdeau is distraught, muttering that the men are in the sap. The left-hand bay has been demolished, sandbags all over the place. Exactly the same scene at No. 4 Post. The firing trench, so painfully constructed, has been flattened. The post has virtually collapsed. The lintel was laden with sandbags and it has almost cracked clean through.

The men have fled.

If the Germans attacked now, what sort of resistance could we put up?

They certainly have no one in front of us.

Matériel! Matériel!

The nights are too short to repair this much damage. I ask for reinforcements and get twenty men from 9th Company, dog tired, dead beat, out on their feet. They've been hard at it since 8.00 am, shifting logs, duckboards and grenades all over the sector.

Just one reserve company to cover 1.5 kilometres of front line!

Tuesday 11 July

5.00 pm. The approach of a Boche Minnie is a terrifying experience. A monstrous, heart-stopping roar, then the deafening crack of the explosion. The whole ground shakes. Pitting our 75s against these enormous footballs is like David battling Goliath. The Minnie appears with the speed of a knock-out punch, offering an irresistible invitation to get down ... and stay down.

Arthur[1] replies to every round.

'Zee, zeee,' he whines, like a yappy little dog.

A trench raid by a party from 124th Infantry is planned for tonight. The 'minor undertaking' has been discussed by division, brigade and regiment for the past week. I don't know the Lieutenant Chardonneau who is supposedly in command, but we think the name is dreadful. It's no 'minor undertaking' when he and his fifty men are risking their lives in a completely pointless operation, announced far too prematurely. The password is no better: 'No fuss'. It's enough to make you squirm. Picking a password like 'No fuss' is no job for some staff officer. A password belongs exclusively to the men.

A poilu involved in the 'minor undertaking' came to the telephonists' dug-out to say goodbye to his chums. According to him, there are only five volunteers among the fifty men taking part. He's a Meudon lad, and his friends also hail from those parts.

---

1. A nickname for the 75.

'Do you know a lass called Georgette?'

'Big Georgette? Your wife, is she?'

'Yes. Say hello next time you're on leave.'

'So you're Georgette's husband. Do you know my sister Alice?'

'Little Alice! Paul Meyer's sweetheart?'

'That's the one!'

''Cos there's a Paul Meyer and a Jules Meyer!'

'She's Paul's girl!'

'So Alice is your sister, eh! ... It reminds me of that trip to Boulogne, lads. Didn't we end up in bother!'

'Damn, I can't wait to go on leave.'

'Well, when you do, don't forget about Georgette.'

'Don't worry! Good as done! Say, let us know if you're wounded tomorrow. Tell us which hospital you're in.'

'Will do! So long then, chum.'

'So long!'

Now there's a man entitled, if he so wishes, to pick a password like 'No fuss'![1]

Wednesday 12 July

1.00 am. Stand to. Mouquet and I tour the posts. Everyone is on the alert.

The Boches know something is brewing. They've been sending up a stream of illuminating rockets near the craters to the west, the planned target of the 'minor undertaking'. We've been talking about it for ever! And their microphones are excellent! They've been opening up thirty minutes to an hour before our artillery for the past three days. It's no coincidence.

Cloudy sky. No stars, but not pitch black – just the normal semi-darkness of a summer night. In the *boyau*, glow-worms are shining at my feet. It reminds me of a song by [Paul] Delmet, *I'll put glow-worms in your hair*. Oh, the distant land evoked by this sweet melody! Montmartre, the cabarets, Legay, Delmet, true poets who conjure up a dreamscape that lends a poignant charm to the modest products of their muse ...

---

1. This dialogue reveals all the stark heroism of the 'rank and file'. A man goes to say goodbye to his chums before the 'minor undertaking'. The telephonists are in the shelter. They know they will survive. He is going to risk his life. He asks them to convey a last greeting to his wife. No grand words. Such is their understanding that the telephonist can mention the possibility of a wound, the salvation craved by all front-line infantrymen. Re-reading this dialogue between working-class men from the Paris *faubourgs* shows the degree of sensitivity hidden behind their normal banter.

Mouquet and I return to our HQ. All we can do is wait. A book is lying on the table: *The Confessions of Jean-Jacques Rousseau*. What a charmer! I come across his time as secretary to Monsieur de Montaigu, the French ambassador in Venice. Some passages are priceless. The ambassador writes his replies on a Thursday to letters that won't reach him until Friday, so there'll be time to encrypt them before the courier leaves again on Saturday! And Rousseau, despite his ambitions in that direction, was obviously not cut out for the diplomatic service.

All in all he was a sorry fellow. Could anything be more pathetic than his affair with Thérèse Levasseur? He was 30 at the time! Falling for a waitress in a Latin Quarter *pension* who divided her favours among all the regulars. It's not hard to guess what happened. His thirty years were excited by her buxom twenty-two. A sordid little episode, nothing to boast about. He was foolish to make so much of it.

You feel somehow that he knows this, but he's like a toddler determined to have his own way. Poor chap, you do feel rather sorry for him. He spouts such drivel, cooing over his inane conquest. Stranger still is the hold he has exerted over several generations. He's become something of a symbol, several groups claiming him as their own. Many of his admirers have never actually read him. Yet he has achieved enormous – and lasting – influence. Very odd. A pathetic creature, soon alienated from society, yet he becomes a demi-god!

Then there's his sudden espousal of virtue. 'I considered myself a member of the Republic of Plato.' Because he abandoned his children! That's a bit rich! And just imagine, Voltaire apart, no one ever made fun of the blighter. The need to find heroes to worship must indeed be deeply rooted within the human psyche for men to raise altars to so singular an apostle. Nowadays you'd find him in the pages of *Le Rire* or *Fantasio*.

3.00 am. The French artillery opens fire.[1] By the first pale light of dawn the green and red rockets soar into the sky. Our 75s are making an infernal din. Our neighbours opposite must be getting a hell of a pasting.

3.11 am. The reply. A shell falls near my HQ.

3.14 am. The first Minnie. Not a small one, either. The gunfire crackles right along the line. The dreadful crack of the Minnies is making my ears ring.

---

1. The start of the 'minor undertaking'.

3.42 am. A lull.

4.00 am. That's it.

I counted fifty-five Minnies falling around our HQ, after the first struck behind and to our right at 3.14 am. A 15-metre stretch of Tranchée 22 has been destroyed. At No. 5 Post the scene is the same as Monday night. Everything flattened. Impossible to make out the shelters. Not a single living thing. The men must be in the sap. Then, from a hole amid the desolation – the northern bay of the post – emerge the haggard features of the indomitable Bourdeau.

Now the sun is blazing down. The remaining stubs of *boyau* are draped with yellow flowers, cornflowers, tuberose, poppies, long blades of grass that whip you in the face. From the silence of this radiant summer's morn comes the sound of birdsong.

And I wonder how many lives the 'minor undertaking' has cost us.

Thursday, 13 July

Rained all day. Another year of this, I keep thinking, perhaps more. Slogging through the mud in search of death!

On these dreary grey days, relieved only by the fussy minutiae of military life, you can understand 'the blues'. No rest, no relaxation, never a moment to settle your nerves.[1] Letters from the rear seem full of dull banter. 'Try not to get wounded!' says one. As if I can do anything about that! 'The war is affecting us too,' reads another. How exactly? Good God! His sheets aren't properly worn in. Try wrapping yourself in a tent section and sleeping fully clothed like me!

Everyone grumbles that the war is going on too long. They all want us to advance towards some point or other. Try coming out here! The combatants are exhausted. They need to be relieved. Inevitably, we have the worst of the billets here. The gentlemen of 14th Hussars have snaffled the few decent ones left by the shirkers. One characteristic of this war is that the less you actually do, the better you get treated – all in accordance with a strict hierarchy.

First come the shirkers able to enjoy the good life in the rear. One friend lives at home and spends 100 francs a month eating in hotels. Another is a private soldier doing better than many a captain. He goes to the factory, does his little job, meals all found, then ambles home. No military discipline for him. He doesn't even wear an armlet. He goes for a spin on a Sunday to get a change of

---

1. No rest: that was the front-line infantryman's chief complaint.

scene and perhaps enjoy a spot of fishing. He wishes me good luck. Still, he is making machine guns.

Next come the shirkers in Paris. Everybody knows a couple of them: the promenaders, the regulars in the fashionable restaurants. Like this chum attached to Val-de-Grâce [Hospital], busy fighting the war in the Sentier de la Vertu, where I bumped into him during my last leave. 'Your chest is pretty well covered,' he moaned. 'At least you've got some decorations! ... Your reputation is safe! Not like ours! ... You have the Croix de Guerre and the cross of the Légion d'Honneur!'

'And the wooden cross, too, my friend! Don't forget that!'

Finally come the shirkers at the front – the medical orderlies, doctors,[1] drivers, artillery park, and so on. They throng the rest areas. They reign supreme in Châlons, Troyes and Sainte-Ménehould. Who are these riffraff from the trenches? These intruders? These hairy, filthy strangers? Send them back at once! We don't want their sort here! They're a blot on the billets!

'I don't want you mixing with those types,' as a hussar major here used to say.

For at the front there is also an outcast, a pariah deserving of any indignity. He is the beast of burden seen on the road on the evening of a relief, festooned with all manner of strange paraphernalia, bowed beneath the weight of his outsized pack, helmet blinding him like a candle-snuffer dowsing a flame. He is the front-line infantryman, the convict, the galley-slave. In all kinds of weather, on roads churned up by guns and by convoys, knee deep in mud, he chunters away over his 20 or 25 kilometres.

'That's it. I'm beat. My pack's too heavy. My boots are soaked with blood.'

'On your feet, you idle beggar! Put that man on report.'

Eventually, he takes up position beneath the shells. A 'minor undertaking' is in the offing.

'You will leave the trench at 9.00 pm and take the trench opposite.'

'What about the barbed wire?'

'There's been an artillery preparation.'

'Ten 75s that all fell behind our own lines. The barbed wire is still intact.'

'I couldn't care less. You're going. The regiment will not be relieved until the trench is taken.'

Et voilà!

---

1. The battalion MOs must be judged an exception to this rule. They did not take part in attacks, or man the loopholes, but they ran the same risks as we did.

If he survives, he's packed off for a few days in the rear. He's chucked into some filthy garret like a bunch of old rags, trampled by rats and devoured by lice.

'There's water coming in through the roof.'

'So what! There are no tiles over my head!'

'This straw's foul.'

'So what! I don't have any straw.'

He starts to nod off. 'On your feet! We're on the move! We have to make way for the next lot.'

Another billet. Another garret. Another pigsty. He's so tired, he's out like a light.

'On your feet! There's a counter-attack.'

'What a life!'

Friday 14 July

It's raining, just for a change. This evening the company did something to celebrate Bastille Day. No shortage of drunks! About time too! Poor sods, it's their only distraction.

Sunday 16 July

The papers today are announcing the death of the Duc de Rohan. Scarcely recovered from a wound received in February at Verdun, he died in action on the Somme on 13 July. What an example! Splendid, the bravery of this young man of 30, worthy of his illustrious name.

Monday, 17 July

The rain is back and so are the blues. The British offensive is unlikely to cheer me up much. It seems to be a big push though. And the two general staffs appear to be getting on well.

Morale is also much improved. We put on a show this evening in a barn in the billets. We compiled a programme without any professionals. Amateur talent was enough, at short notice too. Some of the turns were priceless, my Corporal Sauvage included. The colonel sent over a few bandsmen who rounded off the evening with the *Chant du départ*. The poilus sang along with heartwarming enthusiasm.[1]

---

1. After two years of hardship, their spirit and confidence were a pleasure to behold.

Tuesday 18 July
I went to the hospital to get some bothersome shrapnel removed, left from 9 July.

Wednesday 19 July
Relieved this evening. We're off to Côte 138. A good deal. A lot of work has been done in this sector and it's scarcely recognizable. Instead of the muddy track of last March, we are now following – from Côte 202 to Côte 138 – quite a decent road, in places screened by foliage and shielded from view by strips of canvas. The foul, rat-infested shacks have been replaced with stylish, sandbag-covered arbours – with iron-mesh beds, proper chairs, and flowers on the tables. We gather in a flowery dining-room to take our meals. The dug-outs open on to a nice little terrace, the rather grandly named 'Boulevard Baston', which occupies a ledge halfway up the valley side and is edged with a balustrade of wood and chicken-wire.

Thursday 20 July
Glorious morning. Off to check my posts at 5.00 am. They're not in too much danger here, as we're behind the second line.

The light is an exquisite pink. Through the early morning mist I can observe the whole sector, once so terrible, but today completely peaceful: the plain running down to Virginy, the trees in full leaf in the wooded valley bottom, the ruins of a village, the tragic shell-pocked carcass of a solitary church, red roofs part destroyed. Beyond, a few white walls – Massiges. Behind the village rise the daunting, impenetrable fingers of the infamous Main: the Annulaire, the Médius and, behind and to the left, the 'Index'. The tops are bare. Everywhere is deserted. No sign of life, just a plane rumbling high in the sky. Yet the hills are throbbing with activity, hollowed out like molehills by a whole subterranean population. Pairs of white lines[1] flanking a single dark thread roam in all directions. These are the trenches and the *boyaux*. Between them are patches of leprous grey grass. The hilltops are just bare white earth. Two years ago flocks of sheep were peacefully grazing here. Now these heights are sinister mass graves, incessantly renewed, where men burrow underground to kill and be killed.

At my feet, from Côte 181 to Montrémoy, is the plain. Tall grasses, brambles, bushes, purple-flowered thistles with their spiky, crisp, finely toothed bronze

---

1. The berms or parapets created from the excavated white soil of the region.

leaves – all protected by thin metal barbs. And flowers everywhere: the richly coloured meadow blooms of scabious, wild mallow and buttercups; morning glories, pure white or purple striped; bridal marguerites with their virginal white crowns and golden yellow centres; dazzling poppies. Chaffinch and nightingale sing softly, their chorus punctuated by the clear note of the quail. *Cantus liquidus,* the Romans called it.

In places, shell-holes have killed the greenery. The rumble of the guns is omnipresent. We are at war. Enveloped in pink mist, the Piton de la Justice stands watch on the far horizon, while to my left lies the long, low mound of the Chenille. But the air is fresh and light, filled with song and sunlight. I am seized by an inexpressible delight, the infinite joy of sense and sight. Beguiled by the royal splendour of the blue sky, the bliss of flowers, grasses, trees and birdsong, my soul remains unmoved by the din of guns and shell-bursts, the stupid antics of the anthropoids.

> Yes, Nature laughs to scorn these sufferings of ours.
> Her own sole greatness still to contemplate she deigns.
> Upon all things that be she sheds her sovereign powers,
> And calm and splendour still for her own part retains.[1]

Saturday 22 July
Spirits high, I set off in the cool of the morning with my new lieutenant, D.'s brother. In his mid-30s, bright, energetic, ever cheerful.[2]

Returning from No. 1 Post, we called in at brigade HQ.

[Captain] L[etondot] always wants to let you know how busy he is. Quite comical, m'lud. 'Sorry, sorry. Rushed off my feet.' He bends over his papers.

A young chap – tall, fair, very elegant – has replaced G.

The colonel ... emerged. Tall and lean, hawkish features, pockmarked face. A pleasant enough fellow, normally has a bit about him. Today though he has lost all his go. He talked about the recent trench raid and what our generals view as potential chinks in the German lines. 'We should find out what they have here,' he said, circling Cernay-en-Dormois with his finger. 'It's foolish to be fixed here if there's nothing in front of us.'

'Fine, sir. But what about the barbed wire?'

---

1. Translator's note: Charles Marie René Leconte de Lisle, *Poèmes antiques* (1852). Translated by John Payne, *Flowers of France* (London, Villon Society, 1906) p. 181.
2. Died heroically in Morocco in 1923.

Life is pretty relaxed at Côte 138. The men work every other day. They leave as soon as it gets dark at 10.00 pm, dig under the stars, then return at 2.00 am. It's quite a rest cure. By day, they can enjoy the sunshine and do their washing and mending. It's been quite a while since they enjoyed such a beano. For once, no one is bothering them. They're delighted. Blessings on the captain. Praise from all sides. Leaving men be is such a rarity in the French army.[1]

Tuesday 25 July
A lingering mist allowed me to tour the sector this morning.

Opposite our lines lies the dark mass of the Bois-de-Ville, now in its full summer glory. Beneath its dense canopy of leaves, you imagine the peaceful hum of a forest in fine weather, the delights of a shady wood offering glimpses of blue sky between its branches.

But what is the purpose of these tall plantations, these thin screens of coppice? It is to conceal the feverish activity of the cold blond anthropoids – their vehicles audible all day long – who have visited this green and pleasant land to test weapons capable of wreaking cataclysmic destruction from distances of 10, 12 or 20 kilometres.

Soft sky this evening. The slanting rays of the sun light up the 'Verger', the cherry, pear and apple orchard which once sheltered the ruined house that is now my HQ. The sky is a delicate French blue, stippled with translucent white and grey clouds. The birds are singing, the hushed chorus of a summer's eve. The crickets are chirping, the flies are droning. Is this the peace of the fields, far from the dust and stench of the road? No. It sounds as if railway wagons are rumbling overhead. Thunder shakes the horizon. The anthropoids are here. And the only way to put a stop to their depravity is by repaying them in kind. Nature would be so beautiful if not for these savages.

Wednesday 26 July
I caught a little cat in my dug-out. It spent the night chasing rats and mice. The fearless hunter pricked up its tiny ears, stood stock still, then sprang across the room. Purring, it walked over and rubbed itself against me.

4.15 am. Went to tour the posts.

---

1. I prescribed a halt to all parades and exercises. 'Leave the poilus in peace!' were my orders. And they were followed too – thanks to the tolerance and compassion of Major Fralon, our battalion CO and my superior officer since 8th Company had been disbanded.

7.20 am. Stand-to drill. Every man had to take up his combat position. An excellent notion, but it should have been ordered for earlier in the day. The sun was blazing down. The anthropoids could have picked us off one by one. We were still in the open at 9.00 am, and they sent over a few shrapnel shells.

'That was risky just for a drill, sir.[1] Whatever, it needs to be shorter and held at another time of day.'

'Divisional orders, old chap: "Don't be afraid to show yourselves to keep the Boches on their toes."'

Such are the orders sent from a château comfortably ensconced 10 or 12 kilometres behind the front lines. 'Killing the mandarin,' they call it.

11.15 am. A heavy bombardment, shells exploding all round. Every detonation brings a brief pang of fear. We eat outside, and the men have no shelter, so taking refuge in my dug-out would be very poor form, even though it would offer some protection – from the 77s at least.

Friday 28 July
Relieved by Captain B. of 124th Infantry, a former regular. The easy manner and speech of one who has done his 'full eighteen': strongly built, lively face, prematurely lined, greying hair, fair beard trimmed to a point. He volunteered on the outbreak of war and, as an ex-gunner, requested a posting to the heavy artillery. 'We have more officers than we do guns,' he was told.[2]

Some months later, when we finally got round to creating a heavy artillery, all sorts of tyros ended up as officers.

Sunday 30 July
Lunch with Sergeant Roussel in his mess at Braux. He's an ex-colonial from 124th Infantry, who paints a vivid picture of his time in Chad. He was married for three years to an Arab woman from Fez and apparently still misses her a lot. He lived like a local chieftain, raising taxes, dispensing justice, reviewing troops. He described a parade on 17 July 1900, when his seventy or eighty Senegalese troops marched past him, first on foot, then on camels, and finally on horseback.

---

1. Major Fralon, a graduate of Saint-Cyr: small, trim, energetic, red faced, shrewd, cultivated and exceedingly brave. He simply ignored any danger. Stick in hand, he marched about the lines under the heaviest of shelling with the same measured tread he employs today on the Champs-Élysées. He was seriously wounded in 1917.
2. Our generals in 1914 were incredibly obtuse regarding the value of heavy artillery.

He seems to look back fondly on his life there – a characteristic he shares with many ex-colonials.

Weather fine. I returned at 1.30 pm in bright sunshine.

Dinner this evening with Lieutenant Bourgade and Sous-lieutenant Aubel.

I return at 11.00 pm to find a note ordering me to report tomorrow for a course in Châlons. I have to be there by 3.00 pm. The only possible train leaves Valmy at 5.00 am, so that's another disturbed night. We combatants are like a football thrown between two teams. We're never allowed to touch the ground. No sooner has a kick sent us one way, than another despatches us in the opposite direction.

Monday, 31 July.

I was up at 3.00 am, but I had to settle the company's affairs before leaving, so I missed the 5.00 am train. And Mardochée has gone lame. The farrier damaged his right foreleg while he was being reshod. It took me over an hour to reach Valmy. Luckily, a member of General Gouraud's staff is due to visit the station by car and will give me a lift at 1.30 pm. The lieutenant in charge is a publisher on the Quai des Augustins [in Paris], aged 55 to 60, the air of an intellectual behind his pince-nez. He doesn't seem too anxious. The war can continue. It wouldn't bother him.

Arrive outside Châlons HQ at 3.30 pm. Blazing sun, sweltering heat. The broad avenue is covered in dust that powders the trees like frost. You could be wintering on the Prado in Marseilles. Followed by an ADC, General Gouraud saunters over the road. Tall, erect, slim and elegant, his face is made longer by a beard trimmed to a tightly curled point. He wears the khaki uniform of a colonial, right sleeve empty, kepi tilted to the right. In his left hand he carries a stick to compensate for the slight limp in his right leg. He looks unusually youthful, cool and intelligent.

Under the burning sun Châlons looks as white as any southern town. The houses are low, built of stone or rendered. As I passed the bridge over the Marne, Notre-Dame rose on my left. A very handsome edifice, which I hope to visit at my leisure. I'm billeted with a banker on the corner of the Rue d'Orfeuil and the Rue des Fripiers. Both his sons at the front, leaving him with his wife and a daughter in her mid-twenties. The welcome offered by these wonderful people[1]

---

1. To whom I should like to express my gratitude.

to their unfamiliar guest was very touching, particularly given the number of officers they must have accommodated since the start of the campaign.

My room is lovely, with a high ceiling, a library, a marble fireplace with a Louis XVI clock and, miracle of miracles, a bed – an item of furniture whose function almost escapes me. The walls are adorned with reproduction paintings snipped from the supplements to *l'Illustration*: a young girl by Greuze, two Lancret pastorals and Watteau's *l'Indifférent*, as well as some of his drawings. The room belongs to one of the boys, evidently a lover of eighteenth-century art. Two tall windows open onto the Rue d'Orfeuil, with the green trees of the garden surrounding the apse of Saint-Alpin to refresh the eyes.

The shutters are closed, filling the room with a golden shade. I sink into a comfortable armchair and ponder the words of Thiébault: 'The soldier's life is full of contrasts.'

Tuesday 1 August

7.30 am. Quai Barbot. The hundred captains and lieutenants here to follow the course were carried off by heavy lorries through the dust. We stood in the full sun, on a sort of range, watching grenades being thrown. Nothing new there, but we enjoyed the sunlight.

At 10.00 am, the course director– a major in the chasseurs à pied – turned up on horseback: 'You are going to watch the training programme devised by GQG for a new model infantry company. I ask you to put this into practice. Ignore any other nonsense you may be told. Your companies must be transformed. *Some of you will be heading for the front line* (*sic*). You must do so fully cognizant of the new procedures.'[1]

A fine soldier perhaps, but the major is no orator. 'Some of you will be heading for the front line.' I look around. I'm sure that's where we've all just come from. And that none of us waited for the major's advice before using grenades.

In the afternoon, after a lecture on the [Chauchat] machine gun conducted in the shade of a wood opposite the Cercle [des Officiers], we set off to see it demonstrated on the range. Bouncing around through the sun and dust in the back of a heavy lorry was no fun at all. The [Chauchat] is just a lighter, and

---

1. To deliver this harangue to lieutenants and captains who had all earned their stripes in the field, and nearly all been wounded more than once, was quite grotesque. I later met this major again. He was a good lecturer (if not on 1 August 1916), without ever showing much sign of combat experience. Sadly, this was true of many staff officers.

less accurate, machine gun. Training has not been finalized. The magazine, in particular, is causing problems.[1]

On our return, we wanted something to drink. Impossible. Thirst is not allowed before 6.00 pm.

The public garden, the 'Jard', is very pleasant – long, tree-lined alleys running alongside the stagnant green waters of the Canal de la Marne. All very pleasant and cool, especially in this heatwave.

Thursday 3 August

We are taking our meals at the Cercle [des Officiers]. Dined with a captain from 5th Chasseurs à cheval, a graduate of Saint-Cyr, who left the army after five or six years to go farming in Tunisia. He and three other settlers are planning some big enterprise in Morocco. A thinker and a doer, very sharp. One of his comments made us smile. 'Roman remains? I'm constantly tripping over them. They're a damned nuisance, just stones that damage my ploughs. I'll start taking an interest when I retire.'

This an educated Frenchman speaking. It made his remark even more entertaining. The Americans have no monopoly on the 'Struggle for Existence'. Our men of letters, with their limited horizons, have misrepresented us. Their decadent world of charlatans, loose women, failures, snobs and dilettantes is not France. That much is clear. Strange, the outlook of professional scribes, churning out endless tomes despite their complete ignorance of a subject. Take the present conflict. Which young scribblers are using it as a springboard for their novels and reportage? M[aurice] B[arrès], R[ené] B[azin] and others, happily anonymous, whose pages flood the newspapers. How much fighting have they seen? B[arrès] and B[azin] a few days at the very start; the rest, none at all.

Friday 4 August

Left as usual amid the sun and dust of the Quai Barbot, but at 7.00 am.

We were testing the Walter shield, a kind of steel box that protects the back, head and ribs. Within this carapace, a man can crawl towards the enemy lines safe from any bullets. Walter is an engineer, a reservist captain in a chasseur battalion. He's 30 or so, tall and very thin, with a bushy blond beard. In the dark uniform and silver braid of the chasseurs, he gave a clear, straightforward presentation.

---

1. Since remedied.

'A reservist, is he?' enquired my Tunisian settler.

'Yes!'

'Heavens, finally someone with brains!'

General Gouraud attended the trials, accompanied by an impressive array of generals from IX, IV and XVIII Corps – little P[utz]., with his long moustachios; the restless, jittery T.; the tall figure of H[irschauer], strongly built, bull neck, square head, greying hair, hooked nose, flared nostrils and luxuriant moustache.

And I finally got to see J.-B. Dumas, the butcher of Perthes, the general who ordered all those men to storm the barbed wire. What was he like? A hulking giant like …? A worrier like …? Not at all. An elderly gentleman, small, white haired, puffy red-rimmed eyes, very dapper. You would take him for a small-town dominoes player.

Another old hand is General R., from the Engineers, who came to describe his 'model' shelters.

General Gouraud concluded proceedings. I had a clear view of this fine figure of a soldier, blue eyes, slightly hooded, sharp nose, soft fleshy lips amid a tightly curled fair beard. He looked extremely svelte in his khaki tunic, very elegant and refined. Resting on his stick, he spoke without gestures, in a warm, clear voice: 'Gentlemen, I would like to take advantage of your presence here today to address a few words to you. In all our offensives thus far, particularly in Champagne last September, we have been stymied by barbed wire. Either our guns lacked the power to destroy it or, when it was placed on the reverse slope, they have lacked the range. The Walter shield will solve this problem.[1]

'How many breaches were made on the Somme?' [he asked Walter.]

'At least fifty, sir.'

'Fifty breaches! With only one man killed and four wounded. And that death was caused by our own fire. An unavoidable accident … The trial was conclusive.

'General R. has also presented our current recommendations on shelters. A word on this subject. During the recent action at Maisons-de-Champagne, one battalion was apparently taken prisoner without leaving its shelter, while other, braver companies got away. A counter-attack was immediately launched and the position retaken, but the Germans still had time to evacuate their prisoners. The whole operation lasted no more than fifteen minutes, so the men must have come out quickly enough on the second occasion.

---

1. No. It was just one of many ideas put forward in good faith which subsequently failed in practice.

'It is intolerable for men not to come out and fight yet emerge so quickly in surrender. Officers must take action during an attack to push men out of the shelters. No true soldier would ever accept the time had come when he could do no more! Thank you, gentlemen.'

He declaimed his final words, barking 'no true soldier' in a voice that shook me to the marrow.

He clearly possesses extraordinary powers of persuasion. I began to understand the hold exercised by some military leaders over their troops. I left more stirred than words can say, dazzled by the charisma and unsullied renown of this handsome young general, who bears the scars of wounds sustained while performing his duty with a selflessness unique in military history. All the fatigues of the campaign were forgotten and my soul was prepared for sacrifice.

In the afternoon we visited the camouflage workshop housed in the Indoor Circus. Remarkable.

Military ingenuity has taken a bizarre turn with the war. We saw hollow trees made of painted steel, designed for use as observation posts. A real tree, familiar to the Boches, is removed at night and replaced by a dummy. The steel is covered in cork, all the joints meticulously crafted. It's impossible not to be fooled.

Anything can be turned into an observation post: a telegraph pole, a boundary marker, etc. All is fake here … even the corpses. One body is removed from a line of corpses in no man's land and replaced by a horribly realistic dummy whose head contains the look-out post. The body used as a model is significant. Of course, it's an infantryman. On the back of his greatcoat is the square of white cloth used by the assault waves in Champagne in September 1915.

The Germans use camouflage too. We saw photographs that show how the gun that shelled Châlons was spotted. We saw work getting under way in a clearing, which suddenly was full of pine. The giant gun only managed to fire three rounds – two on a Saturday evening, one to fire the following Monday – before it was destroyed. The gun was spotted by aerial reconnaissance and our next stop was the laboratory that processes the photographs for Central Army Group. In the absence of the lieutenant, the sergeant showed us round. He was 40 or so, obviously a professional photographer, and really knew his stuff. He showed us photos of the Butte de Tahure and the Main de Massiges. Our familiarity with the latter sector made it particularly interesting. Aerial photography is a marvellous way of getting to know the enemy lines. Every hump and bump in our own lines was so clearly delineated that I have every confidence in the information provided about our neighbours. Everything was identifiable … even down to the latrines.

At sunset this evening a little church tour.

Notre-Dame is a handsome building. Of the original late eleventh- or early twelfth-century church, four square towers remain – two flanking the apse, and two the west door. Each tower has three tiers of beautiful Romanesque arcading. The two absidal towers are much less heavily restored, with moss, grass and pigeon nests protruding between the grey and yellow stones. The nave was rebuilt in the mid-thirteenth century with a ribbed vault, possibly due to structural problems with the earlier barrel vault, but also to modernize the church and to introduce more light. The nave is over 30 metres high at the apex of the vault, with a tribune, triforium and clerestory. Very fine. With their geometrical ornament and fantastic bestiary, the capitals of the pillars retain a Romanesque feel, as does the church as a whole. Strange birds, or lions with human heads, crown the responds of the central portal, while squared ashlar corbels emphasize the lines of the building – all typically Romanesque.

Every era has left its mark on the building. The north transept and rose window both date from the fourteenth century. The north portal is obviously later, and was once very finely sculpted, but all the figures on the mouldings, pediment, tympanum and responds have been systematically destroyed (probably by local Jacobins[1]). In the fifteenth century, probably the second half, the bays acquired stained glass windows, some of which survive in the south aisle. In the late seventeenth or early eighteenth century a Baroque façade replaced the narthex. Its fine proportions match perfectly those of the original building, but it does jar a little in style. Statues also graced the portal here, while fragments of a tree on the left, and the Jerusalem discernible on the right, suggest that a fine bas-relief once filled the tympanum. All fell victim to a frenzy of destruction; eternal truths asserted with the blow of a hammer.[2]

The buttresses and flying buttresses, with their pinnacles and crockets, and the huge rose window, ethereal and enigmatic, are flushed by the setting sun. In the tranquil evening light, eight centuries of faith, love and toil endure in stone, while just 30 kilometres away the anthropoids are busy plotting their work of destruction.

Beautiful morning, bright shadows in the Rue d'Orfeuil. With bugle call and roll of drums, the class of 1916 from 17th Infantry march past. The young men

---

1. Or sixteenth-century Protestants. The eternal struggle between Ariel and Caliban. Ariel carefully crafts some celestial figures, only for Caliban to take his club and smash them.
2. Hence the need to cut the number of sacraments from seven to two.

look pretty smart, and their officers – the majority probably reservists – don't seem too out of place.

The country has grown used to the war. No one cares how long it might go on for.

11.30 am. Fled to Paris, where the war could last another hundred years. 'We turned away a real crowd at lunchtime,' said the maître d' at the Boeuf à la Mode.

Sunday 6 August
Back in Châlons by 11.00 am. The Rue de la Marne was dustier than ever. I said goodbye to my charming hosts and caught the 3.00 pm train back to Sainte-Ménehould.

Arrived in Valmy at 8.00 pm. No one was there to meet me. Fortunately, Captain Dupont's orderly had come in a trap.

Monday 7 August
Left for the front at 7.00 am.

[A comrade] and I rode to Araja, via the Berzieux road, with its double screen of quivering pines, and Ville-sur-Tourbe.

Minnies, some a fair size, and 210s are shelling the sector. Our quick-firing 155TR[1] could see off the 210, but it'll be another six months before it reaches the front in sufficient quantity.[2] By then, the Germans will have developed a quick-firing 305, and it will take us another year to respond.

I've had a letter from Mademoiselle L. C. Her uncle has taken in a Red Cross nurse from Douai, previously an internee in Stuttgart, who says that Germany is running out of food. After our vigorous offensive on all fronts, the giant may be starting to totter. Now would be a good time for the Romanians to march.

Tuesday 8 August
Read Hanotaux's article in the *Revue hebdomadaire* of 22 July: 'Theory of the Battle of the Frontiers'. He opens as follows: 'The battle I was first to call the battle of the Frontiers'. He then proceeds to analyse the doctrines current on

---

1. The 155 Filloux.
2. This is August 1916, just over two years into the war.

both sides. Von Moltke, he opines, 'never expected artillery developments to lead to a return to the war of position.'[1]

Yet the war of position as currently conducted cannot be explained by artillery developments alone. Its primary cause lies in the continuity of the front lines, itself a function firstly of the sheer number of troops in the field, and secondly of the machine gun, which spits out 300 to 600 rounds a minute and has made general the use of barbed wire as the principal means of defence. These are the factors that underlie both the current supremacy of the defensive over the offensive and the resulting war of position. In 1885 – when Moltke wrote his final work, cited here by Hanotaux – such machine guns were unknown and barbed wire not yet considered.

Artillery developments play no more than a minor role. Understanding this, however, requires a few short turns in the trenches.

Our leaders should have grasped the importance of machine guns and barbed wire after Mukden and Çatalca. [But] the endless ranks of École de Guerre strategists overlooked these minor details. 'We must not allow the Germans time to deploy,' proclaimed Colonel de Grandmaison in a lecture cited by Hanotaux. 'In the offensive, let boldness be our friend.'

Forward! Forward![2]

We followed this advice at Ethe on 22 August 1914. As did III Corps and the African regiments at Charleroi. The result? We came up against ... barbed wire protecting the machine guns that mowed us down. The 150s were needed only to finish the job.

The École de Guerre was devoted to an uncritical study of Napoleon and the Germans supposed to be his acolytes. But the truth is that in terms of matériel – weapons and communications – we are as far, if not further, from Napoleon than was he from the Romans. From his study of Napoleon's campaigns, Clausewitz identifies 'the predominance of the human factor' in warfare. Our current experience suggests the exact opposite: 'the growing predominance of matériel'. As I write, the anthropoids are rocking my dug-out with 100kg Minnies. I can assure Monsieur Hanotaux that if the enemy opposite had the resources to shell

---

1. Marshal Pétain argues on the contrary that 'it was the lack of artillery that kept both sides pinned to the ground, face to face, for four years' (Fonclare, *L'Infanterie* preface).
2. In Napoleon's words: 'Woe betide any general who arrives on the battlefield with a system.'

us intensively for forty-eight hours, no troops could possibly resist. The few, if any, survivors would be forced to abandon the sector.[1]

The terrific explosion of a projectile and its lingering shrapnel refrain has much to teach the military historian ... Consider this asinine remark: 'The doctrine of the all-out offensive suited the French character.' How does hurling oneself at barbed wire swept by machine-gun fire suit the French character? Monsieur Hanotaux describes this doctrine as 'youthful and dynamic'. It was neither. It was simply ignorant and presumptuous. And none of our leaders was exactly young.

The only youthful and dynamic doctrine is one based upon, and tailored to, the resources available. Whether citing Foch,[2] Bonnal or Grandmaison, Hanotaux seems to be surrounding us with pure theorists. These are questions not for the lecture theatre, but for the trench or the battlefield. Practical experience is what counts, not dissertations.

In the army, as in so many government departments, common sense flew out of the window. No one could see beyond Napoleon, yet his essential precepts were studiously ignored. 'Tactics are a function of armament,' he declared. Simple common sense. But his pale early twentieth-century disciples turned this axiom on its head. For General Langlois, the future lay in 'developing a quick-firing light gun that was fitted with a shield and fired shrapnel shells'.[3] In other words, the 75. A tactic was devised and a weapon tailored to it, forgetting

1. 'And now, ye kings, understand ...' (Psalms: 2, 10).
2. The following passages are taken from *Les Principes de la guerre*, a series of lectures delivered by Foch at the École de Guerre in 1900, published in April 1903, and cited by Jean Norton Cru (p. 76, fn. 3): 'The laurels of victory fly from the point of the enemy bayonets. That is where we must seize them; wrest them, if need be, in hand-to-hand combat ... Charge, but in numbers and *en masse* ... Throw ourselves at the enemy lines and settle matters with cold steel ... Move quickly, preceded by a hail of bullets ... Infantry organized in two ranks will provide fire-power and manoeuvrability ... [Whole] companies in close order (line or column), all fully commanded, will launch the decisive attack ... Everywhere, drum and bugle will sound the 'Charge' ... If the attacking troops outrun the enemy reserves, no matter. We can charge and charge again, from the front, from the flanks, from the rear.'

.   'Charge in numbers and *en masse*!' Throw companies into battle 'in close order'. This was a recipe for disaster even when facing the English bowmen at Crécy. Cru notes rightly that the kind of war described in these lines 'evokes the paintings of war artists, or the novels of Paul Adam'.
3. *L'Artillerie de campagne en liaison avec les autres armes*, vol. 1, pp. 2, 3, 79.

that the enemy could – and would – respond with a more powerful alternative, capable of annihilating both.

'Order your suit and choose your stock accordingly,' advised Napoleon.

Langlois, a self-proclaimed disciple of the Emperor, chose instead to marry his suit to his stock – like a pretty woman ordering a dress to match her hat.

6.00 pm. The Minnies strike with their huge hammer-blows. A burning shell splinter falls in the entrance to the dug-out, demolishing an upright. It's completely green. What on earth is put in these things?

8.00 pm. The moon rises, a golden disc above the ruins of Ville-sur-Tourbe. The tall, shell-ravaged belfry glows pink in the last rays of the setting sun. R[iballier] des Isles and I are on the Servon road, heading for the Verger, doubtless once a lovers' haunt at this time of night. The houses – some well built and obviously affluent (like the notary's house where the colonel is based) – have been reduced to heaps of rubble. All that remains of the little town are fragments of wall and blown-out windows like empty eye sockets. Thus was it willed by the anthropoids, eager to prove to the world the superiority of their ballistics.

Wednesday 9 August

5.50 am. The sun rises over the Bois-de-Ville like a ball of molten silver. The plain is a sea of mist. Clumps of trees emerge from long ribbons of silver dust, and below them, to the south, the ruins of Ville-sur-Tourbe. Shattered walls lurk among the purple shadows. Above them is the belfry – mutilated, blind, like a limbless corpse. The stumps of stone glow pink where they face the rising sun. The light glints off a screen of greenery veiled by gauzy silver mist.

The men are emerging for a coffee.

'Rum?' I hear Pelachon swear at a creole. 'If you want rum, try Martinique!'

Behind the screen of shell-cropped pines are stirring houses with blue roofs and pink gables. Waking, too, is the rifle fire clattering towards the posts.

Friday 11 August

Grey skies.

'Napoleon announced military maxims whenever circumstances dictated, but he never combined them and issued them as regulations, *probably because he didn't have time,*' wrote Marc Villers in the *Revue hebdomadaire*, 29 July 1915.

'Didn't have time?' No! He just wasn't interested, any more than was Rubens in writing a treatise on art.

Tuesday 15 August
We're celebrating the Feast [of the Assumption] this evening by moving into the front line. They're pushing their luck. I'm still exhausted and so are the men. We're off to Maisons-de-Champagne. Lovely spot!

Wednesday 16 August
Maisons-de-Champagne.

12.30 pm. Set off along the Minaucourt road to reconnoitre our new sector. There's not much left of Minaucourt. On reaching the Massiges road, we turn left towards the Ferme de Beauséjour. We halt at the Oasis (!), where a runner is waiting for us, then enter Boyau de Rouvroy. Blazing sun. Heavy atmosphere. Blue sky, but thunder in the air. Interminable trip along the duckboards, turning like mill horses round and round.

'Feeling seasick yet?' asks [Captain] Leblanc.[1]

At last we reach the valley where the mobile cookers are parked!

'We're not halfway there yet,' says the runner.

Thanks, gentlemen!

Back in the *boyau*. Planks stained brown,[2] the odd puddle, splatters on the white walls. There were some accidents here yesterday.

We reach the major's HQ, a proper shelter buried at least 5 metres deep. The major is 50 to 55, solidly built, brush-cut white hair, widow's peak, bushy grey moustache. Very cool and considered. He's ex-colonial infantry and still sports their anchors on his collar.

He's talking on the telephone. A concentrated barrage against Point 829 at 3.00 pm.

We listen in. It is 3.00 pm. A moment later we hear the dull thud of the guns.

'Is that the concentrated barrage?'

'Yes,' he confirms calmly. 'Just wait for the reply.' With that comes a huge explosion right outside the shelter. The lamp goes out. The blast is deafening. We relight the lamp. A stream of explosions follows, rocking the shelter each time.

They obviously have more than just four Minnies to fire.

---

1. A regular captain, a charming fellow.
2. Blood.

Half an hour goes by. Things seem to be calming down. With [Lieutenant] M.D.[1] and a runner, I leave for the HQ of the captain I'm replacing.

The Minnies and the shells start falling again.

The *boyau* caves in. Our guide picks up speed. We follow. A sudden terrifying explosion to my left and I can feel myself flying through the air.[2]

---

1. My new lieutenant.
2. A Minnie had just exploded on the parapet of the *boyau*. In the quarter second of consciousness remaining to me, it felt as if my head, limbs, chest – every part of my body – was being pierced by a thousand jets of intangible, vaporizing gas. I was thrown 5 or 6 metres before hitting the ground. I fainted and came round in an infirmary. I had initially been given up for dead because my head was drenched with blood. Later, I was evacuated to the hospital at Châlons. Thus did the mighty Minnies drive the writer of these lines temporarily from the field. He returned to the front on 15 October 1916. 'They grumbled, but still they marched.'

Names Mentioned in the Text

Abram, Lieutenant: CO, 1st Company, 101st Infantry; wounded and taken prisoner, La Digue, 1 June 1916, Vaux.

Adam, Paul (1862–1920): historical novelist.

Allemand, Captain Charles Jean-Baptiste: CO, 10th Company, 3rd Battalion, 35th Infantry; relieved by Delvert, 18 May 1916, Vaux; killed in action, 7 May 1917, Hôpital de Bouleuse (Marne).

'Arthur': nickname cited by Delvert for the French artillery.

Aubel, Sous-lieutenant: 8th Company, 101st Infantry, November 1915.

Aubry, Soldat de 2e classe: 8th Company, 101st Infantry; one of Delvert's orderlies transferred to machine guns, February 1916, Main de Massiges and Verdun.

Aulard, François Victor Alphonse (1849–1928): historian of the French Revolution; contributor to wartime newspapers and magazines.

Aumont, Soldat de 2e classe Gaston Jules: 101st Infantry; born 28 January 1894, Brienne (Eure); killed in action, 1 June 1916, Tavannes.

'B.', Sous-lieutenant: 6th Company, 101st Infantry; newly promoted on joining the regiment, 21 February 1916.

'B.', Captain: 124th Infantry; his unit relieves Delvert's company, 28 July 1916, Main de Massiges.

'Bamboula': nickname of Soldat Delahaye.

Barbès, Armand (1809–70): republican revolutionary of 1848.

Barrau, Théophile (1848–1913): sculptor.

Barrès, Auguste-Maurice (1862–1923): novelist, journalist and politician of notably right-wing views; stigmatized by opponents as 'chief of the tribe of brainwashers'.

Battesti, Captain Jean-Baptiste: CO, 8th Company, 101st Infantry; born 8 August 1878, Venaco (Corse); killed in action, 22 August 1914, Ethe.

Bazin, René François Nicolas Marie (1853–1932): novelist of provincial life.

Bégert, Captain Valérie Joseph Alphonse Fernand: CO, 1st Machine Gun Platoon, 101st Infantry; born 5 November 1881, Chesly (Aube); wounded 15 September 1914, Ferme des Loges; died of wounds, 17 September 1914, Pierrefonds (Oise).

Benoit, Sous-lieutenant: CO, 4th Platoon, 4th Company, 101st Infantry, August 1914; company mess officer.

Benoit, Major: second-in-command, 101st Infantry; Delvert describes him as 'recently appointed', 9 May 1916.

Bérenger, Henry (1867–1952): writer and politician.

Bernard, Lieutenant Émile Charles André: CO, 8th Company, 101st Infantry; born 16 September 1884, Paris 6e; assumed command of 8th Company on death of Captain Battesti; killed in action, 26 February 1915, Bois-Sabot (Marne).

Bernier, Jean (1894–1975): writer and journalist; author of *La Percée* (Paris: Albin Michel, 1920), an autobiographical novel describing his front-line service, 1914–15.

Bes, Adjudant: CO, 3rd Platoon, 4th Company, 101st Infantry, August 1914.

Bétron, Sous-lieutenant Jacques Alfred Bernard: 7th Company, 101st Infantry; born 20 July 1888, Houx (Eure-et-Loir); killed in action, 3 June 1916, Vaux.

Biancardini, Lieutenant Marius Pierre: CO, 6th Company, 101st Infantry; born 28 March 1879, Vincennes (Seine); killed in action, 2 June 1916, Vaux.

Birot, Jean: statistician; compiler of *La Statistique annuelle de géographie comparée* (Paris: Hachette, 1905–24).

Blaise, Lieutenant: CO, 7th Company, 101st Infantry; wounded, 1 April 1916, Main de Massiges.

Blanqui, Jérôme Adolphe (1798–1854): politician and economist; supporter of the Orléans monarchy during the 1848 revolution.

Blaze, Captain Elzéar (1788-1848): author of *Souvenirs d'un officier de la Grande Armée* (Paris: Fayard, n.d.).

Blum, Sergeant René Aaron: 7th Company, 101st Infantry; born 10 February 1894, Paris 8e; killed in action, 4 June 1916, Tavannes.

Bocage, Soldat de 2e classe: 8th Company, 101st Infantry; Delvert's runner, Main de Massiges, 1915.

Bodin, Sous-lieutenant: 8th Company, 101st Infantry, Main de Massiges and Verdun; replaces Lambert, 24 February 1916; evacuated following gas inhalation, 24 May 1916.

Boisramé, Médecin aide-major: MO, 2nd Battalion, 101st Infantry; captured 7 June 1916, Verdun.

Boitier, Soldat de 2e classe Alfred Edmond: 2nd Platoon, 4th Company, 101st Infantry; born 3 November 1893, Châtillon-sur-Loire (Loiret); positioned beside Delvert, 22 August 1914, Ethe; killed in action, 26 September 1914, Champien (Somme).

Bonnal, Général de division Guillaume Auguste Balthazar Eugène Henri (1844–1917): general of limited regimental experience; prolific writer on military history, tactics, strategy and doctrine.

Bonnieux, Captain Ernest Jean: CO, 12th Company, 101st Infantry; born 23 November 1869, Le Brethon (Allier); killed in action, 22 August 1914, Ethe.

Bouillet, Sous-lieutenant: 1st Company, 101st Infantry; newly appointed, July 1916; previously served as adjudant, Perthes, February 1915.

Bourdeau, Corporal: 1st Company, 101st Infantry; affected by a bombardment, 10 July 1916, Main de Massiges.

Bourdet, Édouard (1887–1945): dramatist and journalist; *Le Rubicon*, originally staged in 1910, was his first play.

Bourgade, Lieutenant: 101st Infantry; dines with Delvert, 30 July 1916.

Bourget, Paul (1852–1935): prolific Catholic writer; his works include the novel *Le Sens de la mort* (Paris: Plon, 1915), featuring the heroic Lieutenant Le Gallic.

Bourguignon, Lieutenant Louis Ferdinand (1880–1957): CO, 1st Platoon, 4th Company, 101st Infantry; wounded August 1914, Ethe; later transferred as captain to 165th Infantry, receiving his majority in 1917; a much-decorated (and frequently wounded) officer, he remained in the army after the war as a member of the French mission to Czechoslovakia; CO, 503rd Tank Regiment, 1932; armour commander, Second Army, 1940; deported by the Nazis to the Eisenberg camp and liberated, 1945.

Boyer, Lucien (1876–1942): popular singer, poet and journalist; author of more than a thousand songs and thirty-nine musical comedies and operettas.

Bragelongne, Sous-lieutenant Marie Joseph Henri Louis de: CO, 4th Platoon, 3rd Company, 101st Infantry; born 18 February 1895, Senlis (Oise); killed in action, 31 August 1914, Halles-sous-les-Côtes; spelt according to the departmental conscription register; Delvert uses Bragelonne.

Branchard, Sergeant: 8th Company, 101st Infantry; one of Delvert's NCOs, 6 April 1916.

Briand, Aristide (1862–1932): politician; several times prime minister (1909–29), including the period of the German offensive at Verdun.

Brunet, Lieutenant: 124th Infantry; brings reinforcements to Delvert, 4 June 1916, Retranchement R.1.

'C.', Sous-lieutenant de: platoon commander, 9th Company, 124th Infantry, 5 February 1916.

Cantenot, Soldat de 2e classe: 8th Company, 101st Infantry; sinks to his waist in mud, December 1915, Main de Massiges.

Cardin, Soldat de 2e classe: 8th Company, 101st Infantry, 15 June 1916.

Carnot, Lazare Nicolas Marguerite (1753–1823): politician and director of the French war effort during and after the French Revolution.

Le Carré: officer, 7th Company, 101st Infantry, 9 January 1916.

Casabianca, Major Louis Anthoine Jacques de: CO, 2nd Battalion, 101st Infantry; born 16 October 1864, Venzolasca (Haute-Corse); joined 75th Infantry, 1883; rose through the ranks to sergent-major; Saint-Maixent 1888–9; commissioned as a sous-lieutenant, 118th Infantry, 1889; lieutenant, 1891; captain, 1901; captain and adjutant, 1912; major, 1914; posted to 101st Infantry, 31 October 1915; transferred to 133rd Infantry, 30 June 1917. Mentioned in Army orders, 18 June 1916: 'a senior officer of rare energy; demonstrated during the fighting of May 1916; possesses many fine military qualities; for five days he and his battalion repelled every German attack on his front, leaving his positions intact for his replacement despite numerous enemy assaults and extremely heavy shelling. Wounded three times during the campaign'. Pejoratively nicknamed 'Consul' by Delvert and his men.

Casimir-Périer, Casimir Pierre (1777–1832): politician and supporter of the Orléans monarchy.

Castelnau, Général de division Noël Édouard de, Vicomte de Curières (1851–1944): commander, Fourth Army (which included Delvert's division), 1914; commander, Central Army Group, 1915; appointed Joffre's chief of staff, 1915; retired, 1916; recalled, 1918.

Cauvin, Captain Jules Joseph Alphonse: CO, 4th Company, 1914; born 6 July 1874, Toulon (Var); Saint-Cyr, 1895–7; served in north Africa, 1900–; joined 101st Infantry, 1912; wounded, 22 August 1914, Ethe; temporary major, 1915; transferred to 102nd Infantry, 1915.

Champ, Corporal: 8th Company, 101st Infantry; seriously wounded, 4 June 1916, Retranchement R.1.

Champion, Soldat de 2e classe: 8th Company, 101st Infantry; bugler, 7 January 1916; accidentally sets off company rocket store, 2 June 1916, Vaux.

Chapelain, Corporal Albert Julien Adrien: 2nd Platoon, 4th Company, 101st Infantry; wounded 22 August 1914, Ethe; listed among the dead by the regimental history.

Chardonneau, Lieutenant: 124th Infantry; commanded a trench raid, 12 July 1916, Main de Massiges.

Charpentier, Soldat de 2e classe: 8th Company, 101st Infantry; Delvert's orderly; wounded, 22 May 1916, Vaux.

Châtenet, Sergeant: 101st Infantry; regimental clerk, 8 June 1916.

Chevaillot, Corporal Émile: 8th Company, 101st Infantry; born 9 December 1895, Paris 12e; killed in action, 2 June 1916, Tavannes.

Chevalier, Soldat de 2e classe: 2nd Platoon, 4th Company, 101st Infantry; Delvert's orderly, August 1914.

Choplain, Sergeant Charles Eugène: 101st Infantry; born 8 September 1894, Puteaux (Seine); commissioned as a sous-lieutenant, June 1916, and appointed platoon commander, 6th Company; killed in action, 27 May 1917, Mont-sans-Nom (Marne).

Choquet, Corporal: 8th Company, 101st Infantry; a company telephonist, February 1916.

Claude, Lieutenant Léon Émile: 18th Company, 298th Infantry; born 8 July 1886, Gérardmer (Vosges); brings reinforcements to Delvert, 3 June 1916, Retranchement R.1; killed in action there, 8 June 1916.

Clément, Sous-lieutenant: 101st Infantry; a regular soldier and ex-NCO; temporary CO, 5th Company, March 1916.

Clément-Thomas, Jacques Léon (1809–71): soldier and opponent of the 1848 revolution; shot by the Communards, 1871.

Clerc, Soldat de 2e classe: 8th Company, 101st Infantry; one of Delvert's runners, Main de Massiges and Verdun; transferred to 1st Company with Delvert, 26 June 1916.

Colette, Soldat de 2e classe: 8th Company, 101st Infantry; one of Delvert's runners, 22 May 1916.

Colombani, Sergeant: 1st Platoon, 8th Company, 101st Infantry, 24 May 1916.

Colonna d'Istria, Médecin-major: regimental MO, 101st Infantry, 17 December 1915.

Colonna d'Istria, Sous-lieutenant Jean-Antoine: 6th Hussars; born 2 May 1879, Sarrola-Carcopino (Corse-du-Sud); died 28 April 1919, Hôpital Militaire de Marseille (Bouches-du-Rhône).

'Consul': the soldiers' nickname for Major de Casabianca; probably in reference to 'Consul the Educated Ape', a pre-war performing animal act.

Cordier: orderly of Lieutenant E. R., May 1916.

Cosset, Company Quartermaster Sergeant Henri Louis: 8th Company, 101st Infantry; born 25 April 1894, Paris 6e; killed in action, 2 June 1916, Tavannes.

Coupry, Adjudant: Engineer NCO, responsible for trench construction, 7 March 1916, Côte 138, Main de Massiges.

Courtonne, Corporal: 8th Company, 101st Infantry, 29 March 1916.

Coutable, Corporal: 8th Company, 101st Infantry, 29 March 1916.

Cru, Jean Norton (1879–1949): veteran and author of a critical bibliography of French war memoirs, *Témoins* (Paris: Les Étincelles, 1929).

'D.', officer: 101st Infantry; described as 'Big D.' by Delvert; serving in Supplies, 1915.

'D.', Captain: Engineers Staff, IV Corps, meets Delvert, 7 April 1916.

'D.', Sous-lieutenant: platoon commander, 101st Infantry, January 1916.

'M. D.', Lieutenant: 1st Company, 101st Infantry; Delvert's 'new' lieutenant, 16 August 1916.

Dantant, Général de division Georges Victor (1856–1925): commander, 124th Division (which included 101st Infantry), 15 June 1915; replaced 8 February 1916 and never employed again.

David, Adjudant Paul Henri Pierre Auguste: 4th Company, 101st Infantry; born Villaines-la-Gonais (Sarthe), 28 October 1888; killed in action, 15 September 1914, Tracy-le-Val; Delvert's company clerk.

David, Soldat de 2e classe: 2nd Platoon, 4th Company, 101st Infantry, 31 August 1914.

Degraf, Soldat de 2e classe: 4th Company, 101st Infantry, 22 September 1914.

Delahaye, Soldat de 2e classe Jean-Baptiste: 8th Company, 101st Infantry; born Thore (Sarthe), 19 February 1895; killed in action, 4 June 1916, Retranchement R.1; nicknamed 'Bamboula'.

Deline, Soldat de 2e classe: 8th Company, 101st Infantry; reported missing after a bombardment, Vaux, 29–30 May 1916.

Delmet, Paul Julien (1862–1904): composer and singer.

Delporte, Corporal: 8th Company, 101st Infantry, 29 March 1916.

Desmoulins, Camille (1760–94): journalist and politician during the French Revolution.

Destival, Lieutenant Colonel Louis François Charles Antoine: CO, 101st Infantry; born 22 August 1863, Miradoux (Gers); died of wounds, 26 September 1915, Camp de Châlons (Marne).

Diafoirus, Doctor: a character in Molière's *Le Malade imaginaire*; a pedant who uses elaborate scientific terminology to disguise his indifference to his patients' health; here, the Engineers insist on using regulation components despite their unsuitability for the task in hand.

Didisheim, Captain Lucien Fernand: CO, 1st Company, 101st Infantry; born 1 February 1873, Guebwiller (Haut-Rhin); died of wounds, 25 November 1914, Hôpital Auxiliaire No. 28, Paris 16e.

Dubuc, Adjudant: platoon commander, 8th Company, 101st Infantry, 29 November 1915.

Dufrenne, Sergeant: platoon commander, 4th Company, 101st Infantry, August 1914.

Dumas, Sous-lieutenant: artilleryman; forward observer, 10 April 1916.

Dumas, Général de division Noel Jean-Baptiste Henri Alphonse (1854–1943): commander, XVII Corps, 1 September 1914–2 May 1917; characterized by Delvert as 'the Butcher of Perthes'.

Dumesnil, Gaston (1879–1918): moderate Republican deputy for Maine-et-Loire; combined his parliamentary duties with active service in 106th Infantry; killed accompanying a parliamentary mission to the front, 8 September 1918.

Dumouriez, Général de division Charles François du Perrier (1739–1823): French general during the Revolutionary Wars; later defected to the enemy.

Dupont, Captain Henri Alphonse: 124th Infantry; born 31 December 1890, Serquigny (Eure); died in hospital of Spanish flu, 9 October 1918, Modane (Savoie); relieves 8th Company, Vaux, 20 May 1916; Légion d'Honneur, 20 June 2016.

Duquesnoy, Général de division Florent Joseph (1761–1801): defeated the royalist Vendée rebellion, 1793–4.

Dutrey, Lieutenant: CO, 1st Platoon, 6th Company, 101st Infantry; assumed temporary command of 6th Company after the battle of Ethe, August 1914.

Elloel, Aspirant: artilleryman; forward observer, 10 April 1916.

Eustache, Soldat de 2e classe: 8th Company, 101st Infantry; one of Captain Delvert's orderlies, responsible for his horses, January 1916.

'F.', Major: staff officer, IV Corps; meets Delvert, 7 April 1916.

Faguet, Émile (1847–1916): prolific writer; like Delvert, a graduate of the Lycée Charlemagne, Paris 4e.

Farret, Colonel Léon Gaston Jean-Baptiste: CO, 101st Infantry; born 23 May 1861, Paris; Saint-Cyr 1879–80; served with a variety of African and Vietnamese regiments, including the Foreign Legion; CO, 101st Infantry, 1913; temporary général de brigade, 13th Brigade (which included 101st Infantry), September 1914; divisional infantry commander, 7th Division, February 1917; 165th

Division, April 1918; divisional commander, 11th Colonial Division, 15 June 1918; remained in the army after the armistice.

Félineau, Colonel (later Général de brigade) Henri François: commander, 14th Brigade, 7th Division; described by Delvert as a 'hapless old stick', 25th August 1914.

Ferran, Lieutenant Colonel François Marc Célestin: 101st Infantry; born 6 April 1865, Gruissan (Aude); Saint-Cyr, 1883; served in a variety of regimental and staff positions; retired, 1909; recalled to 101st Infantry, 1914; killed in action, 17 September 1914, Ferme des Loges.

Fétu, Sous-lieutenant Fernand Florentin: 101st Infantry; born 14 February 1890, Billancelles (Eure-et-Loir); killed in action during a bombardment, 9 January 1916, Main de Massiges.

Feugère, Sergeant: 2nd Platoon, 4th Company, 101st Infantry; wounded, 23 August 1914, Bois de Vezin.

Foch, Général de division (later Maréchal de France) Ferdinand Jean Marie (1851–1929): corps commander, August 1914; army commander, September 1914; pre-war instructor at the École de Guerre, where he became a leading proponent of the 'attack at all costs' school of tactics.

Focillon, Henri (1881–1943): art historian.

Fonclare, Général de division Élie de Riols de (1857–1944): divisional and corps commander; author of *L'Armée française à travers les âges: ses traditions, ses gloires, ses uniformes. L'Infanterie* (Paris: Société des Éditions Militaires, 1930).

Fralon, Major Joseph Théodore Napoléon Augustin: CO, 1st Battalion, 101st Infantry; born 1 September 1869, Ajaccio (Corse-du-Sud); saw pre-war service in Algeria; died 1941.

Frémont, Soldat de 2e classe Charles Henri: 8th Company, 101st Infantry; born 7 May 1895, Saint-Hilaire (Orne); died of wounds, 27 May 1917, Mont-sans-Nom (Marne).

'G.', Lieutenant: CO, 9th Company, 124th Infantry, February 1916.

Gallas, Sergeant: 2nd Platoon, 4th Company, 101st Infantry, August 1914.

Gallieni, Général de division Joseph Simon (1849–1916): retired 1905; recalled as military governor of Paris, 1914; victory on the Marne ascribed by some to his intervention; appointed minister of war, 1915; resigned the following year; his war diaries were published in three volumes as *Les Carnets de Gallieni* (Paris: Albin Michel, 1932).

Gascouin, Général de brigade Firmin Émile: born 1866; experienced artillery officer, best known as the author of *L'Évolution de l'artillerie pendant la guerre* (Paris: Flammarion, 1920).

'Gaspard': the eponymous journalist hero of *Gaspard* (Paris: Fayard, 1915), a novel by René Benjamin (1885–1948); humorous and good-natured, the novel enjoyed great contemporary success but was later dismissed by Jean Norton Cru as the type of book popular only among those unfamiliar with the reality of war.

Gautier, Théophile (1811–72): poet, playwright and critic.

Génin, Soldat de 2e classe René Amédée: 8th Company, 101st Infantry; born 5 January 1888, Amilly (Eure-et-Loir); killed in action, 2 June 1916, Tavannes.

Georget, Soldat de 2e classe: 2nd Platoon, 4th Company, 101st Infantry, 31 August 1914.

German, Captain: territorial officer of Engineers; in charge of stores, 5 March 1916, Virginy.

Glandaz, Sous-lieutenant Lionel Paul Louis: CO, 2nd Platoon, 2nd Company, 101st Infantry, August 1914; later commanded 2nd Company.

Gohier, Urbain (1862–1951): outspoken journalist, anti-militarist, anti-socialist, anti-monarchist; condemned as a collaborator after the Second World War.

Gouraud, Général de division Henri Joseph Eugène (1867–1946): commander, Fourth Army, 11 December 1915–14 December 1916, June 1917–November 1918; lost his right arm during the Dardanelles operation, 1915.

Goutal, Lieutenant: CO, 3rd Company, 101st Infantry; captured 1 June 1916, Retranchement R.2.

Grandmaison, Lieutenant Colonel (later Général de division) François Jules Louis Loyzeau de (1861–1915): notable for a pre-war revision of tactical and strategic doctrine that provided formal justification for the 'attack at all costs' school.

Greuze, Jean-Baptiste (1725–1805): artist noted for genre scenes.

Guibout, Soldat de 2e classe: 8th Company, 101st Infantry; joined the regiment, January 1916; one of Delvert's orderlies.

Guichard, Soldat de 2e classe: 8th Company, 101st Infantry; officer's orderly, April 1916; nicknamed 'Quinze-Grammes' ('Fifteen Grams') on account of his stature.

Hanotaux, Gabriel Albert Auguste (1853–1944): politician and prolific historian.

Hauteclocque, Lieutenant Colonel Wallerand Marie Alfred: CO, 14th Hussars; killed in action, 22 August 1914, Ethe; uncle of Maréchal de France Philippe Leclerc de Hauteclocque (1902–47), a senior Free French commander of the Second World War.

Hébert, Jacques René (1757–94): journalist during the French Revolution.

Herr, Général de division Frédéric Georges (1855–1932): commander, Région Fortifiée de Verdun, August 1915–February 1916; briefly returned to a corps command in 1917, but otherwise served out the war in various administrative posts.

Hillère, Captain Georges René: CO, 5th Company, 101st Infantry; born 12 April 1882, Villejuif (Val-de-Marne); a regular soldier, joined the 101st in 1913; promoted to captain, 13 March 1915; regimental adjutant, 7 February 1917, serving out the war in a number of staff posts; major, 1925 and retired the same year; Légion d'Honneur, 20 June 1916; identified by Delvert in the *Carnets* as X. but elsewhere as Hillère or 'Pansette'.

Hirschauer, Général de division Auguste Édouard (1857–1943): commander, 63rd Division; commander, XVIII Corps, 20 June 1916.

'J.', Captain: staff officer, IV Corps HQ; meets Delvert, 7 April 1916.

Janvier, Sergeant Pierre Jean-Baptiste Alphonse: 8th Company, 101st Infantry; born 26 November 1894, Carnet (Manche); killed in action by a shell, 28 December 1915, Main de Massiges.

Jaurès, Jean (1859–1914): French socialist leader assassinated on the eve of the war; his *L'Armée nouvelle* (Paris: Rouff, 1911) proposed converting the army into a Swiss-style militia.

Jegout, Soldat de 2e classe François Yves: 8th Company, 101st Infantry; born 12 September 1890, Versailles (Yvelines); killed by a shell, 27 January 1916, Main de Massiges; nicknamed 'Pégoud' after Adolphe Pégoud, the first fighter ace; Delvert spells his name 'Jégoud'.

Joffre, Général de division Joseph Jacques Césaire (1852–1931): French commander-in-chief on the Western Front, August 1914; sacked, December 1916.

Kellermann, Général de division François Étienne Christophe (1735–1820): French general of the Revolutionary and Napoleonic Wars; victor of the battle of Valmy (1792).

L., Sous-lieutenant; 142nd Infantry; relieves Delvert's company, 15 January 1916, Main de Massiges.

Lacotte, Colonel (later Général de brigade) Georges (1857–1928): commander, 13th Brigade (which included 101st Infantry), 20 June 1914; replaced, 31 October 1914; briefly commander, 28th Brigade, November–December 1914; retired, April 1917.

Laffitte, Jacques (1767–1844): banker and politician; supporter of the Orléans monarchy.

Lalo, Édouard (1823–92): composer.

Lamartine, Alphonse de (1790–1869): poet and politician; supporter of the Second Republic.

Lambert, Sous-lieutenant Édouard Arthur Louis: born 31 March 1893, Équeurdreville (Manche); enlisted, 26th Artillery; re-enlisted and commissioned, 1914; transferred, 101st Infantry, 6 October 1915; transferred to machine guns, February 1916; died of wounds (Delvert says 'of pneumonia'), 11 June 1916, Hôpital No. 45, Vichy (Allier).

Lancret, Nicolas (1690–1743): rococo artist.

Langlois, Soldat de 2e classe Charles: 8th Company, 101st Infantry; known as 'Charlot'; served, Main de Massiges and Verdun; transferred to 1st Company with Delvert, 26 June 1916.

Langlois, Général de division Hippolyte (1839–1912): soldier, senator and supporter of the introduction of the 75mm field gun; author of a number of books including *L'Artillerie de campagne en liaison avec les autres armes* (Paris: L. Baudouin, 1892).

Lanusse, Lieutenant Colonel Antoine Philippe Joseph: CO, 101st Infantry, 1916; born 13 May 1866, Maubourguet (Hautes-Pyrénées); Saint-Maixent, 1889–90; served with the African Light Infantry and Algerian regiments, not the Foreign Legion as Delvert claims; 101st Infantry, 1913; returned to an Algerian regiment, 1917.

Laporte, Soldat de 2e classe: 8th Company, 101st Infantry; Delvert's orderly, June 1916.

Lascoutx, Médecin-major de 1re classe Léon: regimental MO, 101st Infantry; possibly the 'big, slack-jawed buffoon of an MO' who complained that the regiment was 'overworked', August 1914.

Lauraire, Soldat de 2e classe Louis Marius Jean: 8th Company, 101st Infantry; born 25 February 1896, Ribennes (Lozère); died of wounds, victim of a German sniper, 1 June 1916, Tavannes.

Laval, Sous-lieutenant de: CO, 1st Platoon, 11th Company, 101st Infantry; according to Delvert, killed in action, 22 August 1914; no death by this name appears in the unit war diary or the regimental history; possibly Charles Marie Henri de Lacoste de Laval, born 4 September 1893, Saint-Quentin-des-Isles (Eure); missing in action, 25 September 1915, Mont-sans-Nom (Marne).

Lavalette-Coëtlosquet, Major: 142nd Infantry; welcomes Delvert to the Tavannes tunnel, 17 May 1916.

Lebaud, Major Pierre Émile Charles: CO, 1st Battalion, 101st Infantry, August 1914; born 8 October 1868, Salins (Jura); Saint-Cyr 1887–9; 101st Infantry, 1912; temporary lieutenant colonel, 2 October 1914; confirmed, 3 September 1915; 130th Infantry, 1916; author of *Actes de guerre* (Paris: Éd. Lavauzelle, 1932).

Lecocq, Charles (1832–1918): prolific composer of operettas.

Lecomte, Corporal: 8th Company, 101st Infantry, 3 June 1916.

Leconte de Lisle, Charles Marie René (1818–94): poet.

Ledru-Rollin, Alexandre Auguste (1807–74): lawyer, politician and republican revolutionary of 1848.

Lée, Sous-lieutenant Raymond François Victor: CO, 2nd Platoon, 3rd Company, 101st Infantry, August 1914; born 16 February 1885, Paris 17e; killed in action, 23 August 1914, near Villette (Meurthe); Delvert gives his death as 31 August 1914.

Legay, Marcel (1851–1915): popular singer and songwriter.

Lelièvre, Abbé Pierre (1874–?): Catholic priest and wartime padre; his enquiries are mentioned in his memoir, *Le Fléau de Dieu* (Paris: P. Ollendorff, 1920).

Lély, Madeleine (1878–1961): actress

Lepetit, Captain: staff officer; threatens Delvert, Major Lebaud and Lieutenant Hillère with a court-martial for retreating from Halles-sous-les-Côtes, 31 August 1914.

Leroy, Adjudant (later Sous-lieutenant) Valentin Gustave Aimé: platoon commander, 6th Company, 101st Infantry; born 15 December 1874, Blévy (Eure-et-Loir); killed in action, 1 June 1916, Vaux.

Letondot, Captain Raymond Marie Joseph: regimental adjutant, 101st Infantry; born 5 August 1872, Bayeux (Calvados); Saint-Cyr 1891–3; served with the Foreign Legion, joining 101st Infantry, March 1906; later transferred to 115th Infantry; died of wounds, 23 July 1918; Légion d'Honneur, 1908.

Letondot, Major: battalion CO, 124th Infantry; relieves Delvert's 8th Company, 23 May 1916, Vaux.

Lévêque, Soldat de 2e classe: 101st Infantry, stretcher-bearer, Verdun.

Lévy: 101st Infantry; violinist; attends a musical evening with Delvert, 10 May 1916, Neuville-sur-Ornain.

Liddell Hart, Captain Basil (1895–1970): British military historian and theorist.

Loriot, Soldat de 2e classe Émile Eugène Hippolyte: pioneer platoon, 101st Infantry; born 2 February 1888, Saint-Bomer (Eure-et-Loire); died of wounds, 31 August 1914, Halles-sous-les-Côtes.

Loriot, Sous-lieutenant Serge Gervais: CO, 4th Platoon, 1st Company, 101st Infantry, August 1914; born 7 October 1891, Tuffé (Sarthe); died of wounds, 1 October 1914, Hôpital de Montdidier (Somme).

'M.', Captain: a company CO, 101st Infantry, 23 January 1916.

'M.', Madame: resident of Sainte-Ménehould; describes the German occupation of the town to Delvert, 25 March 1916.

Macler, Lieutenant Fernand Charles Georges: CO, 3rd Machine Gun Platoon, 101st Infantry; born 18 April 1886, Écurcey (Doubs); killed in action, 31 August 1914, Beauclair.

Madelin, Louis (1871–1956): historian; author of *Le Chemin de la victoire* (Paris: Plon, 1920).

Mangin, Général de division Charles Emmanuel Marie (1866–1925): thrusting general with extensive pre-war colonial experience.

Marat, Jean-Paul (1743–93): journalist and politician of the French Revolution.

Marcadet, Sous-lieutenant Nicolas Jules Fernand: 91st Infantry; born 25 May 1884, Château-Regnault (Ardennes); killed in action, 10 August 1914, Mangiennes.

Marçay, Adjudant: CO, 3rd Platoon, 1st Company, 101st Infantry, August 1914.

Marchal, Sergeant: Engineers NCO responsible for trench construction, March 1916, Côte 138, Main de Massiges.

Le Masson, Soldat de 2e classe: 8th Company, 101st Infantry; one of Delvert's runners, 25 January 1916.

Marius, Corporal: 8th Company, 101st Infantry; a company telephonist, February 1916.

Maujean, Corporal: 8th Company, 101st Infantry, 29 March 1916.

Maurec, Maréchal des logis de: cavalryman attached to 3rd Battalion, 101st Infantry, for liaison purposes, 13 May 1916; his lonely hearts advertisement in *La Vie parisienne* attracted over 250 replies.

Maunoury, Général de division Michel Joseph (1847–1923): commander, Sixth Army (which included 101st Infantry) at the battle of the Marne, 6–9 September 1914.

Mélot, Colonel Henry: historian and, as 'H.M.', author of *La Vérité sur la guerre* (Paris: Albin Michel, 1930).

Michelet, Jules (1798–1874): historian of the French Revolution.

Molinier, Lieutenant René Édouard: CO, 1st Platoon, 8th Company, 101st Infantry, August 1914; born 11 June 1882, Paris 6e; killed in action, 22 August 1914, Ethe.

Montesquiou, Léon de (1873–1915): French essayist and monarchist; author of *1870: les causes politiques du désastre* (Paris: Nouvelle Librairie Nationale, 1914).

Mouquet, Soldat de 2e classe: 8th Company, 101st Infantry; transferred with Delvert to 1st Company, 26 June 1916.

Müller: a jocular name for the German artillery.

Musset, Alfred Louis Charles de (1810–57): dramatist, poet and novelist.

Nicolas, Captain (later Major): CO, 3rd Company, 101st Infantry; took command of 1st Battalion, 101st Infantry, after the battle of Ethe, August 1914.

Nicolas, Major: CO, 6th Company, later 2nd Battalion, 101st Infantry, March 1916; two officers named Nicolas served in 101st Infantry.

Nicole, Corporal: 2nd Platoon, 4th Company, 101st Infantry, August 1914.

Nivelle, Général de division Robert Georges (1856–1924): capable artillery commander, appointed French commander-in-chief, December 1916; sacked May 1917.

Nungesser, Captain Charles Eugène Jules Marie (1892–1927): French fighter ace; meets Delvert on a Paris-bound train, 21 April 1916.

'P.', Major: 'a pleasant southerner'; talks to Consul, Ravin des Fontaines, Vaux; perhaps Major Potiez, CO, 3rd Battalion, 35th Infantry, which was relieved by Delvert's battalion, 17 May 1916.

'P.' Lieutenant de: 8th Chasseurs à cheval; plays bridge with Delvert, 8 May 1916.

Paré, Soldat de 2e classe: 101st Infantry, 7 January 1916.

Pelachon, Soldat de 2e classe: 1st Company, 101st Infantry, 9 August 1916.

Pelletier, Sergeant: 1st Company, 101st Infantry; wounded and rendered unconscious by a bombardment, 10 July 1916, Main de Massiges.

Perrin, Lieutenant Marcel Jules Joseph: Machine Gun Company, 101st Infantry; born 14 March 1889, Verchamp (Haute-Saône); killed in action, 11 August 1917, Marmery (Marne).

Pétain, Général de division Henri Philippe Benoni Omer Joseph (1856–1951): commander, Second Army, at the battle of Verdun; later commander-in-chief of the French army on the Western Front; noted for his careful husbanding of manpower.

Pfister, Christian (1857–1933): historian, specialist in the Carolingian period; writes to Delvert, 14 April 1916; lunches with him, 1 May 1916.

Pinel, Soldat de 2e classe Eugène Henri: 2nd Platoon, 4th Company, 101st Infantry; born 19 August 1893, Paris 4e; seriously wounded, 15 September 1914, Ferme des Loges; died 25 September 1914, Hôpital No. 2, Le Havre (Seine-Inférieure).

Pingault, Soldat de 2e classe: 8th Company, 101st Infantry; killed in action, 4 June 1916; no soldier of that name is recorded killed while serving with 101st Infantry; however, Gabriel Henri Pinguenet, 101st Infantry *was* killed on the same day; born 25 February 1893, Ouarville (Eure-et-Loir).

Pionnier, Sergeant: 8th Company, 101st Infantry, 28 December 1915.

Pluyette, Corporal: 4th Company, 101st Infantry, 10 September 1914.

Poincaré, Raymond (1860–1934): politician; president of France, 1913–20.

Pointelin, Auguste Emmanuel (1839–1933): landscape artist, mainly of the Jura.

Provent, Sergeant: 8th Company, 101st Infantry, 19 March 1916.

Prudhomme, Joseph: character created by actor and caracturist Henry Monnier (1799–1877); subsequently used to symbolize a member of the bourgeoisie.

Putz, Général de division Henri Gabriel (1859–1925): commander, IV Corps, 17 June 1915-19 December 1917; his chief of staff was Colonel Jean-Marie Degoutte, perhaps 'the silent staff colonel' who accompanies Putz on his visit to the front line, 28 December 1915, Main de Massiges.

'Quinze-Grammes': nickname of Soldat Guichard.

'R.', Sous-lieutenant: platoon commander, 9th Company, 124th Infantry, 5 February 1916.

'R.', Lieutenant: 315th Infantry; shows Delvert round the Calvaire sector, 8 April 1916, Main de Massiges; they meet again, 29 May 1916, Verdun.

'R.', General of Engineers: describes his 'model' shelter at an officers' course attended by Delvert, August 1916, Châlons-sur-Marne.

'E.R.', Lieutenant: author of newspaper and magazine articles.

Rallier du Baty, Captain Henri Jules Marie: CO, 8th Company, 101st Infantry; born 8 November 1879, Lorient (Morbihan); took command of 8th Company on the death of Lieutenant Bernard; died of wounds, 21 February 1916, Hôpital Complémentaire No. 8, Paris 13e.

Renaud, Sergeant: 8th Company, 101st Infantry; wounded, 19 March 1916.

Reynal, Sous-lieutenant: platoon commander, 101st Infantry, 23 January 1916; a cuirassier who transferred to the infantry.

Riballier des Isles, Sous-lieutenant Raymond Louis: platoon commander, 8th Company, 101st Infantry; born 3 July 1887, Montport (Saône-et-Loire); transferred to 1st Company with Delvert, 26 June 1916. Awarded the Légion d'Honneur: 'An excellent officer in every respect, of unwavering courage and devotion to duty. As battalion adjutant he was seriously wounded en route from his HQ to the observation post to check the situation, the intense shelling suggesting an imminent attack on the front line'; died of wounds, 11 August 1917, Ambulance 3/4, Villers-Marmery (Marne).

Rigallot, Sergeant: Machine Gun Company, 101st Infantry; attached to Delvert's command, 4 June 1916.

Le Roch, Lieutenant (later Captain) Julien Eugène: CO, 1st Platoon, 10th Company, 101st Infantry; born 14 February 1887, Sarzeau (Morbihan); joined 101st Infantry, 1908; Staff, 124th Division, 22 March 1915; member of the French mission to the American Expeditionary Force, 1917, then a liaison officer with 87th US Division; died 19 August 1927, Sarzeau (Morbihan).

Rohan: Captain Josselin Charles Marie Joseph Gabriel Henri de Rohan-Chabot de, 12th Duc de Rohan: 4th Chasseurs à pied; born 4 April 1879, Paris; killed in action, 13 July 1916, Bray-sur-Somme (Somme).

Rousseau, Jean–Jacques (1712–78): writer and philosopher.

Roussel, Sergeant: 124th Infantry; an ex-colonial soldier; dines with Delvert, 30 July 1916.

Rouzeaud, Sous-lieutenant Marcel Léon: platoon commander, 8th Company, 101st Infantry; transferred to 1st Company with Delvert, 26 June 1916; born 5 May 1896, Paris 7e; died 11 August 1917, Moronvilliers, Marne. Mentioned in corps despatches: 'an officer of unwavering courage, always magnificent in action; mortally wounded at his post, 11 August 1917, going to assist an element of his platoon while under intense shelling'.

Rude, François (1784–1855): sculptor.

Ruffey, Général de division Pierre Xavier Emmanuel (1851–1928): commander, Third Army, August 1914; sacked later that month.

Saint-Just, Louis Antoine (1767–94): radical politician of the French Revolution.

Sarraut, Albert Pierre (1872–1962): politician; or his brother Maurice (1869–1943): journalist.

Samain, Albert (1858–1900): symbolist poet.

Sauvage, Corporal: 1st Company, 101st Infantry, 17 July 1916.

Sauviat, Soldat de 2e classe: Machine Gun Company, 101st Infantry; attached to Delvert's command, 4 June 1916.

Savary, Sergeant: 8th Company, 101st Infantry, 30 December 1915.

Schoenlaub, Captain Georges Auguste: CO, 11th Company, 101st Infantry, August 1914; born 8 March 1872, Wissembourg (Bas-Rhin); died 29 August 1914, Arlon (Belgium); Delvert believed him killed at the battle of Ethe, 22 August 1914; his official place of death suggests he may have died in captivity.

Ségonne, Captain Paul: CO, 2nd Company, 101st Infantry, August 1914; born 13 March 1869, Paris; called up into the Administration branch, 1887; Saint-Maixent, 1891; sous-lieutenant, 84th Infantry, 1892; served in north Africa before joining 101st Infantry; wounded, 22 August 1914, Ethe.

Ségur, Philippe-Paul, Comte de (1780–1873): soldier and military historian.

Seigneur, Lieutenant Eugène Louis: CO, 1st Platoon, 1st Company, 101st Infantry; promoted captain and took command of the company, September 1914; born 12 September 1879, Versailles (Seine-et-Oise); died of wounds, 21 September 1914, La Potière.

Serve, Lieutenant Louis Maurice: CO, 1st Platoon, 12th Company, 101st Infantry; born 5 February 1883, Paris 11e; killed in action, 22 August 1914, Ethe.

Sivan, Lieutenant (later Captain) Paul Victor Casimir: supply officer, 101st Infantry, August 1914; regimental machine-gun commander, May 1915.

Sortais, Soldat de 2e classe: 8th Company, 101st Infantry; Adjudant Dubuc's runner, 2 June 1916.

Soult, Marshal Jean-de-Dieu (1769–1851): general of the Revolutionary and Napoleonic Wars.

Susini, Corporal: a colonial soldier; Delvert passes his grave, 9 January 1916, Main de Massiges.

Susini, Captain: CO, 2nd Company, 101st Infantry, 7 June 1916.

'M.T.': 'Big M.T. from 124th Infantry' relieves Delvert in the trenches, 29 February 1916, Main de Massiges.

Tatin, Général de brigade Georges Alexandre Ferdinand (1858–1925): commander, 124th Division, 8 February 1916–28 October 1918, succeeding General Dantan.

Tétard, Sous-lieutenant: platoon commander, 6th Company, 101st Infantry; captured 3 June 1916, La Digue, Vaux.

Théart, Corporal: 8th Company, 101st Infantry, Main de Massiges and Verdun; wounded 19 May 1916, Verdun.

Thibault, Sous-lieutenant: 101st Infantry; signals officer, 22 February 1916.

Thiébault, Général de division Baron Paul Charles François Adrien Henri Dieudonné (1769–1846): soldier and author of several volumes of memoirs and military history.

Thiers, Louis Adolphe (1797–1877): politician and historian, a vocal opponent of Emperor Napoleon III.

Thomas, Albert (1878–1932): prominent Socialist politician, mayor of Champigny-sur-Marne (Val-de-Marne); first director-general of the International Labour Office.

Tisserand, Captain Jules Joseph Ernest: CO, 3rd Battalion, 101st Infantry; born 7 May 1863, La Chapelle-lès-Luxeuil (Haute-Saône); killed in action, 22 August 1914, Ethe.

Touchat, Soldat de 2e classe: 8th Company, 101st Infantry; joined the regiment, January 1916.

Tournery, Sous-lieutenant Louis Anthelme: CO, 7th Company, 101st Infantry; born 18 August 1893, Colomier (Ain); killed in action, 5 June 1916, Vaux.

Toutain, Soldat de 2e classe Alfred: 8th Company, 101st Infantry, 29 March 1916, born St-Rémy-sur Avre (Eure-et-Loir), 5 September 1885; brother of Paul.

Toutain, Corporal Paul: 8th Company, 101st Infantry; born St-Rémy-sur-Avre (Eure-et-Loir), 15 January 1888; seriously wounded, 4 June 1916, Retranchement R.1.

Touveray, Major: 44th Artillery; visits Delvert's positions, 29 March 1916, Main de Massiges.

Tramard, Sous-lieutenant: 8th Company, 101st Infantry, Main de Massiges.

Trentinian, Général de division Louis Edgard de (1851–1942): commander, 7th Infantry Division (which included 101st Infantry), August 1914; Saint-Cyr 1870–2; saw service in the colonies, especially Tonkin, Sudan and Madagascar; not promoted to a divisional command until 1908, perhaps as a supporter of Dreyfus; sacked September 1914, unjustly blamed for the defeat at Ethe, August 1914, and never served again.

'M.V.', Captain: 104th Territorials; messes with Delvert, 3 March 1916.

Vallet, Lieutenant Marie Joseph Raymond: CO, 1st Platoon, 2nd Company, 101st Infantry; born 8 June 1881, Toul (Meurthe-et-Moselle); killed in action, 22 August 1914, Ethe.

Vallet, Captain: 101st Infantry; loses a horse outside Attichy, 13 September 1914.

Vatin, Soldat de 2e classe: 8th Company, 101st Infantry; drummer, 5 June 1916.

Vinerot, Lieutenant (later Captain): 101st Infantry; adjutant, 2nd Battalion, Main de Massiges and Verdun; Légion d'Honneur; identified by Delvert in the *Carnets* as 2, but elsewhere as Vinerot (perhaps a nickname).

Walter, Captain: 21st Chasseurs à pied; inventor of the Walter shield, which he demonstrates to Delvert on an officer's course, 4 August 1916, Châlons-sur-Marne.

Watter, Corporal Hubert; 8th Company, 101st Infantry, 15 June 1916.

Watteau, Jean-Antoine (1684–1721): artist.

Wegener, Gerda Marie Frederikke (1886–1940): Franco-Danish illustrator and artist.

'X.', General: harasses the colonel of 101st Infantry, 15 January 1916; possibly the divisional commander, General Dantant, or the corps commander, General Putz.

'Y.', Captain: 101st Infantry; a regular soldier and machine-gun officer; adjutant, 3rd Battalion, March 1916.

Yver, Colette (1874–1953): Catholic feminist writer.

Places Mentioned in the Text

Les Abris Post (Marne): the 'Petit Poste des Abris', a position overlooking the Creux de l'Oreille; within 101st Infantry positions, Main de Massiges, 19 March 1916.

Araja (Marne): farm behind 8th Company positions, Main de Massiges, January–February 1916.

Argers (Marne): Delvert passes through, returning from leave, 8 May 1916.

Attichy (Oise): 101st Infantry passes through, 13 September 1914.

Aubervilliers (Seine-Saint-Denis): the wounded Delvert is evacuated here by train from Roye-sur-Matz, 25 September 1914.

Azannes (Meuse): 101st Infantry is billeted here, 11–12 August, 14 August 1914.

Barricourt (Ardennes): 101st Infantry passes through, 29 August 1914.

Bastion D (Marne): one of four covering positions, lettered A–D, within 101st Infantry positions, Main de Massiges, 30 March 1916; situated at the junction of the Index and Médius spurs.

Ba-Ta-Clan: music-hall, now spelt Bataclan, still in operation as a theatre and concert venue, 50 Boulevard Voltaire, Paris 11e; it was the scene of a terrorist attack, November 2015.

La Batterie (Meuse): pre-war artillery position south-west of Fort Vaux; 6th Company of 101st Infantry shelters here while in reserve, May–June 1916.

Bayonville (Ardennes): 101st Infantry passes through, 29 August 1914.

Bazar de la Charité: an annual charity event; a fire in 1897 killed over 120 people, including the sister of Empress Sisi of Austria; now the site of an expiatory chapel, Notre-Dame de Consolation, 17 Rue Jean-Goujon, Paris 8e.

Beauclair (Meuse): 101st Infantry passes through, 31 August 1914.

Beauzée-sur-Aire (Meuse): 101st Infantry passes through, going to Verdun, 11–12 May 1916.

Belrupt (Meuse): village and fort situated east of Verdun, used as a storage depot during the battle; Delvert arrives here, 17 May 1916.

Belval-en-Argonne (Marne): Delvert is billeted here, 8–9 May 1916.

Berzieux (Marne): village behind 101st Infantry positions, Main de Massiges; the regiment passes through, returning from rest, 21 February 1916.

Billy-sous-Mangiennes (Meuse): 101st Infantry takes up defensive positions here, 10 August 1914.

Bois de la Caillette (Meuse): wood south of Fort Douaumont, Verdun.

Bois Chausson (Marne): wooded ridge behind German lines, Main de Massiges; known to the French as La Chenille.

Bois Fumin (Meuse): a 'wood' west of Fort Vaux, largely denuded of trees during the battle.

Bois de la Gruerie (Marne): wood near Vienne-le-Château; guarded by Delvert's men, 2–3 September 1914; scene of further heavy fighting, 1915.

Bois de Montrolles (Oise): south of the village of Betz; guarded by elements of 101st Infantry, 8 September 1914; now the site of a small war cemetery.

Bois de Nouelles (Meuse): near Romagne-sous-les-Côtes; 101st Infantry position, 12–14 August 1914.

Bois de la Taillette (Ardennes): 101st Infantry position during the retreat from Ethe, 23 August 1914.

Bois de Vezin (Meurthe-et-Moselle): 4th Company, 101st Infantry skirmishes in the area, 23 August 1914.

Bois de Vieux-Billecoq (Ardennes): east of Buzancy, 101st Infantry passes through, 30 August 1914.

Bois-de-Ville (Marne): wood behind German lines, Main de Massiges; the front line ran between here and Ville-sur-Tourbe.

Bois de Warphemont (Meuse): wood south of Pillon.

Bordeaux (Gironde): Delvert spends time here on leave, 22–23 April 1916.

Boyau Altkirch (Meuse): French communications trench, running from the rear of 8th Company positions in Retranchement R.1, south-west towards Verdun.

Boyau Blanc (Marne): French communications trench, connecting the front line and the Ouvrage Pruneau; within 1st Company positions, Main de Massiges, July 1916.

Boyau Eitel (Marne): French communications trench, leading from 8th Company positions down the Ravin du Médius; Main de Massiges, December 1915.

Boyau de l'Étang (Meuse): French communications trench, running parallel to and west of Boyau Altkirch, from 8th Company positions at Retranchement R.1, south-west towards Verdun.

Boyau Löbau (Marne): German communications trench; Main de Massiges, December 1915.

Boyau de Rouvroy (Marne): French communications trench; within 1st Company positions, Maisons-de-Champagne, August 1916.

Boyau Schultz (Marne): French communications trench, leading from 8th Company positions down the Index spur; Main de Massiges, February 1916.

Boyau Schumann (Marne): French communications trench, running down the Médius spur; within 8th Company positions, Main de Massiges, February 1916.

Boyau Sundgau (Meuse): French communications trench, linking Boyau Altkirch, Boyau de l'Étang and Retranchement R.1; Vaux, May 1916.

Boyau 31 (Marne): French communications trench, leading from the front lines to La Verrue; within 8th Company positions, Main de Massiges, February 1916.

Boyau 32 (Marne): French communications trench, leading from the front lines to La Verrue; within 8th Company positions, Main de Massiges, February 1916.

Boyau 33 (Marne): French communications trench, leading from the front lines to La Verrue; within 8th Company positions, Main de Massiges, February 1916.

Brabant-le-Roi (Meuse): village south-west of Verdun; a Zeppelin is shot down here, 21–22 February 1916.

Brabant-sur-Meuse (Meuse): 101st Infantry stops overnight, heading to the front, 9–10 August 1914.

Brandeville (Meuse): 101st Infantry passes through, 25 August 1914.

Braux-Sainte-Cohière (Marne): village west of Sainte-Ménehould; behind French positions, Main de Massiges.

Brieulles-sur-Meuse (Meuse): 101st Infantry stops overnight, 25–26 August 1914.

Butte-de-Ménil (Marne): French battery position, Main de Massiges, 6 March 1916.

Le Calvaire (Marne): the 'Calvary'; statue sited between the front lines near Ville-sur-Tourbe, Main de Massiges; it lent its name to a sector of the front line.

Canny-sur-Matz (Oise): 101st Infantry passes through, 21 September 1914.

Çatalca (Turkey): city 60 kilometres north-west of Istanbul; site of two battles in 1912 and 1913, during the Balkan Wars.

Cernay-en-Dormois (Marne): village north of the Main de Massiges, behind German lines.

Châlons-sur-Marne (Marne): now Châlons-en-Champagne; Delvert visits here, 19 March 1916; attends a course, 31 July–6 August 1916.

Charency (Meurthe-et-Moselle): 101st Infantry passes through, retreating from Ethe (Belgium), 22–23 August 1914.

La Charmeraie (Marne): site of IV Corps HQ; Delvert visits, 7 April 1916.

Chelles (Oise): 101st Infantry passes through, 12 September 1914.

La Chenille (Marne): 'the Caterpillar'; nickname of the Bois Chausson, a ridge whose shell-blasted tree trunks were said to resemble caterpillar hairs.

Chevert Barracks (Meuse): situated at Belrupt, east of Verdun.

Col des Abeilles (Marne): col at the junction of the Médius and Annulaire spurs, Main de Massiges; literally 'the pass of the bees', but in soldiers' slang *abeilles* were also 'bullets'.

Compiègne (Oise): Delvert is billeted here, 19–20 September 1914.

Côte de l'Étang de Vaux (Meuse): hillside overlooking the village of Vaux and its *étang* (mill-pond).

Côte de Laimont (Meuse): hill crossed by 101st Infantry, going to rest, 9 April 1916.

Côte de Souville (Meuse): rising ground between Fort Vaux and Verdun; site of Fort Souville.

Côte 138 (Marne): hill occupied by 8th Company; Main de Massiges, March 1916, July 1916.

Côte 181 (Marne): hill and battery position south-west of Virginy; behind 101st Infantry positions, Main de Massiges, February 1916.

Côte 199 (Marne): wooded hill where 8th Company dig trenches overnight; Main de Massiges, 5–6 March 1916.

Côte 202 (Marne): hill occupied by 101st Infantry; Main de Massiges, March 1916.

Côte 304 (Meuse): hill on the left bank of the Meuse; scene of heavy fighting during the battle of Verdun.

La Courtine (Meuse): a defensive work outside Fort Vaux, adjoining Retranchement R.1; within 101st Infantry positions, May–June 1916.

Cousance-aux-Forges (Meuse): Delvert attends a bombing course here, 21–24 June 1916.

Le Cratère (Marne): the 'Crater'; created by a German mine, 3 February 1915 on the former Côte 191 at the eastern end of the Main de Massiges; Delvert reconnoitres here, 14 January 1916.

Crépy-en-Valois (Oise): 101st Infantry passes through, 11 September 1914.

Le Creux de l'Oreille (Marne): 'the Earhole'; lower ground on the northern flank of the Main de Massiges; this was no man's land, overlooked from the south by 101st Infantry positions in Tranchée 35 and Tranchée Balcon Ouest, and further to the rear by the redoubt at La Verrue.

Cuise-Lamotte (Oise): 101st Infantry passes through, 13 September 1914.

Dampierre-le-Château (Marne): village and railway station south-west of Sainte-Ménehould, behind the Main de Massiges.

Delut (Meuse): village south-west of the Othain valley; 101st Infantry position, 24 August 1914.

Le Dépôt (Meuse): a pre-war ammunition magazine, south-west of Fort Vaux; site of 101st Infantry's regimental HQ, May 1916.

La Digue (Meuse): the mill-dam of the Étang de Vaux.

Dinant (Belgium): site of an action on 15 August 1914, when a German attempt to capture the town was repulsed.

Dommartin-la-Planchette (Marne): village behind 101st Infantry positions, Main de Massiges.

Dommartin-sous-Hans (Marne): 101st Infantry passes through, going to the Main de Massiges, 2–3 December 1915; the regiment is at rest here, 15–22 December 1915, 1–7 January 1916.

Dommartin-sur-Yèvre (Marne): Delvert is billeted here, 24 June 1916.

Dreux (Eure-et-Loir): one of 101st Infantry's two peacetime depots (see Saint-Cloud).

Dugny (Meuse): 101st Infantry detrains here, going to the front, August 1914.

Dwinsk/Dvinsk (Latvia): now Daugavpils; on 22 March 1916 Delvert discusses a planned Russian offensive here; in fact, the Russians had attacked the previous day, advancing a few kilometres with heavy casualties before losing the ground to German counter-attacks; the Brusilov offensive mentioned by Delvert began in Galicia, 8 June 1916.

École de Guerre (Paris): the French staff college, the École Supérieure de Guerre.

Épinonville (Meuse): 101st Infantry is billeted nearby, 26–27 August 1914.

Étang de Vaux (Meuse): the mill-pond west of Vaux, dammed by La Digue.

Ethe (Belgium): village near Virton where 101st Infantry was heavily engaged, 22 August 1914.

Exermont (Ardennes): 101st Infantry is billeted nearby, 27–28 August 1914.

Feigneux (Oise): 101st Infantry passes through, 11 September 1914.

Ferme de l'Arbre (Oise): large farm between Attichy and Moulin-sous-Touvent; 101st Infantry spends a night here, 13–14 September 1914.

Ferme de Beauséjour (Marne): farm, Maisons-de-Champagne; it became the focus of very heavy fighting; the nearby village of Le Mesnil-lès-Hurlus was destroyed and never rebuilt.

Ferme du Cabaret (Meuse): a farm around 600 metres south of Fort Vaux; 101st Infantry assembles here, going to the trenches, 17 May 1916.

Ferme Haussu (Oise): Delvert holds this position between Roye and Roye-sur-Matz, 22–23 September 1914.

Ferme des Loges, Nampcel (Oise): 101st Infantry sees action in and around this farm, 14–19 September 1914.

Fontaine-sur-Marne (Haute-Marne): 101st Infantry is billeted here, 15–16 June 1916.

Fontainebleau (Seine-et-Marne): the home from 1871 of the army Artillery School, the École d'Artillerie.

Forêt de Belnoue (Meuse): 101st Infantry passes through, going to rest, 9 May 1916.

Fort Douaumont (Meuse): one of the most modern of the Verdun forts; it fell to the Germans on 25 February 1916 within days of their initial attack.

Fort Souville (Meuse): one of the inner line of right-bank forts, lying between Fort Vaux and Verdun; the site of several French artillery batteries.

Le Fourneau (Meuse): hamlet south-west of Billy-sous-Mangiennes, now Le Haut Fourneau; Delvert and his men are billeted here, 10–11 August 1914.

Fresnières (Oise): 101st Infantry falls back here after fighting around La Potière, 21 September 1914.

Garches (Hauts-de-Seine): site of 101st Infantry's firing ranges on the outskirts of Paris.

Givry-en-Argonne (Marne): Delvert rejoins 101st Infantry here, 11 November 1915; he passes through again, going to Paris on leave, 27 June 1916.

Gomery (Belgium): village on the battlefield of Ethe, 22 August 1914.

Grandcourt (Belgium): 101st Infantry passes through, 22 August 1914.

Grimaucourt-en-Woëvre (Meuse): 101st Infantry passes through, 11 September 1914.

Gymnase (Paris): an old-established theatre, now the Théâtre du Gymnase Marie Bell, 38 Boulevard Bonne-Nouvelle, Paris 10e.

Halles-sous-les-Côtes (Meuse): 101st Infantry passes through, 30–31 August 1914; Delvert's company remains behind to defend the village from German advanced elements.

Hardaumont (Meuse): wooded area, including a redoubt, between Fort Douaumont and Fort Vaux.

Haudainville (Meuse): 101st Infantry passes through, 16 May 1916.

Ippécourt (Meuse): 101st Infantry passes through, heading to Verdun, 15 May 1916.

Joinville (Haute-Marne): Delvert visits the town, 18 June 1916.

La Justice (Marne): wooded ridge, behind the German front line but overlooking French positions, Main de Massiges.

Laheycourt (Meuse): 101st Infantry passes through, going to rest, 9 April 1916.

Laimont (Meuse): 101st Infantry passes through, going to Verdun, 11 May 1916.

Landrecourt (Meuse): 101st Infantry is billeted here, going to Verdun, 15–16 May 1916.

Lempire-aux-Bois (Meuse): 101st Infantry passes through, leaving Verdun, 15 June 1916.

Louppy-le-Château (Meuse): 101st Infantry passes through, going to Verdun, 11 May 1916.

Le Luat (Oise): 101st Infantry is billeted here after the battle of the Marne, 10–11 September 1914.

Maffrécourt (Marne): village behind French positions, Main de Massiges; 101st Infantry passes through, returning from rest, 21 February 1916.

Main de Massiges (Marne): 'the Hand of Massiges'; a ridge feature with south-west facing spurs resembling splayed fingers, named Pouce (Thumb), Index, Médius (Middle) and Annulaire (Ring); within German lines until September 1915, when the French recaptured the lower parts of the ridge, spurs included; the higher ground remained in German hands until 1918.

Maisons-de-Champagne (Marne): farm north of the Main de Massiges; the scene of heavy fighting during the French Champagne offensive, September 1915; battery position, March 1916.

La Malmaison (Meurthe-et-Moselle): hamlet near the Belgian border; 101st Infantry is billeted here, 21 August 1914, 22–23 August 1914, before and after the battle of Ethe.

Mangiennes (Meuse): 1st Battalion, 101st Infantry is positioned here, 14–15 August 1914.

Marville (Meuse): Delvert is wounded here, 25 August 1914.

Massiges (Marne): village behind French lines, south of the Main de Massiges.

Minaucourt (Marne): village behind French lines, south-west of the Main de Massiges; destroyed during the war and rebuilt in 1922–3.

Mont Têtu (Marne): eminence straddling the French and German front lines, Main de Massiges; the 'summit' lay within German lines and was known to them as the Kanonenberg.

Mont Trémois (Marne): isolated hill behind French lines, east of Virginy, Main de Massiges.

Montigny-devant-Sassey (Meuse): village south-east of Halles-sous-les-Côtes; Delvert expects the Germans to attack from this direction, 31 August 1914.

Morte-Homme (Meuse): hill on the left bank of the Meuse; the scene of heavy fighting during the battle of Verdun.

Moyenneville (Oise): 101st Infantry is billeted here, 20–21 September 1914.

Mukden (China): now Shenyang; site of the last major land battle of the Russo-Japanese War, 20 February–10 March 1905.

Nampcel (Oise): 101st Infantry takes part in clashes nearby, during and after the first battle of the Aisne, 13–17 September 1914.

Nanteuil-le-Haudouin (Oise): 101st Infantry disembarks here, prior to the battle of the Marne, 8 September 1914.

Neuilly-Plaisance (Seine-Saint-Denis): 101st Infantry pauses here, 7 September 1914.

La Neuville-au-Pont (Marne): Delvert spends two periods at rest here, January 1916, April 1916.

Neuville-sur-Ornain (Meuse): Delvert is billeted here, 9–10 May 1916.

Noisy-le-Sec (Seine-Saint-Denis): 101st Infantry disembarks here, prior to the battle of the Marne, 7 September 1914.

L'Oasis (Marne): feature in 1st Company positions, Maisons-de-Champagne, August 1916.

Offémont, Parc d' (Oise): 101st Infantry rests here briefly, 14 September 1914.

L'Oreille de Massiges (Marne): see Creux de l'Oreille.

Ouvrage Martin Saint-Léon: trench work at the eastern end of the village of Massiges; within 8th Company positions, Main de Massiges, January 1916; perhaps 'Ouvrage M' as mentioned, 5 March 1916.

Ouvrage Pruneau (Marne): trench redoubt, north-west of Ville-sur-Tourbe; within 8th Company positions, Main de Massiges, July 1916.

Paris: Delvert spends time on leave here, 22 April, 24 April–1 May, 27 June–1 July 1916.

Perthes-les-Hurlus (Marne): 101st Infantry suffers very heavy casualties in a poorly planned and disastrously executed attack on German front lines here, 25 February 1915.

Pillon (Meuse): village 4 kilometres north of Mangiennes; Delvert is billeted here, 16–17 August 1914.

Plessis-Belleville (Oise): 101st Infantry is billeted here after the battle of the Marne, 9 September 1914.

Le Poncelet (Marne): behind French positions, just outside Courtémont, south of the Main de Massiges; the regiment passes through, going to rest, 29 February 1916.

La Potière (Oise): 1st Company launch a surprise attack here, at the start of the Race to the Sea, 21 September 1914.

Puisaleine (Oise): Delvert is billeted here, 18–19 September 1914.

La Râperie (Oise): a sugar-beet works near Silly-le-Long; 101st Infantry position, 10 September 1914.

Ravin des Abris (Meuse): see Ravin des Fontaines.

Ravin du Bazil (Meuse): valley leading west into the French right-bank positions at Verdun; the continuation of the Ravin de Vaux.

Ravin du Bois Fumin (Meuse): valley leading south from the Étang de Vaux, with Retranchement R.1 at its head.

Ravin de l'Étang (Marne): valley between the Pouce and Index spurs, Main de Massiges; named after the Étang stream at its foot.

Ravin de la Fausse-Côte (Meuse): valley leading south from Fort Douaumont towards the Étang de Vaux.

Ravin des Fontaines (Meuse): valley leading south-west from the Digue towards the Côte de Souville, outflanking the French positions around Fort Vaux; Delvert has a shelter here, 29 May 1916; alternatively 'Ravin des Abris' or 'Ravin de la Mort'.

Ravin du Médius (Marne): valley between the Médius and Annulaire spurs, Main de Massiges.

Ravin de la Mort (Meuse): 'Valley of Death'; four valleys were so baptized by soldiers on the Verdun front; see Ravin du Bois Fumin, Ravin des Fontaines.

Ravin des Tombes (Marne): valley west of the 'Hand', Main de Massiges.

Ravin de Vaux (Meuse): valley leading west into the French right-bank positions at Verdun; continued by the Ravin du Bazil.

La Redoute: pre-war shelter DV4, designed to hold fifty men, and shown on some trench maps as Abri 4595; situated west of Fort Vaux, it was incorporated into Retranchement R.1 and used as an aid post during the German assault, 1–5 June 1916.

Reichshoffen (Bas-Rhin): one of the opening battles of the Franco-German War, 6 August 1870; scene of a gallant but doomed charge by the French cuirassiers to disengage their infantry.

Reims (Marne): 101st Infantry passes through, going to the front, August 1914.

Rembercourt-aux-Pots (Meuse): 101st Infantry passes through, going to Verdun, 11 May 1916; Delvert visits the church of Saint-Louvent, 13 May 1916.

Retheuil (Aisne): 101st Infantry passes through, 11 September 1914.

Retranchement R.1 (Meuse): one of a series of trench redoubts west of Fort Vaux, overlooking the village of Vaux and the Ravin de la Mort; R.1 lay closest to the fort and faced down the valley; the work consisted of a trench faced on one side in brick and stone, with a pre-war shelter, La Redoute; it was garrisoned by 8th Company, 101st Regiment, 31 May–5 June 1916.

Retranchement R.2 (Meuse): one of a series of trench redoubts west of Fort Vaux, overlooking the village of Vaux and the Ravin de la Mort; situated on the western side of the ravine, R.2 fell to the Germans, 1 June 1916, threatening 8th Company with encirclement.

Retranchement R.3 (Meuse): one of a series of trench redoubts west of Fort Vaux, overlooking the village of Vaux and the Ravin de la Mort; R.3 lay north of R.2, overlooking the Digue.

Revigny-sur-Ornain (Meuse): small town and important railway junction, 60 kilometres south-west of Verdun; Delvert leaves by train, going to Paris, 27 June 1916.

Riga (Latvia): on 22 March 1916 Delvert mentions a planned Russian offensive here; the Russians had attacked the previous day, advancing a few kilometres with heavy casualties before losing the ground to German counter-attacks.

Roye-sur-Matz (Oise): Delvert is evacuated here, 23 September 1914.

Roilaye (Oise): 101st Infantry passes through, 13 September 1914.

Ruette (Belgium): village on the southern edge of the Ethe battlefield; the French retreat through here, 22 August 1914.

Saint-Bertrand-de-Comminges (Haute-Garonne): a small town in the foothills of the Pyrenees.

Saint-Cloud (Hauts-de-Seine): one of 101st Infantry's two peacetime depots (see Dreux); the regiment assembled here on mobilization.

Saint-Cyr (Yvelines): former home of the French military academy, the École Spéciale Militaire, since 1945 based at Coëtquidan (Morbihan); cadets spent two years here before receiving their commission; *Les Marie-Louise* graduated in summer 1914; in August 1914, the three current classes – *Montmirail, La Croix du Drapeau* and *La Grande Revanche* – were deemed commissioned and the men posted straight to regiments.

Saint-Juvin (Ardennes): 101st Infantry halts here, 1 September 1914.

Saint-Maixent (Deux-Sèvres): home of the École Militaire d'Infanterie, the officer's training school for infantry NCOs admitted after a competitive exam; up to 60 per cent of officers were commissioned via this route.

Saint-Mard-sur-le-Mont (Marne): Delvert attends a company commander's course here, 15 September 1915.

Sainte-Ménehould (Marne): 101st Infantry entrains here for the battle of the Marne, 3 September 1914; Delvert makes several subsequent visits – 21, 24, 25 March 1916.

Samogneux (Meuse): village on the right bank of the Meuse, north of Verdun; within French lines but beyond the outer ring of protective forts.

Saumur (Maine-et-Loire): home of the École d'Application de la Cavalerie, where cavalry officers were trained.

Sentier de la Vertu (Paris): one of the main promenades in the Bois de Boulogne.

Sevastopol (Ukraine): Crimean port and site of the famous siege (September 1854– September 1855).

Sèvres (Hauts-de-Seine): 101st Infantry passes through, going to the front, August 1914.

Silly-le-Long (Oise): 101st Infantry positioned here during the battle of the Marne, 9 September 1914.

Souville (Meuse): see Fort Souville.

Tahure (Marne): the adjoining villages of Tahure and Somme-Py lay behind German lines, north-west of the Main de Massiges; the scene of heavy fighting throughout the war, they were finally liberated in September 1918, but Tahure was never rebuilt.

Tailly (Ardennes): 101st Infantry passes through, 31 August 1914.

Tavannes (Meuse): the Tavannes railway tunnel, carrying the line to Étain, lay east of Verdun; its eastern end was blocked by the German advance and it was used as a storage and rest area for Verdun's right-bank defences; Fort Tavannes lay on the ridge above.

Tracy-le-Val (Oise): 101st Infantry takes part in clashes nearby, during and after the first battle of the Aisne, 13–17 September 1914.

Tranchée Balcon (Marne): front-line trench, within 8th Company positions, Main de Massiges, December 1915; continued westwards by Tranchée Balcon-Ouest.

Tranchée Balcon-Ouest (Marne): see Tranchée Balcon.

Tranchée Bismarck (Marne): German trench, Main de Massiges, December 1915.

Tranchée Doerflinger (Marne): trench within 101st Infantry positions, Main de Massiges, April 1916.

Tranchée Fumin (Meuse): trench within 101st Infantry positions, Bois Fumin, south-west of Fort Vaux, Verdun.

Tranchée Merlonnée (Marne): trench within 8th Company positions, Main de Massiges, December 1915.

Tranchée Nord (Marne): trench within 8th Company positions, Main de Massiges, January 1916.

Tranchée du Plateau (Marne): trench within 6th Company positions, situated at the junction of the Annulaire and the main Main de Massiges ridge, March 1916.

Tranchée du Saillant (Meuse): trench in the Ravin de Vaux; opposite 101st Infantry positions.

Tranchée Sarajevo (Meuse): German trench, west of Fort Vaux, Verdun; opposite 8th Company positions at Retranchement R.1, June 1916.

Tranchée Vix (Marne): trench within 8th Company positions, Main de Massiges, February 1916.

Tranchée de la Voie Ferrée (Meuse): trench within 101st Infantry positions, Ravin de Vaux, Verdun, May 1916; it ran alongside a pre-war narrow-gauge railway line.

Tranchée 21 (Marne): trench within 1st Company positions, Main de Massiges, July 1916.

Tranchée 22 (Marne): trench within 1st Company positions, Main de Massiges, July 1916.

Tranchée 35 (Marne): trench within 8th Company positions, Main de Massiges, February 1916; it was a spur off Tranchée Balcon-Ouest, overlooking the Creux de l'Oreille.

Tranchée 36 (Marne): trench within 8th Company positions, Main de Massiges, February 1916; also known as Tranchée Kellermann, it was a cover trench behind Tranchée 35 and Tranchée Balcon-Ouest.

Val-de-Grâce (Paris): French military hospital; HQ of the army's medical branch.

Valmy (Marne): village behind French positions, Main de Massiges; the French defeated the Prussians here in 1792.

Vaux (Meuse): village on the right bank of the Meuse, north of Verdun, completely destroyed by the fighting.

Venzolasca (Haute-Corse): village just outside Bastia.

Verdun (Meuse): heavily fortified city on the right bank of the Meuse.

La Verrue (Marne): 'The Wart'; a trench redoubt within 8th Company positions, Main de Massiges, January 1916; held by a different company, April 1916; the redoubt was situated on a slight rise at the junction of the Index and Médius spurs, close to the Col des Abeilles.

Vichel (Aisne): 101st Infantry passes through, 12 September 1914.

Vienne-la-Ville (Marne): 101st Infantry halts here, 8 August 1914.

Vienne-le-Château (Marne): 101st Infantry halts overnight here, 2–3 September 1914.

Ville d'Avray (Hauts-de-Seine): 101st Infantry passes through, going to the front, August 1914.

Ville-sur-Tourbe (Marne): village near the front lines, Main de Massiges; 101st Infantry takes up positions here, 8 April 1916; and again, July 1916.

Villefranche (Meuse): 101st Infantry is billeted nearby, 28–29 August 1914.

Villers-le-Rond (Meurthe-et-Moselle): 101st Infantry passes through, during the retreat from Ethe, 22 August 1914.

Villers-lès-Mangiennes (Meuse): 101st Infantry is billeted here, 18–21 August 1914.

Virginy (Marne): village immediately behind the front lines, Main de Massiges; it was destroyed in the fighting but reconstructed after the war.

Vitry-le-François (Marne): Delvert passes through, going to Paris on leave, 21 April 1916.